PUTNAM COUNTY, TENNESSEE

MISCELLANEOUS RECORDS

1771-1872

Including

Diaries, Letters, Wills, Indentures, etc.

Originally Prepared By:

The Historical Records Project
Transcription Unit
Division of Women's and Professional Projects
Works Progress Administration (WPA)

JANAWAY PUBLISHING, INC.
SANTA MARIA, CALIFORNIA

> *Notice*
>
> This book has been reproduced from carbon-copies of the original transcriptions of court records by the Works Progress Administration (WPA) in 1930s. In many instances, the resulting text is light, the documents are physically flawed, and foxing (or discoloration) occurs. The pages of this reprint have been digitally enhanced and, where possible, the flaws eliminated in order to provide clarity of content and a pleasant reading experience.

Putnam County, Tennessee, Miscellaneous Records 1771-1872;
Including Diaries, Letters, Wills, Indentures, etc.

Originally transcribed by:

Works Progress Administration (WPA)
1936

Reprinted by:

Janaway Publishing, Inc.
732 Kelsey Ct.
Santa Maria, CA 93454
(805) 925-1038
www.JanawayGenealogy.com

2006, 2014

ISBN: 978-1-59641-038-1

Made in the United States of America

Putnam Co., TN Miscellaneous Records

transcribed by Mrs. Rhea E. Garrett and Ms. Matilda A. Porter for the Works Progress Administration, 1936, reprinted by Byron Sistler & Associates, 1998

The transcript this book was printed from is a carbon copy typed on onion skin paper over 60 years ago. The print quality varied throughout the work--this would seem to be due to the wear on the carbon paper. We have made an effort to make all the print as legible as possible. This is a second generation copy of the original, and there will be a few places where the writing cannot be made out.

We would like to thank Jean Sugg and Chuck Sherrill of the TN State Library and Archives for their kind loan of the original book.

TENNESSEE

RECORDS OF PUTNAM COUNTY

MISCELLANEOUS RECORDS
(DIARIES, LETTERS, WILLS, INDENTURES, ETC.)

COPIED UNDER WORKS PROGRESS ADMINISTRATION

HISTORICAL RECORDS PROJECT
Official Project No. 65-44-1487

MRS. JOHN TROTWOOD MORE
STATE LIBRARIAN & ARCHIVIST, SPONSOR

MRS. ELIZABETH D. COPPEDGE
STATE DIRECTOR OF WOMEN'S & PROFESSIONAL PROJECTS

MRS. PENELOPE JOHNSON ALLEN
STATE SUPERVISOR

MRS. RHEA E. GARRETT
MISS MATILDA A. PORTER
DISTRICT SUPERVISORS

COPYISTS

MISS PEARL KUYKENDALL
MRS. ALLIE LOFTIS
MRS. JOHN RICHARDSON

AUGUST 1936

PUTNAM COUNTY

MISCELLANEOUS RECORDS
DIARIES, LETTERS, WILLS, INDENTURES, ETC.

INDEX

A

Abingdon, Virginia, 107
Academy St., 15
Adcock, James W., 24
Alabama River, 105
Alcorn, John, 11
Alex, 139
Alexan, John William, 52
Alexander, Wm., 41
Alexandria, 140
Alexandria, Joel, 42
Algood, 19,23
Algood, (Mrs.) 22
Algood, A., 18
Algood, Alfred (Mrs.)1,5,9
Algood, Elizabeth, 21,22
Algood, Joe, 45
Algood, Joel, 8,13,14,15,16,17,18,
　　19,21,24
Algood, Lula (Mrs.) 1,2,3,4,6,7,8,
　　11,12,13,14,15,16,17,18,19,20,
　　21,22,23,24,25,26,27,28
Algood, Nancy (Mrs.) 27
Algood, Sam. A., 35
Algood, Wm., 7
Algood, William, 1,2,3,4,5,6,7,11,
　　12,18,24
Allcorn, 6
Allcorn, John, 3,4,5,10
Allison, Robert D., 133,135
Allison, Robert Dallisro, 133
Alton, John, 7
Ament, I., 85
Ament, J., 85
Ament, John, 85
Amonet, 80
Amos, 51
Anderson, 100
Anderson, Jacob Jr., 99
Anderson, James, 98,99,100
Anderson, John, 98,99,100
Anderson, John A., 96
Anderson, Josiah, 99
Anderson, Preston, 98,99
Anderson, Rebecca, 98

Anderson, G., 33
Anderson, William P., 31
Ann, 139
Ann, Eslenor, 120
Anna, 138
Apple, M., 85
Apple, O., 85
Appomatox, 109
Archer, A. M., 127
Arichet, 85
Arkansas, 95,104,139,141
Arks. (Arkansas) 117
Arks, Kate, 120
Arnell, 118
Arnold, Cora, 126
Ashgrove, 13
Atlanta, Georgia, 105
Austin, F., 86
Austin, G., 86

B

Bable, Wm., 3
Baby, (Miss) 116
Baker, 85
Baker, W., 133
Baker, William, 30,32,46,97,133
Bald Knob, 54
Ballard, A., 86
Ballard, J., 86
Ballard, Jo., 86
Ballard, Polly, 33
Baltimore, 79
Bardstown, 106
Barnes, 44
Barnes, John, 57
Barnes, Thomas, 44
Barnes, Thomas (Esq.)45
Barnes, Thos., 43
Barnes, W. H., 135,136
Barnes, W. H., Sr., 136
Barr, 122
Bart, 125
Bartlett, Joseph, 57

Bartlett, Nathan, 28,67,68
Bate, (Col.) 104
Battle, Joel, 103
Batton, J. W., 38
Bauman, John, 3
Baxter, (Tenn.) 84
Beachen, J. R., 14
Bean's Station, 107
Bear Creek, 13,17,20,25,67,69,93,98,
    100,101
Beauregard, (Gen.) 105
Bell, B. T., 14,16,35
Bell, Benjamin, T., 16
Bell, J. T., 14
Bell, John, 13
Bell, W. T., 25
Bell, William T., 25
Bell, Wm. T., 35
Benson, E., 35
Benson, S., 85,86
Berk, F., 86
Berryville, Ark., 96
Bet., 127
Bever Creek, 131
Bill, 127,141
Billsworth, B. T., 16
Black Stables, 49
Blackburn, 87,89,91,92,94,95,128
Blackburn, Benjamin, 128
Blackburn, Benjamin J., 128
Blackburn's Fork, 90
Black Smoke Hills, 49
Blakemore, S. L., 5
Blair, George, 61,77
Bledsoe, 124
Blount, W. G., 31,56
Blount, W. T., 70
Blount, Willie, 70
Blount, Willie (Gov.) 31,56,71
Blunte, William, 71
Bohannon, Lewis, 99
Bolivar, 53
Borne, Lornes, 131
Bostick, L.H., 27
Bowling Green, 103
Boyd, A., 86
Boyd, Alexander, 83
Boyd, E. J., 86
Boyd, I., 85,86
Boyd, J., 85
Boyd, J. W., 83
Boyd, James S., 83
Boyd, John, 85
Boyd, L. J., 85
Boyd, Mary A., 83
Boyd, T. J., 85
Bradley, George, 24

Bragg, 106,107
Bragg, (Gen.) 106
Bragg, Braxton, (Gen.) 105
Brasel, C., 86
Breckenridge, J. C. (Gen.) 106
Brewington, Henry, 20,25
Bridges, Shadwick, 80
Brien, 104
Brien, (Capt.) 105
Brien, M. M. (Capt.) 103
Balley, (Mr.) 64
Brinley, B. F., 61
Bristol, 107
Bristol, Virginai, 143
Brock, 130
Brook, James, 130
Brown, Eake, 71,73
Brown, Eale, 70
Brown, Gideon, 78
Brown, Gifion, 74
Brown, Hezakiah, 62,76,74,77
Brown, James, 131
Brown, M., 63
Brown, Marlin, 75
Brown, Martin, 62,63,73,76
Brown, N. T., 20
Brown, Neil S., 20,81
Brown, S. W., 19,45,135
Brown, Stephen W., 135
Brown, Steven W., 19
Brown, T. N. W., 136
Brown, W., 36
Brown, William, 81
Brownlow, M. G., 110
Brunswick, 50
Buok, Isaac, 94,97
Buck, Jon. Jr., 24
Buckhanon, M., 118
Buckner, (Gen.) 105
Buell (Gen.) 105,106,145
Buffalo Valley, Tenn.,31,32,33,35
Buford, John H., 7
Bullington, L. M., 29,30
Bullock, Jess, 99
Bullock, John, 30
Burford, L. M., 90
Burnside, 107
Burnsides, 107
Burnsides, (Gen.) 106
Burton, A., 85
Burton, C. F., 85
Burton, S. D., 8,26
Burton, Stephen D., 24
Burton, Steven, 23
Butler, B. F. (Gen.) 107
Butler, C. F., 85
Butler County, 79,80

Byers, 52
Byrne, 82,138
Byrne, Ann, 131,139
Byrne, Brice, 139,140,141
Byrne, Dallas, 86
Byrne, L., (Esq.) 139

C

Cadmus, 47
Cage, John, 2,3
Cain, John, 36
Cahahan, W. M., 16
Calhan, W. W., 14
Camard, W., 86
Cameron, A., 86
Cameron, Mo., 89
Cameron, S., 86
Cameron, S. O., 86
Camp Chattanooga, 145
Camp Trousdale, 142,143
Campbell, 53
Camson,, S., 86
Cane Creek, 53,54,56,79
Caney Fork, 29,31,47,60,82,99,129, 136
Cannon County, 103,115
Cannon, N., 69,91
Cannon, N. (Gov.) 54
Cannon, Newton, 61,69,91
Cannon, Newton (Gov.) 54
Caplinger, Samuel, 11
Capner, Samuel, 15
Car, Elijah, 96,97
Carden (Lieut Col.) 103
Carland, J., 85,400
Carland, James, 85
Carlen, J., 85
Carlinger, Samuel, 6
Carlisle, Simon, 58,59,61
Carlton, John M., 101
Carnes, Becton, 104
Carr, C., 13
Carr, Henry, 55,77
Carr, James, 55
Carr, W. H., 94
Carr, William, 95
Carroll (Gov.) 88
Carroll, William, 67,72,78,88,91, 92,94
Carroll, William (Gov.) 28,40,41, 44,68
Carroll, Wm., 28,73,78,92,94,95
Carroll, Wm. (Gov.) 30,41,44,67, 129
Carson, George, 79,80
Carson, James, 80

Carson, Nathan, 80
Carsons, Nehemiah, 79,80
Carter, F., 96
Carter, F. C., 96
Carter, Sion, 96
Carthage, 47
Cass, Lew, 66
Cassetty, S. W., 101
Cassetty, Sampson W., 101
Cates, Thomas, 101
Cath, Mary, 122
Crowell Catholic Cathedral, 49
Carve, C., 17
Cedar Bridge, 37
Cedar Creek, 12,15,24
Chaffin, 107
Chanard, W., 86
Charley, 125
Chattanooga, 105,106,107,110
Chesapeake Bay, 109,112
Cheatham County, 103
Chestnut Mound, 72
Chestnut Mound, Tenn., 58
Chicamauga River, 106
Chind (negro) 98
Choat, John, 57
Choate, Thomas, 92,94,95,97
Claborn, W., 122
Claiborn, A., 122
Claiborn, Amelia Weldon, 118
Claiborn, Bettie, 127
Clark, 3,18,136
Clark, Benjamin, 1,3,6,18
Clark, Gilbert, 1
Clark, Henry B., 70
Clark, Isaac, 88,96
Clark, J. D., 65
Claysville, 84
Cleburne's Brigade, 10
Cleghorn, John, 43
Clement, Ann H. (Mrs.) 126
City Point, 109,112
Cobey, Fern, 83
Cofeld, Willis, 12
Cofell, Willie, 10
Cofell, Willis, 9,10
Coffee County, 103
Coffeld, Willis, 12
Cole, Anderson, 98
Cole, Josiah, 32
Coleman, Jim, 110
College Grove, 106
Collins, 91
Collins, William, 76,77
Columbia, Tenn. 118
Confederate Army, 111
Cook, C. W., 51
Choat, Austin, 98

Cook, Calvin Whitley, 51
Cook, Charles, 133
Cook, Jess A., 52
Cook, Margaret, 51
Cook, R. F., 51
Cook, Richard C. M., 52
Cook, Richard, F., 54
Cooks, Richard F., (Maj.) 91
Cook, Richard F. C. M., 53
Cookeville, 106
Cookeville, 129
Cookeville, Tenn., 1,5,9,12,13,15,21, 29,30,34,35,36,37,38,39,40,41,42, 43,44,45,46,47,52,55,56,57,79,83, 85,89,90,102,111,112,114,115,116, 118,119,120,121,122,124,126,127, 128,130,131,132,133,135,137,139, 140,142,143,144,145
Cooper, 136
Corinth, Miss., 103,104,105,106
Corley, Nathan, 6
Cornwell, David, 86
Cornwell, E., 86
Cornwell, Rich., M., 80
Covington, 127
Covingtons, 111
Cowen, B. C., 38
Cragwall, W. J., 21
Crook, Charles, 133
Crooked Creek, Ark., 139,140
Crooms, Peter, 81
Crowell, J., 86
Crutcher, Fly, 15
Crutcher, I. W., 19
Crutcher, J. W., 135
Crutcher, Joseph W., 135,136
Cullem, George, 55
Cullom, George, 77
Cullom, J. H., 86
Cumberland, 47
Cumberland Gap, 103
Cumberland Mountain, 84
Cumberland River, 21,61,65,70,71,72, 74,103
Cumming, Wm. B., 96

D

Dalton, Georgia, 106,107
Dan, 51
Dandridge, 107
Daniel, Graham, 72
Davidson, H. L., 22
Davidson, H. L. (Hon.) 21
Davidson, Hughes L., 21
Davis, (Dr.) 116
Davis,(Maj.) 103

Davis, J. J., 106
Dawson, W. M., 35
Day, John T., 90
Dearing, J. P., 130
Debrell, 99
Decatur, Alabama, 104
Deer Creek, 120
DeKalb County, 88
Dennison, Joe,99
Denny, J., 85
Denny, S. J., 85
Denny, Virgil, 31,32,33,
Dick, 124
Dick, (negro) 58
Dillard, J. L., 18
Dillard, John L., 18
Dillard, William, 24
Dillard, Wm., 25
Dillon, John, 18
Dillon, John J., 18
Ditty, A., 53
Ditty, John, 79,135
Doak, 111
Doak, Andy, 111
Dodson, 130
Dodson, James, 130
Donnell, 15
Donnall, George, 15
Dorcus, 139Dorinda, 49
Dorinda, 49
Double Springs, 52
Double Springs, Tenn., 53
Douglas, 11
Douglass, Burchet, 7
Douglas, Burchett, 11
Douglas, Elmore, 1,3,4,5,6
Douglas, Ennis, 5,12,24
Douglass, J. M., 97
Douglas, John, 13,17
Douglas, Monroe, 15
Dowell, John, 92
Drapers, 29
Drury's Bluff, 108
Dry Fork, 40
Duncan, G. A., 17
Dunivan, C., 85
Dunnivan, E., 81,85
Dyer, Robison, 133

E

Eatherly, Jonathan, 21
Eaton, 120
Eaton, Lou,124
Edmonson, Catsby, 110
Edwards, J. L., 66
Eldridge, Calvin, 40

Elen, 116
Elgin, Geo., 62,63,76,77
Eli, 117,120
Elias, 52
Elizabeth, 53,139
Elkhorn, 146
Ellison, 53
Ely, Lewis Fletcher, 65
Elylas, 123
Embry, Patsy, 129
England, 104,146
Ensor, (Tenn.) 81,82,83
Ensor, W., 85
Ethiopia, 138
Evans, E., 85
Evans, G., 85
Evans, J., 85
Evans, T., 85
Everlance, Bolivar, 52

F

Fain, R. E., 85
Falling Waters, 7,30,41,44,55,
   56,130
Fane, Larester, 124
Fannie, 117
Fayetteville, 104,109
Fent, 117
Fergerson, 35
Ferrell, Andrew, 4,5
Ferrell, Jefferson, 75
Ferry, Hart, 18
Fisk, 96,100
Fisk, Amul, 88
Fisk, Arnol, 87
Fisk, Madison, 132
Fisk, Moses, 88
Fisk, Omel, 88
Fisk, Sarah Perry, 88
Fats, T. W., 13
Fletcher, J., 85
Fords, (Col.) 103
Ford, C. L., 85
Ford, C. R., 85,135
Ft. Donaldson, 103,104
Ft. Sanders, 107
Fowler, Jonathin, 26
Fowlers, 131
Fox, C., 86
France, 146
Francis, 138
Frasier, Henry, 132
Frasure, Henry, 132
Freeze, J. C., 34
Fulton (Col.) 109

G

Gailbreath, William, 58,59
Gainsboro, 54,59
Garack, T. M., 94
Gardenshire, Benjamin, 57
Garland, J., 85
Gee, John M., 1
Gentry, L., 86
Gentry, S., 86
Gentry, Silas, 86
Gentry, W., 86
George, 117,120,121,122,123,125
George, Will, 111
Georgia, 66
Gillehan, Thomas, 78
Gillen, Elizabeth, 141
Gilliam, G. Edemound, 21
Gilmore, James, 37
Gipson, John M., 101
Girard,(College) 125
Gishen, 50
Glade Creek, 55
Glasgow, Kentucky, 106
Gleaves, Guy J., 21
Gleaves, W., 86
Gleaves, W. L., 86
Glenn, Giles, 15
Glenn, Giles H., 15
Goldron, Jno. M., 15
Goodbar, J. M., 94
Goodgains, Sallie, 52
Gore, William, 131
Goss, 111
Grace, C., 86
Gracie, (Gen.) 107
Graham, Daniel, 28,30,31,44,60,67,
   68,72,74,78,88,92,129
Grandville, 65
Grant, 104,105
Grant (Gen.) 107,108,109
Grant, U. S., (Gen.) 110
Green, Fannie, 116,120,123,124
Greensville, 124
Griffireth, George, 99
Goshen, 50,51
Gus, 117

H

Hail, Moody P., 11
Hall, William B., 99
Ham, J. E., 104
Hambleton's (line) 3
Hamier, Bobby H., 126
Hanbery, Meshack, 71
Hancock, (Gen.) 108

G

Hancock County, 137
Hanna, (negro) 58
Hardee, (Gen.) 105
Hardester, Samuel, 128
Hardyer, Alfred, 128
Hare, Saml. E., 79
Harvey, M., 85
Harp, 19
Harp, Burton, 19
Harriett, 52
Harris, E. K., 119
Harris, F. (Judge) 34
Harris, Isham G. (Gov.) 8
Harris, John, 101,129
Harris, Lewis, 11
Harrison, Samuel, 36
Harrison, Stith, 94,129
Hatton, Robert (Col.) 103
Hawes, D. W., 26
Hawes, I., 85
Hawes, J., 85
Hawes, John, 85
Hawkins County, 42
Haws, William Oscar, 52
Hays, Narcissa, 88
Helens, Ruth, 33
Hendersonville, 64
Henrian, 127
Henry, John, 37
Henry, Joseph, 37
Hensley, John, 129
Herbert, J., 85
Herd, Jo., 99
Hern, Jacob S., 21
Hicksford, 124
High, Dave (Mrs.) 79,81,82,83,
    85
Hill, (Col.) 104
Hill, Thomas, 37
Hill, William, 99
Hillham Road, 89,90,92,102
Hills, W., 99
Hodge, 116
Holdman, Reech A., 3
Holey, Henderson, 15
Holliday, J., 85
Holliday, T., 85
Hollis, 111
Hollis, James, 111
Hollis, M. L., 104,105,111
Hollis, Will, 111
Holloway, Richard, 21
Holoman's, 29
Hookery, Jonathan F., 11,21

Hooks, Isaac, 5
Hoolman, John, 15
Hopkins, Thomas, 30,41
Houston, 49
Houston, James, 60
Houston, Sam., 74
Houston, Sam. (Gov.)130
Houston, Samuel, 60
Howard, James, 99
Howard, John (Mrs.) 35,36,37,38,39,40
Howard, William, 99
Howe, William (Esq.) 43
Huddleston, 44
Huddleston, B. C. (Judge) 41,42,43,44,
    45,46
Huddeston, B. C.(Mrs.) 47,48,49,50,51,
    52,53
Huddleston, Charles, 30,41,42,43,44,45
Huddleston, Charley, 42
Huddleston, Chas., 45,46
Huddleston, David, 46
Huddleston, Davis, 30
Huddleston, Hugh G.,95
Huddleston, Isaac A., 30
Huddleston, Isaac L.,30
Huddleston, J. A. 85
Huddleston, J. E., 85
Huddleston, J. L., 30
Huddleston, J. L. H., 94
Huddleston, J. T., 85
Huddleston, John C.,42
Huddleston, John L., 30
Huddleston, Jordan F., 45
Huddleston, Lewis, 30
Huddleston, S. E. H., 85
Huddleston, Thos. C., 45
Hudgens, Dudley, 57
Hufey, Robert G., 74
Hughes, Gideliah, 13
Hughes, John P., 13
Hughes, Wm. L., 13
Hulit, 120
Hunter, Hardy, 4
Hunter, Joseph, 130
Hunter, William, 43
Huntsville, Alabama, 104
Huston, Sam, 92
Hyder, J. D., 135,136
Hyder, Joseph, 135
Hyder, Joseph D., 136

I

Illinois, 111

Indian Creek, 29,60,61,70,71,72,
　73,74,75,76,77,78,82,86,141,
Indian Mad Waters, 49
Indiana, 110
Ingram, Thomas, 42
Ingram, Thos., 45,46
Ingram, William, 42
Ingram, Wm., 42
Irwin, Rashford, 42
"Isaac of York", 122
Isle of Wight, 123
Italian Opera, 125

J

Jackson, A. A. (Gen.) 127
Jackson, C. W., 22
Jackson, Calvin W., 22
Jackson County, 29,30,44,46,52,54,
　58,59,60,61,62,63,64,65,66,70,
　71,72,73,74,75,76,77,78,79,81,
　82,87,89,92,93,94,95,97,98,101,
　128,130,91
Jackson, Daniel, 10
Jackson, Job M., 37
Jacob, 48
Jake, 96
James, 58
James, Alston, L., 5
James, J., 85,107,108,109,112,128
Jared, B. B., 86
Jared, Douglas, 2,
Jared, J., 85,86
Jared, John, 2,32,85
Jared, Joseph, 139,140
Jared, Lawrence Byrn, 82
Jared, Lorance, 140
Jared, Malinda, 82,84,137,138,139,142
Jared, Martha R., 82
Jared, Mat R., 82
Jared, Matthew, 82
Jared, Moses, 33
Jentry, R., 86
Jared, R. F., 144
Jared, Robert F., 144
Jared, S. A., 85
Jared, S. R., 85
Jared, William, 82,140,141
Jared, Wirt Jones, 2
Jeffries, (Capt.) 118
Jeffries, Benjamin C., 41
Jennings, W. B., 21
Jentry, W., 86
Jernigan, A. J., 110
Jerusalem, 138
Jimmie, 118,127
Jimmy, 116

Jinny, 120
John, 50,51,142
John, Frisk, 12
John, Jared, 86
Johnney, 118
Johns, Elijah, 25
Johnson, 107,139
Johnson, (Mr.) 64
Johnson, A. S. (Gen.) 103
Johnson, Andrew, 90
Johnson, Andrew, (Gov.) 136
Johnson, Byrum C., 36
Johnson, Daniel, 15
Johnson, Joseph, 21
Johnson, Lamb, 43
Johnson, M. Samuel, 43
Johnson, Robert, 21
Johnson, Samuel, 40
Johnson, W., 85
Johnson, W. J., 85
Johnson, William, 15,85
Johnson, Z., 14
Johnson, Zealous, 14
Johnston, (Gen.) 104
Johnston, A. S., 105
Johnston, Bushrod (Gen.) 105
Jones, Elijah, 13
Jones, James C., 13,17
Jones, John, 86
Jones, McClellon, 61
Jones, William (Esq.) 41
Jonnie, 122
Jonny, 117,120
Joseph, 58,137
Josiah, 58
Justice, Albert, 108

K

Kate, 127
Kate (old) 96
Keeble, R. H. (Lt. Col.) 105
Keeble (Col.) 109
Keith, F. G., 92
Kennedy, John, 131
Kentucky, 79,80,103,105,106,110
Kerr, A. F., 85
Kerry, A. K., 85
Keykendall, Jess, 91
Kings River, 140
Kingslow, Bird C., 52
Kirby, Henry W., 64
Kizzie Ray, 51
Knoxville, 41,106,107
Knoxville, Tenn., 106
Kovers, John, 74
Ku Klux Klan, 111

Kuykendall, Jess, 91,97
Kuykendall, Mathew, 92,93
Kuykendall, Noah, 100
Kuykendall, Peter, 93

L

L. V., 139
Land of Nod, 48
Lane, A. R., 42,86
Lane, J. Turner, 45
Lane, Jacob A., 42
Lane, Turner, 45
Larence, 139
Laycock, Martin, 102
Lea, Luke, 30,54,61,69,91
Lebanon, 15,27
Lebanon, Tenn., 21
Ledbeter, Charles, 9,10
Lee, 108,113
Lee (Gen.) 107,109,112
Leftwich, W., 85,86
Leftwich, William, 85,86
Lester, Sterling H., 55
Legrange, 125
Leiper, H., 124
Lewis, (negro) 58
Ligeard, Henry, 37
Lincoln,(Pres.)109,145
Little Caney Fork, 30
Little, Leroy B., 87
Livingston, 23
Livingston Co., Missouri, 47
Loe, (Miss) 124
Logan, 51
Longstreet, 107
Longstreet (Gen.) 106
Louisa, 50
Louisville, Ky., 65,106,110,113
Low, (Capt.) 105
Low, A. R., 42
Low, E. P., 17
Lowe, A. R., 85
Lowe, H. R., 86
Maclinburg, 119
Maddux, D., 86
Maddux, G., 85
Maddux, G. H., 86
Maddux, G. J., 85
Maddux, George, 85
Maddux, H., 86
Maddux, J. G., 85
Maddux, J. H., 86
Maddux, J. M., 86
Maddux, S., 86
Maddux, S. H., 86

Maddux, T. J., 85
Malinda, 141
Malone, D., 85
Malone, G., 85
Malone, Vance, 85
Malone, Y., 85
Mamie, 127
Manassa, 146
Manns, Robert H. M., 99
Marchbanks, 13,23,31,131
Marchbanks, Burton, 17
Marchbanks, Josiah, 139
Marchbanks, William, 28
Marchbanks, Wm., 131
Maria, 50
Marley, Young, 86
Martha, 138
Martins Creek, 81
Martin, George, 13
Mary, 22,116
Maryland, 79,112
Masidonia, 53
Massa, H. Y., 15
Massa, John, 55
Massa, O. D., 55,56
Materia Medica, 119
Matthews, A., 85
Maupin (Dr.) 122
Maxwell, J., 86
Maxwell, Samuel, 54
Mayhew, John, 38
McAuly, John, 99
McCall, 127
McCallahan, P., 86
McClain, J. L., 18
McClain, J. T. 15
McClain, Joseph L., 14
McClain, Josiah L., 18
McClain, W. S., 57
McClelland, 50
McClelland, John, 50
McClendon, Thomas, 1
McClinttock, David, 29
McColitus, 14
McCormack, John, 96
McCullough, Bell, 110
McCullough, P., 86
McDaniel, 2
McDaniel, Daniel, 55
McDaniel, H. C., 65,66
McDaniel, H. L., 55,66
McDaniel, Henry L., 66
McDaniel, Henry L, 66
McDaniel, J. W., 83,86,135,136
McDaniel, James W., 83,135
McDaniel, Jas. W., 83

McDaniel, R. B., 19,135
McDaniel, Stephen, 7
McDaniel, Steve, 7
McDaniel, W., 135,467
McDonald, A. J., 16,18,25
McDonald, Andrew, J. M., 21
McDonald, Stephen, 7
McDonald, W. F., 25
McDowell, J. W., 86
McDowell, R. W., 85
McGavock, D., 30
McGavock, Alex., 88
McGavock, D., 73
McGavock, D. M., 31,41,60,70,71
McGavock, D. R., 67
McGavock, D. W., 68
McGavock, H. W., 44
McGavock, T. M., 129
McGavock, Wm., 88
McGavock, W. M., 72
McGhee, George, 131
McKee, J., 86
McKee, J. G., 86
McKee, J. Y., 86
McKee, Leaner, 33
McKenney, James, 131
McKesicks, Daniel, 12
McKinley, 17,55,59,60,61
McKinley, Eliza, 65,74
McKinley, Hays, 74
McKinley, Henry, 13,17,69
McKinley, James, 19,25,61,62,63,
    64,65,70,75,76,77,79,80
McKinley, James M., 26
McKinley, Mathew, 58,60,79,80
McKinley, Mollie (Mrs.) 58,60,61,
    62,63,64,65,66,67,69,70,71,72,
    73,74,75,76,77,78
McKinley, P. G., 74
McKinley, R. B., 61
McKinley, R. M., 59
McKinley, Robert, 58,59,62,72,78
McKinley, S. M., 74
McKinley, Sally, 58
McKinley, Sarah, 74
McKinly, James, 55
McKinney, 17
McKinney, Henry, 13,67
McKinney, James, 7,23,25
McKinny, 135
McKinny, Henry, 17
McKinny, James, 135
McKinny, James M., 136
McLelon, Thomas, 6
McMinn, Joseph (Gov.) 41,55
Mechlinburg, Va., 118
Meeks, (Journal), 53
Meeks, Wm., 52

Methodist, 49
Methodist Episcopal Church, 9
Mexico, 53
Mexican War, 52
Miariam, 139
Mill Creek, 92
Miller Bro. & Sister, 35
Miller, James M., 37
Miller, J. M., 35
Miller, Jno. (Capt.) 38
Miller, John, 40
Miller, Robert, 36,37
Miller, Samuel, 36
Milly, (negro) 58
Mine Lick Creek, 129
Miranda, 51
Mires, Bashaba, 84
Miriam, Price H., 141
Mississippi Gap, 103
Mississippi River, 103
Missouri, 50
Miss (Mississippi) 145
Mitchell (Gen.) 145
Mitchell, Daniel West, 115
Mitchell, J. A., 110
Mitchell, Myra, 111
Mitchell, Myra Anne, 115
Mitchell, William, 42
Mobile, Ala., 105
Monroe, 35
Montgomery, 105
Montgomery, Alex., 82
Montgomery County, 36
Montgomery, Robert, 132
Moore (Capt.) 105
Moore, R., 33,97
Moore, Robert, 75
Moore, Russell, 19,30,32,33,36,39,
    45,83,97,133,135,136
Morgan, John, 81
Morgantown, 80
Morris, T. E., 13
Morris, T. E., 13
Morrison, R. C. E., 80
Morristown, 107
Mount Richardson, 60,79
Mumfordville, 106
Murfreesboro, 72,103,104,105,106,109,
    110
Murfreesborough, 41,44,55,67
Murmsey, W. B. A., 20
Murphey, 96
Murphree, 131
Murphree, Enoch, 131
Murphy, John (Sergt.) 105

N

Nails Schook, 35
Nancy, 50
Nashville, Tenn., 8,13,30,31,38, 49,54,60,65,83,91,92,94,105, 106,110,113,129,130,136,146
Nawvou, Ill, 137
Nawvou Mormonism, 137
Neal (Col.) 104,105
Ned (negro) 58
Neely, M. C., 110
Neely, Med., 110
Neese, Dora, 84
Nelson, M., 92
Nelson, R., 13,17,46,69,70,74,91, 92,130
Nelson, R. N., 78
Nelson, Richard, 46
Nelson, T. R., 91
Nelson, W. E., 13,17,100
Netherton, Mary, 37
New, J. C., 104
New, J. C. (Lieut.) 105
Newman, E. J., 85
Newman, J., 85
New York, 112
Nicholas, Thomas, 87,90,91,92,93, 95,98
Nichols, Betsy Ann, 83
Nichols, D., 85,86
Nichols, D. H., 143,144
Nichols, Dave, 82
Nichols, Davey (Mrs.) 81,83
Nichols, David, 85,137,144,145, 146
Nichols, J. P., (Mrs.) 84
Nichols, John H., 143
Nichols, M. J., 142,145,146
Nichols, Moses Joseph, 142,146
North Carolina, 1,41,55,64
Northview, 126
Noussa, Lawson, (Dr.) 132

O

Oaks, H., 86
O'Connor, M. F., 8
Ohio, 49,110
Old Tipton, 120
Oldham, Nicholas, 100
Oliver, John, 90
Organ, (Oregon) 52,53
Orleans, 49
Osage River, 140
Ott, Capt., 106
Ott, W. A., (Capt.) 105
Overall, Jon., 86
Overton County, 13,17,20,25,28,36,40, 67,68,69,89,131
Owen, A. H., 89
Owen, Susan S., 88,89
Owens, A. H., 88
Owham, N., 132
Owham, Nicholas, 132

P

Pace, John, 80
Page, John, 37
Pall Ridge, 54
Palmer, J. B., 103
Panco (Father) 49
Parched, E., 86
Pareu - Adeu, 48
Parker, William, 99
Patrick, J. A., (Lieut.) 105
Patross, John, 89,90,94
Patross, Matthew, 93
Peak, W. M., 79
Peak, Wm. P., 53
Pearce, Walsey, W., 42
Pearson, Bob, 87,88,90,92,93,102
Pearson, I., 96
Pearson, J., 96
Pearson, Jo., 98
Pearson, Joe, 88
Pearson, Joseph, 89,90,92,94,95,96,97, 98,100,101,102
Pearson, N. J., 97
Peek, (Dr.) 123
Peek, James, 20,96
Peek, Robert, 20,25,57
Pekin, 65
Pennington, John, 99
Pennsylvania, 110
Perkins, Betsy, 51
Perkins, John, 52
Perkins, Louisa, 52
Perkins, Ruben, 50,51
Perkins, Reubin, 128
Perryville, 106
Peter (slave) 99
Petersburg, 107,108,109
Petersburg, Va., 112
Petree, John, 89
Peyron, James, 104
Phillips, 138
Phillips, 88
Phillips, Charles, 101

Phy, Josiah, 95
Phy, Phillips, 94
Phys, Phillip, 93
Pigeon Creek, 130
Pigeon Roost Creek, 128
Pittsburg, 49
Pittsburg Landing, 103,104
Platte, 50
Pleasant Grove, 85
Pleasant Grove Fountain, 49
Plunket, J., 85
Point Lookout, 110
Point Lookout, Maryland, 109
Point Lookout Prison, Md., 113
Point Lookout Prison, 112
Pointer, John B., 98
Polk, James K., 61
Polk, James K. (Gov.) 30,46
Polly (negro) 96
Pool, J. O., 65
Port Melthall Junction, 107
Poteet, Thomas J., 136
Poteet, Thos. J., 134
Potiphars Prison, 148
Potomac River, 109,110,112
Potts (Squire) 21,22
Prairie Township, 140
Price, 15
Prichet, 86
Prim's Corner--
Prim, James, 1, 5
Princeton, P. O., 53
Pris (negro) 58
Providence, 11
Providence Camp, 18
Pulium, J., 85
Putnam County, 65,85,86,94,102
Pys, Phillips, 89

Q

Quarles, 8,23
Quarles, Ann, 28,57

R

Rainey, John, 92
Ramsey, George, 133
Ramsey, James, 133
Ramsey, John, 87,91,94,97,131
Ramsey, Randolph, 87
Ramsey, W. B. A., 81
Ramsey, William, 100
Randolf, John, 39
Randolf, Lancaster, 36
Randolph, Mary, 39

Raulston, C., 85
Ray, James, 79
Ray, Joseph, 54
Ray, O. W. R., 8
Ray, Wm., I., 79
Rays, Samuel, 53
Ready, Horace (Maj.) 105
Remsey, John, 87
Rhea, 50
Rhea, Nancy, 53
Rhea, R. S., 100
Rhea, S., 53
Rhea, Seabird (Col.) 52,53
Rhoulstons Stand, 79
Richard, Isaac, 95,98
Richmon, 146
Richmonds, Isaac, 90
Richmond, 107,108,109
River, J. L., 37
Roan (Dr.) 116
Roaring River, 86,88,89,90,92,97
Rock Island, 67
Roger, C., 86
Roberts, Jo. W., 132
Roberts, Robert, 37
Roberts, William, 99
Robertson, Ann, 71
Robertson, Christopher, 71
Robertson, Elijah, 71
Robertson, Elizabeth, 71
Robertson, L. W., 21
Robertson, Mary, 71
Rock Springs, 77
Rock Spring Creek, 55,60
Rock Spring Valley, 60
Rockey Springs, (Tenn.) 85
Rosencrantz, (Gen.) 106
Ross, H., 11
Ross, Henry, 1,3,4,5,7,10,12
Ruben, 50
Rushing (Capt.) 104
Rushing, John R., 104
Rushing, M. R., (Capt.) 103
Rutherford County, 103,105

S

St. John, H. J., 103
St. Joseph, 52
St. Louis, 49,50
St. Paul, 137
Samuel, 137,138
Sandy, Daniel, 99
Sarah, 139
Savage, William R., 90
Savage, Wm. A., 131

Sawyer, D., 86
Scanland, C. R., 29
Scanland, William, 93
Scarlet, 132
Scarlet, I. M., 133
Scarlet, M. N., 133
Scott, James, 98
Scott, R., 85
Scott, Ralph, 35
Scott, V. R., 85
Scruggs, 113
Scudder, B., 85
Scudder, M., 85
Searcy, Bennett, 56
Searcy, Robert, 41
Searly, Robert, 70
Seartland, 53
Seartland, John (Col.) 53
Selby, John, 23
Seleys, 24
Selvy, J. J., 19
Selvy, John J., 19
Selvy, Loyd S., 19
Settle, Leroy B., 93
Shelbyville, 104,106
Shelton, William, 87,91
Sherly, Noah, 40
Sherlys, John J., 24
Sherman (Gen.) 107
Shiloh, 111,146
Shirley, John W., 8
Shirley, Rebecca, 36
Shoat, Thomas, 89,90
Shoats, Austin, 91
Simpson, John W., 29
Sims, 99
Sims, W. G., 46,99,100
Sims, William G., 98,99,100
Smith, (Dean) 115
Smith, Austin, 115
Smith, Austin W., 103,111,112
Smith, Austin Wheeler, 114
Smith, Billy, 117
Smith County, 5,11,64
Smith, J. G., 108
Smith, John, 111
Smith, Myra Anne, 114
Smith, R., 100
Smith, R. G., 103,104,105,106,
    107,109,110,111,112,115
Smith, T., 85
Smithland, 49
Solomon, 49
Somervell, A. C., 122,124,125
Somervill, Augustine C. (Dr.)
    116,117,118,120,122,124,125,126
Somervell, Fannie, 122,124

Somervell, Gus. A. Claiborn, 121
Somervell, J. J. (Rev.) 126
Somervell, John W., 123
Somervell, John W. (Capt.) 127
Somervell, Kate, 118
Somervell, Mary B., 126
Somervell, Wm., 126
Sons of Europe, Asia, Africa, 48
Souger, D., 86
South Carolina, 109,145
South Street, 135
Sparks, Wm., 40
Sparta, 23,41,49,64,98,100,102,106,
    132,144
Sparte, 52
Spencer, 106
Sperry, C. R., 132
Sperry, Charles, 132
Sperry, Charles R., 132
Spery, V., 86
Spivy, V., 86
Spring of Castalia, 49
Spring Street, 135
Stamps, James, 37
Stamps, School, 37
Stamps, William, 37
Stark, George, (Dr.) 124
Stewarts, 10
Stipe, Rebecca, 96,102
Stokes, W., 85
Stokes, William J., 38
Stone, E. H., 34
Stone, Joshua R., 98
Sullivan, Jordan, 61,74
Sumner, I. J., 30
Sumner County, 13,64,103
Susan, 51
Swan, Moses M., 88
Sweats, 56
Sweats, Isaac, 56
Swinney, William, 14
Sypert, Lorance, 21

T

Tally, Christiany, 40
Tary, Somervell, 118
Tarry, Lem., 118
Tarry, Mollie, 118
Taylor, George Anderson, 116,117,118,
    120,122,123,124,125
Taylor, I. J. (Mrs.) 123
Taylor, Isaac, 56,99
Taylor, Isaac (Junior)56
Taylor, Mary H., 127
Taylor, Mollie, 116
Taylor, Nathaniel, 44

Taylor, Sam., 126
Taylor, Tom, 120
Taylorsville, 14
Ted, 121
Temple, Charlotte, 57
Tenn. Polytechnic Inst., 111,115
Tennessee, James W., 40
Tennessee River, 103,104,106
Terry, 90
Terry, Benton (Mrs.) 116,118,119,
    120,121,122,124,125,126,127
Terry, Curry, 93
Terry, Curtis, 57,101
Terry, George, 120
Terry, James, 89,91,93,94,95,98
Terry, John, 95,133
Terry, John, (J.P.) 92
Terry, Ninson M., 101
Terry, William, 20,25,26
Terry, Wm. A., 95
Texas, 52
Thomas, James B., 21
Thompson, 51
Thompson, Regin (Dr.) 22
Tinsley, H., 25
Tipton County, Tenn., 126
Tom, 96,127
Tousans, James, 128
Townsdon, William, 53
Townsend, James, 56
Travis, Jeremiah, 101
Trigg, Stephen, 36
Trousdale, (Camp) 103
Trumit, H. T., 8
Trumit, P. P., 8
Tullahoma, 106
Tupelo, Mississippi, 105
Turner, Edward, 64
Turner, J. S., 66,79,82,87
Turner, John S., 66,82
Turner, John T., 79
Turner, S., 87

U

University of Va., 116,118,120,
    122,124
Uthey, Jeffries (Col.) 120

V

Vaden, Altha, (Mrs.) 128,130,131,
    133
Vaden, Altha Denton, 129,131,134,
    135,136
Vally, S., 35
Van Buren County, 96

Vance, William R., 82
Vandever, 35
Vandever (Mrs.) 35
Vannerson, Alf, 64
Vannerson, Alfred, 58,59
Veniery's, 53
Vice, (negro) 99
Vick, A. W., 14,18
Virginia, 51,106,107,109,143,145
Vivian, 138
Vass, Jno. F., 20
Vass, John F., 134

W

Walla Walla Valley, 52
Wallace, Jane, 73
Wallace, Mathew, H., 95
Wallace, Matthew, 97
Wallace, Nathan W., 95
Wallace, Samuel, 65,66
Wallace, Wade H., 55
Wallace, Sarah, 55,61,77
Wallam, J., 74
Walter, 127
Walton, 79,80
Walton, Isaac, 70
Walton Road, 61,64
Ward, Bryan, 14
Ward, Stevenson D., 130
Warren, 99
Warren County, 64
Warrentown, 117,122
Wartrace, 106
Washington, 52,118
Washington City, 110
Watts, J. H., 61
Watson, 49
Wayman, Albert H., 15
Webb House, 108
Welch, John, 95
Welch, John W., 8
Welches, 41
Well, 122
Wesley Chapel, 86
West, (Mrs.) 142
Wheeler, David, 25
Whitaker, Jacob, 5
White, 15
White County, 30,31,41,42,44,45,54,
    55,56,79,84,95,96,98,100,130,132
    144
White, E. A., 15
White, Edward, 15
White, George, 9,10
White, John, 16
White, L., 15

White, L. H., 15
White, L. W., 15
White Plains, 8
White, S. W., 15
White, S. W., 15
White, Samuel T., 12
Whiteacer, James, 37
Whitefield, Jim, 51
Whitehead, H., 85
Whitley, 52,53
White Plains, 57,90,96,102
White River, 140
Wilcher, 111
Wilhite, Solomon, 99
Wilkerson, 136
Will, 120
William, 139
William, George, 10
Williams, Absolom, 101,130
Williams, Henry, 55
Williams, J. W., 126
Williams, Jobe, 116
Williamson County, 106
Will's Valley, 106
Wilson (Col.) 104
Wilson County, 1,2,4,5,6,7,9,10,
    11,12,14,16,18,22,24,25,103
Wimberly, Alf., 108
Witherspoon, J. M. (Lieut)105
Wood, Granville (Capt.) 103
Woodard, (Hezekiah, 9
Woodbury, 103,110
~~Woodbury, Tenn., 110~~
Woodcock, James, 12
Woods, Lurary, 12
Woodstock, James, 12
Wrather, B., 5

Y

Yates, Dow, 85
Yates, W., 85
Yates. Woodson, 85
Young , 31,78
Young, 138
Young, A. D., 138
Young, C., 86
Young, David, 31
Young, Effie Boyd, 139,140
Young, Effie Boyd (Mrs.) 137,142,144
  145
Young, Felix R., 86
Young, Hayden (Mrs.)143

Young, Jacob, 55,61,75,77
Young, J. E., 86
Young, J. H., 86
Young, John, 102
Young, Jno. G., 46
Young, Jon C., 17
Young, L., 86
Young, Mark, 33
Young, Marley, 86
Young, P., 86
Young, R. B., 138
Young, Robert, 86
Young, Roda Byrne, 137
Young, Sam, 73

PUTNAM COUNTY

FAMILY RECORD
JAMES PRIM – WILLIAM ALGOOD MONTGOMERY DEED
1808

Owned by Mrs. Lula Algood and Mrs. Alfred Algood, Cookeville, Tennessee.

Copied by Miss Pearl Kuykendall, Mrs. Allie Loftis, Mrs. John Richardson.

This indenture made this eleventh day of July in the Year of our Lord One thousand Eight hundred and Eight Between James Prim of the County of Wilson and State of Tennessee of the one part and William Algood Montgomery County and State of North Carolina of the other part witnesseth that the said James Prim for and in consideration of the sum of Two hundred and Thirty five Dollars to him in hand paid on or before the Sealing or delivering of these presents the receipt of is hereby acknowledged by the aforesaid James Prim unto the aforesaid William Algood and the said James Prim for himself his heirs doth hereby bargain sale and convey and confirm unto him the aforesaid William Algood his Heirs Executors Administrators and assigns forever a certain tract or parcel of Land situated in Wilson County and State of aforesaid and bounded as follows viz: Beginning on a poplar at the South west corner of the field in Benjamin Clarks line and running from said poplar North Seventeen degrees West twelve poles to a Hickory & whit Oak Thence North Seventy degrees west forty poles to a small Hickory on the top of a ridge thence North sixty five poles to a dogwood thence East forty two poles to a dogwood thence North Twenty four poles to a beach thence East fifty Two poles to a stake thence South one hundred and eighty poles to a stake said Prims Corner thence West to the beginning by estimation fifty five acres and one half including the plantation whereon Thomas McClendon now lives be the same more or less which trade or parcel of Land with all and every of its appurtenances thereunto belonging or otherwise appertaining the said James Prim for himself his heirs Executors Administrators or assigns hath hereby sold Conveyed Released and confirmed unto the said William Algood his heirs Executors Administroators and assigns and the said James Prim for himself his heirs to and with the said William Algood his heirs & that the said James Prim his heirs & shall warrent and forever defend the same Land with all and every of its members from all Lawful claims or Claim of any Person or persons unto the said William Algood and his heirs assigns forever in witness whereof I have hereunto set my hand and Seal the day and year above wirtten in presents of John M Gee

James Prim (X) his mark SEAL

Elmore Douglas   Ackd.
Gilbert Clark

State of Tennessee Wilson County 1, Henry Ross Register of said County I do hereby certify that the written Deed is duly Registered in Book D. P, 298 the 25th February 1811.

Henry Ross Register

James Prim 55½ acres
    Deed to
William Algood
Recorded in Book D. Page 198

RECORDS OF MRS. LULA ALGOOD (CON)

    This Indenture made this fourth day of December in the Year of Our Lord onr Thousand Eight hundred and Eleven Between John Cage of the County of Wilson and State of Tennessee of the one part and William Algood of the County and State aforesaid of the other part Witnesseth that the said John Cage for and in the consideration of the sum of five hundred Dollars to him in Hand paid the Receipt whereof is hereby acknowledged hath bargained Sold conveyed and comfirmed unto the aforesaid William Algood a certain tract or parcel of Land lying in the County of Wilson and Tennessee near the Cumberland River and bounded as follows Beginning on McDowells South Boundry line of a six Hindred andforty one acre Tract on an E---- and running South one hundred and eighty four poles to as ash and hickory thence East one Hundred and Eighty poles to an Hickory thence North two Hundred and twenty eight poles to a white oak Thence West one hundred & fifty six poles to a Hickory on McDanials East boundry line thence South with said line forty four poles to said McDanials corner thence poles to the Beginning and Joining Twenty five Acres be the same more or less which said tract or parcel of Land with all and every appurtenances thereunto belonging to said John Cage for himself his Heirs Executors Administrators or assigns hath hereby sold delivered conveyed and confirmed to the said William Algood his heirs ececutors Administrators or assignsand said John Cage doth for himself his heirs Executors and Administrators hereby cevenant with the said William Algood his Heirs Executors Administrators or as assigns that the said John Cage his Heirs Executors Administrators will war rent emebers and appurtenances thereunto belonging free from all claims of any person or Persons whatsoever unto the said William Algood his heirs Executors Administrators or assigns forever In witness whereof the said John Cage hath set his Hand and affixed hsis seal the day and Date above written Signed Sealed and Delivered in the Presance of Wirt Jones Jared John Jared
                     Douglas Jared   (SEAL)

State of Tennesse Wilson County
  Of said County certificate Duly Registered
13- 1813

RECORDS OF MRS. LULA ALGOOD (CON)

This Indenture made this fourth Day fo November in the Year of Our Lord one Thousand Eight hundred and Twelve between Benjamin Clark ofdthe County of Wilson and State of Tennessee one part and William Algood of t the county and State aforesaid of the other part. Witgss that the said Benjamin Clark for and in the consideration of the sum of five Hundred and Eight Dollars him in Hand paid the Receipt whereof is hereby acknowledged hath bargained sold conveyed and confirmed unto the afoteseid William Algood a ceratin Tract or parcel of Land Lying in the County of Wilson State of Tennessee and B unded as follows on a Whiye oak in the Road leading from Said Clarks to the place where John Cage formerly Resided Belonging to William Algood and Running South thirtytwo degrees West fifty nine Poles to a post oak and Hickory in Hambletons line Thence East twenty two Poles to a Hickory and black oak said Clarks North west corner of a hundred Acres purchased of Humbletons Thence South one hundred and Clarks North West corner of a hundred Acres fiekd East one hundred snd forty poke to an ash and fourteen poles to a Hickory and Sugar tree thence to a black oak said Hambletons North East Corner of a six hundred and forty poles/ Acre Tact thence West fouteen Poles to a Hickory and Dogwood thence North fifty nine Poles to a Spanish oak and two Ironwoods on Elmore Douglas line thenceWest three Degrees South one Hundred and twenty six poles to the beginning- Including one Hundred and forty Acres of Land be the same more or less, which said tracctor parcel of Land with all and every appertenanceh thereunto belonging the said Bagarning Clark for himself his Heirs Executors Administrators and Assigns hath hereby Sold delivered conveyed and confirmed the William Algood administratots and assigns hathhbreby Sold dellivered the said Benjamin Clark doth for himself his heirs there administrators Executors or assigns hereby covenant with the said William A;good his heirs Executors Administrators and assigns that the said Benjamin Clark his Heirs Executors Administrators and Assigns Shall and willwarrent and defend forever the said trade or parcel of Land with all and every of its members and Appertenances thereunto belong free from Claims of any Person or Person whatsoever unto the said William Algood his Heirs Executors Administrators or Assigns for ever In witness whereof the said Benjamin Clark hath set his Hand and Affixed his S al the day and Date Above written
Signed Sealed and Delivered in the Presance of
           Reech A. Holdman
          Wm Bable
          John Bouman
            Benjamin Clark SEAL
           Ackd

State of Tennessee Wilson County March Term 1813
   The within deed of bargain and Sale from Benjamin Clark to William Algd for 140 acres of land was duly acknowl edged in open court by said Clark ordered to be Registered
         Test- John Allcorn   Clerkof Wilson County
State of Tennessee Wilson County Registers office Aprile lo, 1813
I, Henry Ross Register of Wilson Countydo hereby certify thatthe forsgoing deed is certificate are duly registered in Book E. Page 138
       Test- Henry Ross Registered of Wilsoh County
Benjamin Clark to Deed William Algood
Registered in Book E. Page 138 Deed 14 acres

RECORDS OF MRS. LULA ALGOOD (CON)

    This Indenture made this fifteenth D ay of June in the Year of Our Lord one Thousand Eight hindred and Fourteen between Elmore Douglas of the County of Smith and State of Tennesseeof the one part and William Algood of the County Wilson and State of Tennessee of the other part Witnesseth tht the Said Elmore Dpuglas for and in the Consideration of the Sum of fifty Dollars to him in hand paid the receipt where of is hereby acknowledged hath bargained Sold conveyed and Confirmed unto the afore said William Algood a certain Tract or parcel of Land lying in the County of Wilson and State of Tennessee and Bounded as follows beginning on a sugar Tree Hardy Hunters corner in Elmore Douglas West boundry line and Running South between eighty and one hundred Poles to a Stake nine poles and three Quarters North of he spring thence West to a Stake thence North to Hardy Hunters line thence East to the beginning including Eight acres and sixty four poles of Land be the same more or less which said Tract or parcel of Land with all and veery appertunencethereuntobalonging to the said Elmore Douglas for himself his heirs Executors Administrators or Assigns hath hereby Sold delivered conveyed and confirmed to the said William Algood his heirs Executors Admifistrators or assigns hereby covenant with the said William Algood his heirs Exors Administrators or assigns that the said Elmore Douglasm his, heirs & C shall and will warrent and defenf forever the said Tract or parcl of Land with all and every of to numbers and appertenences from all claim of any person or persons whtso ever unto the said William Algood his Heirs & C forever ,

    In witness whereof the said Elmore Douglas hath set his Handn and affixed his seal the Day and Date above written

    Signed and Sealed and De ivered in the Presance

                                                 Elmore Douglas   (SEAL)
                                                 Acked.

State of Tennessee Wilson County Court June Term 1814, Thw within Deed of barganer and Sale from Elmore Douglas to William Algood was duly acknowledge in the open court by the bargainer and ordered to be Registered

                                       Attest-John Allcorn Clerk of Wilson County

State of Tennessee Wilson County Registers office the 5th of August 1814

   The Weather deed of a bargain and Sale and clerk certificate thereon are duly Registered in Book E. Page 341

                                       Attest-Henry Ross Register of Wilson County

Deed   8-64poles
Elmore Douglas
   To William Algood   107
Registered in Book E. Page 341

RECORDS OWNED BY MRS. ALFRED ALGOOD, COCKEVILLE, TENN

This Indenture made this twenty fourth of December in the year of Our Lord one thousand eight hundred and fiveteen between Elmore Douglas of the county of Smith and State of Tennessee of the one part and William Algood of the County of Wilson State of Tennessee of the other part-
Witness that the said Elmore Douglas and in the consideration of the sum of Fifty Dollars to him in Hand paid the receipt whereof is hereby acknowledged that bargainedshould conveyed and confirmed unto the said William Algood a certin tracct or parcel of Land lying in the County of Wilson and State of Tennesseeand bounded as follows: beginning at the SouthEast Corner of a fifty five and one half acre Tract Deeded to said Algood by James Prim at a stake near saidAlgoods stable and running East fifteen and three fourth poles to a Popular in the Elmore Douglas line thence North four degrees East fifteen poles to a Stake on the North sided of the Spring and near the Spring so as to divode the Spring equally between said Douglas and Algood and their Heirs or assigns forever and both the parties are hereby bound never to dig about said Spring so as to alter its present Judit (?) or stop any way to the same or in any other respect to injure said Spring thence North eighty two degrees east two poles to a black gum thence north thirtyf five Degrees East twenty one poles to a Chinquapin white oak thence North thirty three degrees West twenty six poles to a white Oak thence South thirty and one half poles to a Stake nine poles and three fourths of the Spring thence West fifteen poles and three quarters to a Stake thence North twenty fourPoles to the beginning including four Acres and ywenty one and one fourth ploes be the same more or less which said Tract or parcel of Land with alland every eppurtenances thereunto belonging in the siad Elmore Douglas for himself his Heirs executors Administrators or assigns hath hereby should delivered conveyed and confirmed unto the said William Algood his Heirs Executors Administrators or assigns and the said Elmore Douglas doth for himself his Heirs & C. hereby covenent with the said William Algoos his Heirs & C that he said Elmore Douglas his Heirs & C shall and will forever Warrent and defend the said Tract or Parcel Land with all and every member and Appurtenances the unto belonging or in any wide appertaining free from all and every claim or claims of any person or persons what so ever unto the said William Algood his Heirs Executors Administrators or Assigns forever In Witness whereof the said Elmore Douglas hath hereunto set his Hand and affixed his seal the Day and Date above written Sogned Sealed and Delivered in the Presence of intered the words belonging
             Elmore Douglas (SEAL)

Test S. L. Blakemore
Alstone L. James
Ennis Douglas
B. Wrather Jurant
Isaac Hoaks Jurant
State of Tennessee, Wilson County Court May Term -The mentioned Deed of bergained to William Algood from Elmore Douglas for four acres of land was exhibited in open court and proceed by the oaths of Baker Whitker and Isaac Hooks two of the subscribing witness thereunto and ordered to be registered
Test- John Alcorn Clerk of Wilosn County (Clk)
State of Tennessee, Wilson County I Henry Ross Reg. of said Coujty do hereby certify that the within Deed is truly rogistered in Book G. Page (?)---
May 1818   Henry Ross Reg.
Elmore Douglas To Deed 4 Acres
William Algood   E. M. Registered Book G. Page

RECORDS O.NED BY MRS. LULA ALGOOD, COOKEVILLE, TENN.

This Indenture made this the thirteenth Day of December in the Year of Our Lord one thousand eight hundred and Sixteen between Benjamin Clak of the County of Wilson and State of Tnnssee of one oart and Willian Algood of the county and State aforesaid of the other part witness that the Said Benjamin Clark for and in the consideration of the sum of Eighty Dollars to him in Hand paid the Receipt whereof is hereby acknowledged hath bargained sold conveyed and confessed unto the aforesaid William Algood a certain Tract or parcel of Land lying in the County of Wilson and State of Tennesseeand Bounded as follows Beginning on a poplar said Algood South boundry line of a sixty six Acre Tract Purchased of Thomas McClelon and Running on a poplar saidAlgoods South boundry line of a sixty six Acre Tact and Running South sixty degrees forty poles East to a stake in Elmore Douglas West boundry line thence North eleven Degrees East twenty poles with said Douglas line to a corner North Poplar East of the Meeting House thence West forty poles to the Beginning including two and one half Acres of Land be the same more or less Which said Tract or parcel of Land with all and every appurtenances thereunto belong the said Benjamin Clark fro himself His heirs Executors Administratos or assignshath sold delivered conveyed and confirmed unto the said William Algood hid heirs Executors Administrators or assugns and the said Benjamin Clark doth fot himself Heirs & Evernly cocenant with the said William Algood his Heirs & C that he the said Benjaimn Clark his heirs & C phlland will warrent and forever defend the said tract or parcel of Land with all and every of its membered and Appertenances thereunto belonging any wise Appertaining free from a;; lawfull claim or claims of any person or persons unto the siad William Algood his heirs Executors Administrators and assignees forever In witness whereof the said Benjamin Clark hath'st his Hand and affixed hisnSeal the day and Date above with signed and sealed and delivered in the presents of Nathan Corley, Samuel Carlinger Jurant at Sept Term 1817

            Benjamin Clark (Seal)

State of Tennessse Wilson County Court May Term 1819

The with in Deed ofbargain in Clarks to Wm. Algood for the 2½ acres of land qwas exhibited 12 of Court and fully proved by the oath of Nathn Croley are of the witness thereunto and ordered to be registered

Test   Allcorn Clk. of Wilson County Court

Benjamin Clark To Deeds 2½ acres
Wm. Algood
  Deed Benjamin Clark
    To
 William Algood

RECORDS OF MRS. LULA ALGOOD, (CON)

This Indenture made this second Day of June in the Year of Our Lord, one thousand eight hundred and Eighteen between Stevem McDaniel of the county of Wilson and State of Tennessee of the one part and William Algood of the county and State aforesaid of the other part witnesseth ayat the said Stephen McDanial for and ni consideration of the sum of the Seventeen Dollars to him in handnpaid the receipt whereof is hereby acknowledged hath bargained sold conveyed and confirmed unto the siad William Algood a certain tract or parcel of Land lying in the County of Wilaon and State of Tennessee adn bounded as follows viz, beginningon a Dogwood said Algood south west corner in said Mc- Danial East boundry line and running East Forty one Poles to a popularin Sd Algood line thence & North twenty Seven Poles to a cornerBeavh in Sd Algood line thence south fifty Degrees West to the beginningin and lying three acres and Seventy three and one half Poles be the same more or less which said Tract or parcel of Land with all and every appertenances thereuntobelonhgig or in any wise appertaining to the said Stephen McDanial for himself Heirs Executors Admijistrators or assigns heth hereby sold delivered conveyed and confirmed unto the sáis William Algood his Heirs Executors Administrators or assigns and the said Stephen McDanial doth hereby for himself his Heirs & C Hereby covenant with th said William Algood hid Heirs & C, that he the said Stephen McDanial hid Heirs & C shall and will warrent and forever defend the said Tract or parcel of Land with all and every of its members and appertenences thereunto belonging or in any wise Appertaining free from all claims of any Person or persons whatsoever un to the said William Algood his Heirs & C forever In witness ehereof the said Stephen McDanial hath seth his hand and affixed his seal the Day and Date above written
Signed Sealed and Delivered in Presance

              Stephen McDonald (SEAL)
              Acked
John H. Buford   Deed 3 acres
 Burchet Douglass   Stephen McDanial
               To William Algood R B Page 260

State of Tennessee Wilson County C Court Feb Term 1819
The within Debt of bargain and sale from Stephen McDanial to Wm A;good for was exhibited in open court ack by the said Stephen and ordered to be Registered
Tæst-   John Alton Clerk
State of Tennessee Wilson County This Deed is Registered in Book p9 26
             Henry Ross Registered

The State of Tennessee
To all to whom these presents shall come Greetings
  Know ye that by virtue of Entry No 131 mede in the office of the Entry Taker of Putnam County and Entered on the 3 day of Aprile, 1860 pursuant to the provisions of an Act of the General Assembly of said Satet passed on h the 9th day of January 1830 There is granted bt the State of Tennessee uhto Joel Algood a certain parcel of Land containing Fifty nine acres 3 roads & poles by survey bearing date the 30th day of Aprile 1860Lying in the said county on the waters of Falling Waters Beginning at a stake and Blck oaks pointers the South West corner of a tract of Land purchased bt said Algood of James McKinney Running East with his South Bpundry line crossing the

RECORDS OF MRS. LULA ALGOOD (CON)

cpuntry Road at 70 poles crossing the Road to the whits plains at 16 poles in all 113 poles to two Chestunts and 2 Black oaks Algoods corner tnhence North with another of his lines 51 poles to a stake and 2 Black oaks pointers thence East to poles to a stake in the Road leading to Quarles thence South 25- East with said Road 53 poles to a stake and 3 Black Jacks pointers thence South qith another of his line 87 poles to 4 post oaks & Black Jack another of his corners in S. D. Burtons line thence West with his line 36 poles to a Post oak & Black Jack his North West corner South 2 poles to a stake & Black Jack John W.,Welches corner west with his North Boundry line crossing the Road to White Plains at 46 poles crossing the Cantucky Road at 90 poles inall 110 poles to 4 Black Jacks Welchs corner in John W Shirley line North with his lines 58 poles to the Beginning with the hereditaments d and appurtenances To have and To hold the said Tract or parcel of Land with its appurtenences to the said Joel Algood in witness whereof Isham G. Harris Gov. of the Sate of Tennessee hath hereunto set his hand and caused the great Seal of the State to be affixed at Nashville on 10 day of Apr. in the Year of Pur Lord one Thousand and Eight Hundred and Sixty one and of the Independance of the United States the 85 year

By the Govnor-Isham G. Harris
O. W. R. Ray
Secretary.

Joel Algood is entitled to the within described tract of Land
P. P. Trumit
per H. T Trumit

Recorded in the office for the Mountain District in Book by page 262
Register Mountain District

Grant No 12332
Joel Algood Putnam County 59 a, 3 R 3$ pr

RECORDS OF WILSON COUNTY
OWNED BY MRS. ALFRED ALGOOD, COOKEVILLE, TENN.

This in made this twelfth day of November Eighteen hindred and eighteen between George White of Wilson County and State of Tennessee of the one part and Charles ledbeter Hezakiah Woodard and Willis Copied trustees in t trust for the uses and purposes herein mentioned All of the within State of aforesaid George White for and in consideration of the sum of eight dollars specilas to him in hand paid at and upon the sealing and delivering of these presents the receipt whereof is hereby acknowledge hath or have given granted bargained sold released confirmed and convey and bythese presents doth or do give grant bargain sell release confirm and convey unto them the said Charles Ledbetter Hezakiah Woodard and Willis copied and their successors trustees in trust for the uses and purposes herein after mentioned and declaired all the estate title interest propertyclaim and dem mandwhatsoever either in lawe or equilty which he the said George White hath or have into or upon all and singular a certain lot or acres of ground situated lying and being in the County and District of bounded and bounded as follows to wit beginning on white aok and Sasafras at the South West corner of said George White's land and running East twenty six poles to a popular tyence North six and one fourth poles to an sourwood thence west twenty six poles to a stake, thence to the Beginning containing and laid out for one acre of ground to gather with all and singular the houses and woods water ways privileges and appurtenances then to belongingor in any wise appurtaining to have and to hold all and singular the above mentioned and described lot or acres of ground situated and lying and being as a foresaid together with all and singular the houses wood water ways and privileges there to belonging or in assesingasserteining unto them the said Charles Ledbetter hezakiah woodard Willis copied and their successors in office forever in trust that they shall erect and build or cause to be Erected and built there on a house or place of worship for the use of the members of the mentioned Episcopel Church of the united State of America according to the rules and disipline which from times to time may agree upon and by ministers and preachers of the said Church their general Conferences in the United States of America and in futue trust and confidence that they shall at all times forever hereafter permits such ministers and preachers belonging to said Churches shall from time to time be duly authorized by the general conferences of the ministers and preschersof the said presches for by the Yearly conferances authorized by the said conferences to preach and expound therein and in further trust and condidence that aa often as any one or more of the trustees herein before mentioned shall die or cease to be members of the said church 9ror dissopline as a' foresaid there and in such cases it shall be the duty of Stationed ministers or preachers authorized as before said who shall have the personal charge of the members if the siad church to call a meeting of the remaining trustees as soon as conveniently may be and whenso ever the sai ministers or preacher shall proceed to niminate one or more persons to fill the place or places of him or them whose offuce has or have been vacated as a aforesaid provided the person or persons to nominate shall have been one year a member or members of the Said church immediately proceeding such nomination and of at least of twenty one years of age and the said trustees so assembled shall proceed to Elect and by a majority of votes appointed the person or persons so nominated to fill such vacancy ordanesnse in order to keep up the members of three trustees forever and in cases of any equal member vote for and against the said mentioned the Stationed ministers or preacher shall have the electing vote provided nevertheless that if the said trustee p

WILSON COUNTY RECORDS (CON)

any of them or their successors have advanced or shall advance any sum or sums of money or shall be responsable for any sum of money on account of said premises and they said trustees or their successors be obligated to pay the said sum or sums of money they or any party of them shall be authorized to rais the said sum of money by a mortgage on the said premises or by selling the said premisses of the after notice given to the pastor or preacher who has the oversight of the congregation attending service on the said premises of the money due be notpaid to the said trutees or their successors with in one year after such notice given and if such sale takes place the said trustees or their successors afterpying the debt and all other expenses which were due from the money arising from such sale shall deposit the remainder of the money produced by the said sale in the hands successors after paying the debts and all other expenses which are due from the money arising from such sale shall deposite the remainder by the said sale in the hands of the Stewarts of the society belonging to or attending devine service on the said premises which urplus of the produce of such sale so deposited in the hands of the said steward or stewards shall be at the disposal of the next yearly conferance authorized as aforesaid which said yearly conferance shall dispose of the said momey according to the best of thereJudgment for the use of the said Society and the said George White doth by these presents warrent and forever defend all and Singular the before mentioned and described lot or acres of ground with the appurtenances thereunto belonging unto them the Said Charles ledbetter Hezakiah Woodward Willis Cofled and their suaccessors chosen and appointed as a foresaid from the claimor claims of him the said George White his heirs and assigns forever Testimony whereof the said George White have had unto set myhand and caused/ seal the day and year a foresaid

            George William
            Daniel Jackson

Received the day of the date of the above written endenture the consideration ther in mentioned in full
Test, George White (SEAL)
   George Williams & Danial Jackson Intrust
State of Tennessee, Wilson County

           I Henry Ross Register
I do hereby certify that the White and in duly Registered in Book H. Page 134 this 24th day of March 1820
Test- Henry Ross Registerof Wilson County
 State of Tennessee Febuary Term 1820 Wilson County The within and of bargain & sale from Georgw White to Charles Ledbetter Hezakiah Woodard ' Willie Cofell was exicuted in open court and Proven by the oaths of George William and Danial Jackson the subscribing witness thereunto and ordered by the Court to be Registered
George White (SEAL)   Test- JohnnAllcorn Clerk of
                Wilson County court
DEED-George White for land to build a meeting house
        Registered in Book H. Page 134

RECORDS OF MRS. LULA ALGOOD (CON)

This Indenture made this twentyfourth day of January in the Year of Our Lord Eighteen hundred and twenty four Between Samuel Caplinger of the County of Smith and the State of Tennessee of the one part and William Algood of h the County of Wilson and the State aforesaid of the other part Witness that bthe said Samuel Caplinger for and in consideration 66the sum of Seventy five dollars and twenty cents to him in hand paid the receipt where of is hereby acknowledged and himself to be therwith fully satisfied contented and paid Hath given granted bargained sold offered and conformed unto the said William Algood his heirs ans assigns the following descrebed tract or parcel of land situated in the county of Wilson aforesaid Beginning at a poplar Stump lying and being in the county of Wilson aforesaid Beginning at a poplar stump South East corner of the tract of land where as the said William Algood now lives Running South fifty degrees East twenty five and one half poles to a stake North West corner of Providence meeting House lot therewith seventy seven degrees East with the north boundry line of siad lot Eleven poles to a Stake Thence North six degrees West Douglas line sixteen poles thence North ten degrees East with said line ten and one half poles 24 links to a stake thence North 62 West with the south boundry line of the tract whereon the said Algood now lives forty poles to a Stake thence West to afores aid place Beginning 34 poles containing nine acres and 64 square poles to have and to hold the above described parcel of land with its appertenances to the said William Algood his heirs and assigns and the said Samuel Caplinger doth further consort compromise and assign to and with the said William Algood that he the said Samuel Caplinger his heirs and assigns will forever warrent and defend to the said Algood his heirs and the aforesaid tract of Land with all the Appertenances thereunto belonging ahainst the aforesaid tract of Land with all and every person or person in the within whereof shall hereto set my hand and affixed my seal the day and date above written signed sealed and delivered in the

presence of   Burchett Douglas (Juror)
                                       Moody P Hail
                                       Lewis Harris J rant
                                       Samuel Caplinger (Xhis mark)
                                                 (SEAL)

State of Tennesse Wilson County Court June Term 1824
The with in deed of bargain and sale from Samuel Caplinger to William Algood for nine acres -poles of land was produced in open court and proven by hhe Oath of   Burchett Douglas &
                                       Lewis Harris Subscribing witness
thereto and ordered to be Registered
                                       Neil John Alcorn Clk of said County
In the office the 29th July, 1824
                                       H.,Ross Register
Tennessee, I, Henry Ross Reg, of Wilson Co. do hereby certify the the within deed and certificate proven thereon and Registered
Deed 9. A. 64 P.
Samuel Caplinger
    Deed To William Algood
    & -64
      E. M. Registered in Book No Page 125

RECORDS OWNED BY MRS. LULA ALGOOD, COOKEVILLE, TENN.

      This Indenture made the Twenty Second Day of Oct. one thiusand eight hundred and twenty four between Willis Cofeld of the County of Wilson and State of Tennessee of the one part of William Algood of the County of state aforesaid of the other part Witnesseth that hte said Willis Cofeld for and in consideration of the sum of two hundred and fifty Dollars to him in had paid the receipt whereof is whereby acknowledged with granted bargained and sold and delivered and by these presents doth grant bargain sell and deliver unto the said William Algood his Heirs Excns Administrators or assigns a certain Tract or Parcel of Land situated lying and being in the cpunty of Wilson on the waters of Cedar Creok containing Sixty ywo Acres be the sa same more or less neginning at a Cedar N. W. at corner of a survey of Daniel McKesicks and RunningWest 34 poles to a Stake thenceNo C. poles to a Sassafas thence South & 5 Degrees West 45 poles to a stake thence 2½ poles to a stak thence West 27 Poles to a white oak and Sassafras, thence South 105 poles toa cedar thence East 110 poles to a stake thence North tb the begin ning which peace or parcel of Land with all the apertenances and improvements thence unto belonging or in any wise appertaining the said Willis Cofeld for himself his Heirs exctrs administrators orassigns doth forever warreht and defend the title against the claims of all and every preson or persons what so ever to the sais William Algood his Heirs Exors Sdmins or assigns forever , In witness where of the said Willis Cofeld hath unto set his Hand and affixed hisSeal the day and date above mentioned . Signed Sealed and delivered in the presents of

Samuel T. White   Lurary Woods Clk Jurant SEAL
Ennis Douglass Jurant

State of Tennesse Wilson County Court, March Term 1825
Bargain & Sale from Willis Coffeld to William Algood for 60 acres of land was duly proven in open court by the oaths of James Woodcock & Ennis Douglas two of the Subscribing witness thereto and ordered to be Registered.
                                                              Alcorn Clerk
                         Frisk John of said Court
Tennessee Wilson County, I, Henry Ross Register of said County do hereby certify that the weather report and probate are duly Registered in my office this 9th day of May 1825
                Test-Henry Ross Regs.

Deed from Cofeld to
Willaim Algood 26 acres
Registers in Book K. Page 355

RECORDS OF MRS. LULA ALGOOD, COOKEVILLE, TENN.

State of Tennessee No 8833-
To all to whom these present shall come Greetings- Know ye, that by virtue of Entry No 1804 made in the office of the Entry Taker of Overton County en and entered on the 6th day of May 1842 pursuant tot eh provisions fo an Act of the General Assembly of said State passe don the 9th day of January 1830 there is Grantee by the said State of Tennessee uhto Henry McKinlwy a certain tract or parcel of Land containing firty Eigth acres by survey bearing date the 66ht day of May 1842 lying in said County abthe Waters of Bear Crek Beginning at a post aak two Spanish Oak pointers the North West corner of C Carr, Tract on which the said McKinley now lives Running East with the Noth boundry of said tract one hindred and six poles to a hickory and pointe corner to said McKinleys two hindred acre Tract Then North with the same sixty six poles to a chestnut and four Black oaks pointers Burton Marchbanks corner Thence West with said line one hundred and sixteen poles to a post oak and two Hickory pointers Marchbanks coener Thence South with John Douglas line sixty five poles to a hickory Thence East ten poles to the beginning with the hereditaments and Appurtenances to have and to hold the siad tract or parcel of Land with its appurtenences to the said Henry McKinley.
In witness whereof James C, Jones Govnor of the State of Tennessee has hereunto set his hand and caused the Great Seal of the State to be affixed at Nashvielle, on the 20th day of Aprile 1843 and of America Independance the 67th year.

           James C. Jones Gov.
           Jon. S. Young, secretary.

Henry McKinley is entitled to the within described land.
    R. Nelson, Register of the Mountain District
Recorded in my Office Book L. page 278-279
      Nelson Register of the Mountain Dis.
     By W. E. Nelson, D. R.

No 8833 Henry McKinney 48 acres
   Overton County.

           Ashgrove- Aprile 21st, 1845
I was called on with T. W. Fits of Summer County to settle a disputed line between Joel Algood and Wm. L. John P end Gideliah Hughes and after examining the boundry of the two tracts and the title papers and taking evidene of John Bell, Elijah Jones and George Martin upon oath came to the conclusion that the line that Algood claims was the original line and the line that the former owners of the land claimed to and Jurisdiction to and acknowledged to be the line for many years Given under my hand this date above written.
           T. E. Morris

RECORDS OF MRS. LULA ALGOOD (CON)

I, Zealous Johnson Administrator P. C of Wiliam Swinney deceased do hereby virtue of the power in me vested by law and in complyance with the last will and testament of said William Swinney convey hereby to Joel Algood he being the highest and best bidder for the consideration of two hundred and eighty two dollars and sixty cents to me this day paid by said Algood a tract of land in the Satet of Tennessee wilson County District No. 7 containing by estimation thirty acres and one hundred and forty two poles be the same more or less and boundee as followsBeginning at a rock Bryans Wards cornor with an Elm Black and White oak pointer and running thence South with the said Wards west boundry seventy six and three quarter poles to a stake and h hickory and Blck Lacust pointers it being the North East corner of the tract willed by the said Swinney to his widow thence West seventy nine and a half poleswith said widows North boundry to a stake in the East boundry of the heir of W. W. Calhan deceased Thence North with thw road from Taylorville to McCalitus fifty three poles to a stake Thence East fifty seven and a half poles to a Hickory Thence North twenty one poles to a sugar tree on said road Thence East one poles to the beginning The title to which land I here bind the heirs of the said William Sweeney to warrent and defend tot eh said Algood againdt the lawful claims of all persons are fully and effectually as their could be bounded if the said Sweenying had executed this deexd himself according to the power invested Given under my handand sael this 20th day of August

              Zealous Johnson Adms of this surveyed
Deed   SEAL
Signed sealed & delivered in our presence the day and date above written
       J. T. Bell proven 1856
       J. R. Beachen
State of Tennessee Wilson County Personaly appeared before me Joseph L. McClain clerk of the county Court of said County of Wilson Zealous Johnson the within named Administrator a bargeiner with whom I am personally acquainted and whom acknowledged that he executed the within Deedfor the purpose therein contained witness my hand at office this forst day
              J. L. McClain Clerk

Deed- Z. Johnson Adm PC
  To
Joel Algood 30 acres , 142 poles
Proved by B. T. Bell Sept, 1, 1856 Act Sept 1856
Revd for Registration Sept 1, 1856 at 12, O'clock W
            A. W. Vick Reg

State Tax 5.
Reg fee 1.00 paid
Clerk fee 25

   132

DEED
OWNED BY MRS. LULA ALGOOD, COOKEVILLE, TENN

I L. White Trustee for Edward White this day bargained and sold and do hereby transfer and convey to Joel Algood an his heirs forever for the consideration of Three thousand and two hundred and seventy five Dollars to me paid one lot in the town of Lebanon representatives in the plot of said Town as lot No 6 also one other lot representative of lot No 7 in the North Square of said Town boundry ob the South by the land that Jno. M. Goldron nw lives on an the lot belonging to John Hoolman on the east by Academy street an on the West by Main North Street & on the North by two acres of land the residence of the said E. A. White said lots are conveyed to E. A. WHite by Albert H. Wayman and Fly Crutcher and Monroe D ouglas also lot or parcel of land bounded as follows Beginning at the North West corner of lot N . running North to to the said South West corner of George Donwalls lot thence east with said Donnells line on the school lands to the street thence South with Academy Street to the North Corner of lot No 7, thence West wit h the boundry of lots No 7 to the beginning about two acres it being the place Whom the said E. A. White now lives also the one half of an hundred tract of land lying in the County of Wilson and State of Tennessee on the wateer Cedar Creek for the consideration of four hindred dollars to me paid the said land is bounded as follows on theNorth by the land of Henderson Holey on the East by the land of H. Y. Massa on the South by the lands of Daniel Johnson on the Wesy by the lands of Daniel Johnson and Samuel Capner ths h whole of said tract of land is estimated to containing two hundredand ten acres said land was deeded to White and Price by William Johnson theone half of the above mentioned two hundred and ten acres is hereby conveyed tot the saod Joel Algood to have and to hold the above describeed Town property and tract of land to said Joel Algood his heirs and assghs forever I thei said L. W. WHiteTrustee for said do covenent with the said Joel Algood, the I am lawfully seized of said land and town property, have a good right to convey it and that the same is unincumbered I do further covenant and bind myself my heirs and representatives as trustee of aforesaid to warrent and forever defehd the title to the above described property portion thereof to the said Joel Algoodhis heirs and assigns against the lawful claims of all persons whatsoever this the 8th day of December on ethousnad eight hundred and forty one the above dollars entitles before signed

S. W. White, Trustee (SEAL)
for E. A. White & I. W. White

State of Tennessee Wilson County Personally appeared before me Josiah McClan Clerk of the County Court of said Wilosn County the with in L. W. White whthi whom I am personally acquainted and acknowledged that executed the with in deed for the purpose therein contained Witness my hand at office this 8th day of December 1841

J. T. McClain Clerk

State of Tennessee I Giles Glenn Register of Wilson County do hereby certify that the within deed and certificate ofacknowleddgment thereon duly Registered in my office in Book F. Page 397 witness my hand at office this 15th day of December A. D. 1841

Giles H. Glenn Reg.

L. W. White
    Deed
Joel Algood
Register Fee 1.75

RECORDS OF MRS. LULA ALGOOD (CON)

I bind myself to pay John White eight hundred and thirtyeight dollars The condition of this obligation is such that whereas the said John White has this day purchased of me four hundred and eighteen dollars and seventy cents on the following payments and third due July 1st 1845 , 1st July 1846 and C due third July 18st, 1847 for which note underseal have been this day executed to me a tract of land in Wilson County State of Tennessee District No 7 and biunded as follows Beginning at a hickory Marchsuns South West corner in B. T. Billsworth boundry Thence North sixty poles b to two Hickorys and two Beeches Thence West forty poles to a mulberry and sugar tree Thence South fifty fourdegrees West thirty five poles to a white oak and poplar Thence West thirty four poles to a stake a little north of a branch Thence South fifty and a half degrees West twenty seven poles to a walnut Thence South twenty poles to a beech and C. two Hickory Thence South sixty four degrees West forty poles toma Hickory Black Gum and Dogwood Thence Southtyo and a half degrees West tyirty two poles to a Black and White Oak and Elm Thence East ninty two poles to a Black walnut B. T. Bell south west corner Thence north one degree East with Bairs Bells west boundry forty poles to a Ironwood and Hickory said Bells norh west corner Thence East seventy poles to the beginning Law if I shall mk make or cause to be made to the said John White his heirs or assigns a godd and sufficient title in fee simple with generly wardly to the said tract o of land on the making of last paymentthere this obligation to be void
This November 7th 1844

                                    Joel Algood (SEAL)

Test-A. J. McDonald, Ben. T. Bell

Bond -Joel Algood To John White 62¾ acres

I, Joel Algood Bind myself to pay Benjamin T. Bell nine hundred and twenty dollars . The condition of this obligation is such that whence the said Benjamin T. Bell has this day purchased for me the same of four hun- sixty dollars on the following payments One hundred and fifty three dollard and 33¼ due on the 25th day of January 1852The same amount due on the 25th day of January 1854 & the for which his notes under seal have this day been executed to me a tract of Land in the State of Tennessee Wilson County District Np 7 containing by estimation sixty two acres and one hundred and twenty poles be the same more or less and bounded as follows to wit: Beginning at a Hickory in said Bells South boundry which is W. M. Calahan sobh west corner and running thence North west corner Thence &set forty poles to a mulberry and sugar tree Thence South fifty four degrees west thirty five poles to a white oak & poplar Thence West thirty four poles to a stak near a branch Thence South fifty & a half degrees west twenty seven poles to a walnut and said branch thence South twenty poles toa beach & hickory Thencesouth sixty four degrees west forty poles to a Hickory Black Gum & D Dogwood Thence South two and : half degrees west th rty two poles to a blac and white oak & Gum Thence East ninty two poles to a small Black walnut said Bells south west corner Thence North one degree East forty poles to an ironwood & Gickory thence wsst seventy poles to the beginning now if I shall make or cause to make to the said Benjamin T. Belll his heirs and assignd a good right and sufficient title in fee simple with general

RECORDS OF MRS. LULA ALGOOD, (CON)

waranty to the said tract of land an the making of last payment then this obligation to be void This day 25th of January 1851

            Joel Algood (SEAL)

Entitle before assigned
Test-, E. P. Low, G. A. duncan

State of Tennessee-No 8833.
To all to whom these presents shall come Greeting: Know ye That by virtue of Entry No 1804 made in the office of the Entry Taker of Overton County and entered on the 6th day of May 1842 pursuant to the provisions of an Act of the General Assembly of said State passed on the 9th day of January 1830 there is Granted by the said State of Tennessee unto Henry McKinley a certain tract or parcel of land containing forty eight acres by survey bearing date the 6th day of May 1842 lying in said county on the waters of Bear Creek Beginning at a post oak two Spanish oaks pointers the north west corner of C. Carve Tract on which the said McKinley now lives Running East withthe North boundry of said tract one hindred and six poles to a hickory and pointer corner to said McKinneys two hundred acre Tract Then North with the same sixty six poles to a chestnut and four Black oaks pointers Burton Marchbanks corner Thence West with the said line and one hundred and sixteen poles to a post Oak and two hickory pointer Marchbanks coener The ce South with Jihn Douglas line sixty five poles to a hickory Thene East Teh poles to thebgginning with the hereditaments and Appurtenences to have and to hold the said tract or parcel of Land with its appurtenences to the siaid Henry McKinny In witness whereof James C, Jones Govnor of the State of Tennessee has hereunto set his hand and caused the Great S al of th State to be affixed at Nashville on the 20th day of Aprile 1843 and of America Independence the 67th year

            James C. Jones
            Jon. S. Young Secretary

Henry McKinney is entitled to the within described land
            R. Nelson Register of the Mountain
              District

Recorededim my office Book L. Pages 278-279
            Nelson Register of the Mountain District
    by W. E. Nelson, D. R.

No 8833
Henry McKinny 48 acres
Overton County

RECORDS OF MRS. LULA ALGOOD (CON)

I, John L. Dillard have this day bargained and sold and do hereby transfer and convey to Joel Algood and his heirs foeever for the consideeration of five hundred abd forty six dollars a tract of land in the State 6f Tennessee Wilson County District No 7 containing by estimation ninty five acres be the same more or less and boundes as follows Beginning on a Black oak said Algoods North East coener of a tract of land purchased by William Algood cf Benjamin Clark and running thence South eighty seven degrees west one hundred and forty two poles to a large white oak and Beach said Algoods South West corner of tract above named bought of Clark Thence North forty seven degrees West twenty six and a half poles to a stake a large white oak and Beach said Algoods South West corner of a tract abovenamed bought of Clark Thence North forty seven degrees West twenty six and a half poles to a stake a large white oak and small walnut and Hickory pointers Thence Norh two degrees East two hundred and four poles to a stake two ash and two locust pointers Thence North forty five degrees East fifty seven poles to a beach and Hickory on the road lead from Hart Ferry to Road Thence South seventeen degreed East two poles to a stake Thence South forty eight degrees East seventy four poles to the boundry of Providence Camp ground Thene with the west and south boundry of said Camp ground to the South East coenr of said ground Thence South five degrees east about sevnenty poles to a stk Burch and sugar tree pointers Thence South seventy degreesEast forty poles to the beginning To have and to hold the same to the said Joel Algood his heirs and assigns forever I do covenent with the said Algood that I am lawfully seized of said land have agood right to survey it and that the asame is unincumbered I do further covenent and bind myself my heirsand representative forever to warrent and defend the title t to the said land and my part thereof to the said Algood his heirs and assigns against the lawful claims of all persons This Nov, 9th 1844

Test- A. J. McDonald   J. L. Dillard (SEAL)
    John J. Dillon

State of Tennessee Wilaon County Personally appeared before me Josiah L. McClain clerk of the County Court if said Wilson County A. J. McDonald and John Dillon subscribing witness to the within and who being sworn depose and say they are acquainted with the named Jihn L, Dillard the bargner with whom I am (?) and that he acknowledged the same in their presence to be his act & deed upon the day it bears date witness jy hand at office this 27th day of January 1845

                          J. L. McClain Clerk

State of Tennessee Wilson County , I, A. W. Vick Registrr of Wilson County do certify that the within Deed and certificate are duly Recorded in my office in Book V. Page 182-183 January 28th 1845 at 1 OClock P. M.

                          A. W. Vick Register

Deed
J. L. Dillqrd
    To
Joel Algood
Clerks Fee   .25
State tax   .14
    - -----
    paid 394

Rec for Registration January 28th, 1845 at 1' oclock P. M.
               A. W. Vick Reg
               fees 1.00 by A. Algood

RECORDS OF MRS. LULA ALGOOD (CON)

I, John J. Selvy have this day bargained and sold and do hereby transfer and convey to Joel Algood his heirs and assigns for the consideration of one hundred and ninty dollars to me paid a tract of land in the State of Tennessee Putnam County District No 1 containing by estimation thirty eight acres be the same more or less and bounded as follows to wit: Beginning on the South West corner of a twenty acre tract conveyed by me to said Algood the 27th of November last and running thence west sixty ywo and a half poles to two chestnut pointers eight or ten poles South of Burtons Harps south east corner Thence North nine degrees west and with said Harps east boundry line eighty poles to three Black oaks and a post oak pointer Thence East seventy five and a half poles to the North West coener of said twenty acre tract Thence North fifteen and a half poles to a small Black Jack Chestnut and Hickory pointer Thence east forty poles the south west coener of a five hundred and fifty acre tract conveyed by James McKinley to said Algood Thence South fifteen and a half poles to a Black Gum pointer Thence West forty poles to two small Persimmons pointers Thence South eighty poles to the beginning to have and to hold the same to the said Algood his heirs and assigns forever I do covenent with the Algood that I am lawfully seized of said land have a good right to convey it and that the same is unincumbered I d do further covenent and bind myself my heirs and representatives forever to warrent and defend the title to the said land andevery part thereof to the said Algood his heirs and assigns against the lawful claims of all persons This day of December 1858

John J. Selvy (SEAL)

Test-I. W. Crutcher, R. B. McDnial, Loyd S. Selvy

State of Tennessee Putnam County Personally appeared before me Russell Moore Clerk of Putnam County Cpurt John J. Selvy the within bargainer with whom I am personally acquainted and who acknowledged the due Execution of the within deed of conveyance to be his act and deed for the purpose and things Therein contained which is recorded witnessed my hand at office the 27th day of December 1858

Russell Moore Clerk

State of Tennessee Putnam County , I, Steven W. Brown Register of said county do hereby certify that the within deed of conveyance was filed for Registration on the 28th day of Dec. 1858 & was noted on filation Book A. pg 82-82 at 3 o'clock P. M. and was Registered on Book C. Pages 135& 136

S. W. Brown
Register

Deed
J. J. Selvy
  To
Joel Algood 38 acres
State Tax   5.00
Clerks fee   .25
Reg. fee   1.05

Ack 27th Dec. 1858

RECORDS OF MRS. LULA ALGOOD, (CON)

The State of Tennessee-
To all to whom these presents shall come Greetings:

    Know ye that in consideration of Intry No 1612 Made into the office of the Entry Taker of Overton County and entered on the 1st day of May 1837 Pursuant to the provisions of an Act of General Assembly of said State passes on 9th day of January 1830 Thereunis Granted by the said State of Tennessee unto William Terry assigned of James Peek a certain Tract or Parcel of Land containing Thirty acres by Survey bearing date the Fifteenth day of January 1839 lying in Overton County on the waters of Bear Creek Beginning at a small hickory and three white oaks pointer the North East corn of a fifty acre Survey made in the namr of Robert Peek and now owned by James Peek Running nine and one half poles to a smallBlack oak a post oak and two black oak pointers coener to Henry Brewington fifty acrevTract Thence West with the same one hundred and ten poles to a black oak on the banks of Bear Creek in a line of Robert Peeks Tract South with the same seventeen poles to a stake and white oak pointer corn to the same West seven and s fourth poles to a stake South ninty two and one half poles to a Stake a blck oak and hickory pointer East thirty three poles to a stake a hickory post oak and black oak Saplin pointer Northpassing the Siuth West corner of said Peek's fifty acre tract at two poles and with the same in all one hundred and two .poles to a hickory Peeks corn East with the same fifty p poles to the Beginning with the hereditaments and appurtenances To have and To hold the said Tract or Parcel of Land with its appurtenences to the said William Terry and his heirs forever In witness whereof Neil S Brown, Govnor of the State of Tennessee hath hereunto set his hand andcaused the Great Seal of the State to be affixed at Nashville on the Twenty fifth day of August in the Year of Our Lord one Thousand eight hundred and forty nine and of the Independance of the United States and Seventy Fourth year

                                              W. B. A. Murmsey
                                    By the Governor N. T. Brown

William Terry is entitled to th e within Described tract ojf Land
                                        Jno F. Vass Register Mountain District
Recorded in the Registers office for the M untain District in Book W. Page 137
                                        JohnFT Vass Register Mountain District
No 10119William Terry 311 acres Overton County

WILL
RECORD OWNED BY MRS. LULA ALGOOD, COOKEVILLE, TENN.

State of Tennessee Wilson County, At a circuit court of the Fifth Juducial circuit began and held in and for the County aforesaid at the Court House in the town of Lebanon on the third Monday in January in the Year of Our Lord Eighteen hubdred and fifty three and of America Independance the 77th President the Hon. Hughes L. Davidson , Judge of said Court Squire Potte vs Joel Algood Come the parties by there Attornies and thereupon came a jury of good and lawful men to wit James B Thomas 1 W. J. Cragwall 2 Jonathan Eatherly 3, L.W. Robertson 4 Richard Hollaway 5 W. B. Jennings 6 Larance Sypert Robert Johneson 8 Guy J Gleaves 9 G Edemound Gilliam Jonathan F. Hookery 11 and Joseph Johnson who being elected tried and sworn the truthto sapek upon the issue joined on there oaths do say tha the proper writing in the pleadings mentioned is not the last will and testament of Elizabeth Algood deceased, It is therefore consideredby the coutt that the said paper writing August 12, 1848 is not the last will and testament of the said Elizabeth AlgoodIt is therefore considered by the Court that the defendant recover of the Plaintiff the costs of this suit and that exeduto issue &C Squire Potts VS Joel Algood Be it remenbered that this course come on this day 12th January 1853 to be heard before the Hon. H. L. Davidson Judge and a jury where the plaintiff introduced Andrew J. M. McDonald one of the subscribing witnesses to the paper writing purporting to be the last will and testament of Elizabeth Algood deceased, who stated that he had been aqquainted with Elizabeth Algood for a great many years He signed a paper at the request of Mrs. Algood and which she said was her act and deed. The paper was folded partly he did not read it nor did she say what it was. Nothing more was saidabout a will at the time he signed it. The paper writing purporting to be thw will was there shown to him and he said that his name signed as witness there to was his handwriting and he supposed it was the same he had signed at her request. At the time he signed her name as witness to the paper he thought she was of sound mind He had but little conversation with her at the time nor at any other since then he has heard read the paper purposing to be her will and has seen a copy of the will of William Algood her husband and seeing that she had willed away property that did not belong to her He had his doubts wheather shy was of sound mind at the time when he witnessed the paper that Joel Algood her son was always very kind and affectionate to his mother as far as he knew The Plaintiff then introduced Jacob S. Hern the other witness to the paper, who stated th thathe had known Elizabeth Algood a great many years and for the last twenty yearsbefore her death he had visited her at least once a year at her request he had witnessed the paper writing purporting to be her will now produced She said it was her will is not certain that he read it but thinks he did She said her husband in his life time had said that the Negro woman Jane had come by her and wants to be permited to labor for herself. She called him into the Garden and seemed disposed to be very secret he thinks he signed his name in the garden, he conversed with her on religious subjects She said she was seeking sanctification of her soul and ask him to pray that she moght obtain that grace. She would frequently repeat the same thi things over and thought she talked foolish from these two last facts and her Disposition to be very secret and from the contents of the will itself he had his doubts as to wheather she was a sound mindat the time he witnessd the paper the Plaintiff then ceased his indeir and by consent was permittd

WILL-RECORDS OF MRS. LULA ALGOOD (CON)

to read to the jury the paper writing purporting to be the last will and testament of Elizabeth Algoods'elect to exceptions The Defendantthen introduced Dr. Regin Thompson a practicing Physician who stated that he had known Mrs. Algood for twenty years before her death Saw her frequently for the first two years of his acquaintance butnot so frequently for the last tenyears of his life She had consulted him about a mole on his face thinking it would turn to be a cancer. He assured her there was no danger, thati was nothing but a mole During the first of the his acquaintance with her this assurance seemed to satisfy her but during the last ten years of her life she consulted him about the mole every time he saw her and would ask about it several times during the same conversation seeming to forget she had mentioned it before she would also consult him abput her negroes but pa patticularly about a woman named Mary In the same conversation shw would repeat over the same question and after he had told herwhat she wanted to know she would follow when he statted off and after he had gotten on his horse would some times detain him an hour asking him the same questions she had asked him just before. She had a parcel of old medicine wraped up in old paper She would get this out and show them to him and ask him what they were good for He told her they were no account and advised her to throw them in h the fire She would fold them carefully and put them away The next time he would visit her the same thing would occur in regard to the medicine When there she slept in a little room with a great many shelves in it having on them a great amny articles and among them rest a variety of victuals that seemed to be old and had been there a long time When he would start pff she would insist upon him to take some biscuit and would give him some old hard dry biscuits that no person could eat He called there one night in the absence of her Son Joel and she seemed to be alarmed and asked why he had come there after night She seemed to be so much alarmed that he left and went to a neighbors house and stayed all night He was related to her by marriage and she shwmed to have confidence in him This seemed about four years before hi death. From all the circumstances and from her appearance he is satisfied that she had for ten years before death been of unsound mind that the reason Judgment and memory had been declining that she was very old when she d died which hapened in January 1852 That a neat tombstone had been put over the grave of her husbandseveral years before her death This was done shortly after his deathand before the date of the will This was all the proof in the cause. The Court charged the Jury that if they believed that Elizabeth Algood wwas of sound mind and deposing mind " memoryat the time the paper purporting to be her will was witnessed it would be her will and to find for the plaintiff but if the proof did not show that she was of sound mind and disposing mind and memory at the time it was witnessed It would not be herw wil and they ought to find against it and in favor of the defendant and that how the facts where they must Judge from the proof. This is in Substance the charge without stating it fully. The Jury returned a verdict for the defendant. The Statement of the proof in the cause and the proceeding had there in made and signed by the presiding Judges and ordered to be spread upon the minutes of the Court by the request of Joel Algood the defendant in this

H. L. Davidson (SEAL)

State of Tennessee Wilson County I Calvin W. Jackson Clerk of the Circuit Court for the county of Wilson I state aforesaid do hereby cert fy that the foregoing is a true and perfect copy of the Judgment in th case heretofore prosecuted and delivered in said court wherein Squire Potts, Plaintiff and J Jole Algood Deft and the evidence in said cause as the same remain of recoded in my office Witness my hand at office the 11th Oct 1853

C. W. Jackson Clk

RECORDS OF MRS. LULA ALGOOD, (CON)

I, James McKinney have this day bargained and sold and do hereby transfer and convey to Joel Algood and his heirs and assigns for the consideration of Twenty seven Hundred and fifty dollars to me payed a tract of land in in the State of Tennessee Putnam Founty District No 1 on both sides of the road leading from Sparta to Livingston containing by estimation five hundred and fifty acres be the same more aorless and bdunded as follows, Beginning on a post oak one of Steven Burtons corner in his North boundry andu running thence West one Hundred and thirty eight poles to a stake and thene to Post oak pointers on the esat side ofma glade Thence North fofrty poles to the road Quarles Thence North twenty five degrees West with said road fifty three poles to a stake Thence West ten and a half poles to a stake and Bkack Jackaand Black Oak pointer Thence South twenty eight poles to.a Stake and chestnut Post Oak and Black oak pointers Thence West crossing the road leading to Livingston one hundred and seventeen poles to a stake and Black Oak pointer in John Selbys east boundry Thence North eighty eight poles to a stb stake and Black oak and Black Jack pointers Thence East one hundred and seven poles to a Stake Thence North one hundred and eighty poles to a Stake and Hickory and bkack oak Pointers Thence West eighty poles to two white oaks Thence North one hundred and eleven poles to a smallpost oak and Black gum Thence East eighty poles to two Small beach oaks Thence South and eighteen poles to a Hickory Poast OakMarch BanksSouthWest corner Thence East one hundred and sixteen poles crossing the Road leading to Livingsten to four Black oaks Thence North five poles to a post Oak and Hickory Thence East sixty two poles to a Hickory and post Oak thence SouthThirty seven poles to a stake Thence East fifty poles to a stake Thence South twenty poles to a s take Thence East one hundred poles to a Spanish Oak and two Chestnuts pointers Thence South one hundred and thirty poles to a Post Oak and Black Gum Thence West two hundred and thirty six poles to a Black and P st oak Thence South twenty two degrees East forty four poles to a Black and post oak Thence South fifty degrees East thirty poles to a Walnut Thence South forty five degrees West six and a half poles to twoBkack oaks Thence South thirty n nine Degrees East twelve poles to the BeginningTo have and to hold the same to the siaid Algood his heirs and assigns forever I do covenant with the said Algood that I am lawfully seized of said land have a good right to convey it and that the same is unincumbered I dofurther covenant and bind myself my heirs and representatives to warrent and defend the title to the said land and every part thereof to the said Algood his heirs and assigns against the Lawful claims of all persons This day of Aprile 1858
                                                                            SEAL

(THE end of this one)

RECORDS OF MRS. LULA ALGOOD, (CON)

This Indenture made this day 22 of Oct, Eighteen hundred and twenty four between William Dillard of the County of Wilson and State 6f Tennessee of the one part and William Algood of the county and state aforesaid of the other part witnesseth that the said William Dillard and for consideration of the sum of two hundred and twenty five Dollars to him in Hand paid the Receipt whereof acknowledged hath granted bargained sold and delivered and by these presents doth grant bargain sell and deliver unto the Said William Algood his heirs Exor. Administrators or assigns a certain tract or parcel 6 Land situayed lying and being in the county of Wilson on the waters of Cedar Creek containing forty six acres and sixtypoles beginning at a Red bud and white Oak in George Bradleys North West corner running 126 poles to a ced cedar Thence East 6¼ polos to a stake thence South to an ironwood and Elm on a Branch procseding from a Pond just above thence with the meaders of a Branch down to a barnbeam thence South 78 Degrees West to the beginning containing 46 acres and 60 poles be the same more or less which piece or parcel of Land with all and every improvement and appertance of Land with all and and evrery improvement and appertenance therein to belonging or in any wise appertaining the said William Dillard hath hereby Should for himself his Heirs Exor. Administrators or assigns and doth forever waerrentd and defend the title of said Land unto the Said William Algood his heirs Exors adm or assign free from sall and every claim or claims of any person p or persons what so ever to the onlyuse and behalf of him the Sd William Algood his Heirs Exors Adminst or assigns forever

In witness where of the Said William Dillard hath hereunto Set his Hand and affixed his Seal the day and date above written or mentioned
Signed Sealed and delivered in presents of

               William Dillard (SEAL)

Jurat- Ennis Douglas
James W. Adcock

DEED NO 113

Joel Algood enters Three hundred acres of land in Putnam County on the waters of the Falling waters Beginning on John J. Srlys South East corner ad and running thence West with his line Thence South Thence East Thence North With Stephen D. Burton's west boundry of said Algoods South bpundry Thence with said line to said Seleys East boundry Thence South with his East boundry to the Beginning

              This July 13, 1858
A copy Tast   Joel Algood Locator
 Jon Buck Jr.
Entry Taker of Putnam County

DEED
RECORDS OF MRS. LULA ALGOOD (CON)

Deed- Made to A, J. McDonald who purchased of W. F. Sept 7th 1853 I witnessed by said Bell & Wm Dillard I bind myself to pay William T Bell four hundred and sixteen dollars The consideration of the obligation such that whereas the said Bell for this day purchased of me for two hundred and eight dollard and sixty five cents on the following payments to wit one hundred andfifty four dollars the 25 day of December next and fofty four dollars andsix ty five cents on the 25 day of January 1853 which his note under seal have this day Exarated to me a tract of land in the State of Tennessee Wilson County District bounded as follows Beginning on a black d and white oak & a black Gum in Elijah Johns North boundry and thence East seventy two poles to a dogwood and Box Elder Thence North two degrees wast i thirty one poles to two ten pointers in a hollar Thence west twelve poles to two poplars pointers Thence forty and a half degrees West thirty poles to a sugar tree Thence South fourteen poles to a Samall Black Walnut on a large Branch Thence South seventy five degrees West twenty poles down said branch Thence North sixty four degrees W st with said brancgh twelve poles Thence West four and a half poles to a Stake in Daid Wheeler East boundry Thence South two and a half degrees west ninty two poles to the beginning cantaining twenty three acres and twenty and nine poles be the same more or less if I should make or cause to be made to thesaid Wm h s heirs or assigns a good and sufficient title in the simple with general warrentty on the making of the past payment Then this obligation to be void ThisNov the 1st i 1657

H. Tinsley Bond-
B. T. BEll Sam A, Algood
    To Wm T. Bell
23 acres deed made to A. J. McDonald who purchased of W. T. Bell Sept, 7th 1853

I William Terry I have this day Bargained and sold and hereby transfer and convey to James McKinley and his heirs forever for the consideration of Twenty five Dollars to me paid a tract of land in the State of Tennessee Overton County and District number 1 containing by estimation Thrty acres be the same more or less and bounded as follows on the waters of Bear Creek Beginningat a small Hickory and three white oaks pointers the North East corner of a fifty acre survey made in the name of Robert Peek and nowowned by said William Terry running nine and one half poles toma small Black oak a post Oak and two Black oaks pointers corner to Henry Brewingtons fifty Acre tractthence West with the same one hundred poles to a Black oak on the Banks of Bear Creek in a line of Robert Peeks tract south with the same seventeen poles to a stake south ninety two and one half poles to a stake a Black oak and Hickory pointers thence East thirty three poles to a stake a Hickory post oak and Black oak saplins pointers thence North passing theSouth west corner of said fifty acres tract at two poles and with the sm same in all one hundred and two poles to a Hickory Peeks corner East with the same fifty poles to the Beginning To have and to hold the same to the a said James McKinny his heirs and assigns forever I do covenant and bind myself my heirs and Representatives to warrent and defend the title of said land to James McKinney his heirs and assigns forever against and claims tob be madeby myself or any person claiming through or under me but nofurther

RECORDS OF MRS. LULA ALGOOD (CON)

this day of August 1850

William Terry (Xhis mark)   SEAL

Attest
D. W. Hawes
S. D. Burton
Jonathin Fowler

William Terry
    To Deed 50 acres
James M. McKinloy

RECORDS OF MRS. LULAA LGOOD (CON)

Lebanon June 21st 1865

Mrs. Nancy Algood,
Madam;

    I commence suit on a number of notes belonging to your Husband estate before the war commenced Nothing has been done the breaking out of the war but now I suppose the courts will be held reguelrly and I wish to prosecute the suit most all my papers notes & c were destroyed and I will be obliged to you if you will send me a copy of the receipt you have of mine for the notes placed in my hand for collections. I have copies of all the notes so that nothing will be lost I will have to only have to swear to the amount of ech note which I can easily do as I took the precaution to take copies I wish the copy of my receipt to compare with my copies and see if there are any notes that I havent copies ofLet me hear from you at your earliest convenience.

                                 Respectfully & C
                                 L. H. Bostick

RECORDS OF MRS. LULA ALGOOD (CON)

State of Tennessee No 2886
To all to whom These Presents shall come, Greetings:
Know ye, That for and in consideration of the sum of twelve and one half cents per acre paid in the office of the Entry Taker of Overton County and entered On the 29th day of June 1824 pursuant to provisions of an Act of the General Assembly of saidState Passed on the twenty second day of November, one thousand eigth hundred and twenty three by No 166 there is granted by the said State of Tennessee unto Nathan Bartlett A certain tract or parcel of Land containing fifty acres by survey bearing date the 23 day of July 1825 lying in said county on both siades of the road leaving from William Marchbanks to Ann Quarles and bounded as followsto wit: Beginning at hickory at h the foot of a mountain running South 23 d East with the mountain forty poles to a post oak Thence South 40 Eadt with the mountain forty poles to a post oak Thence with one hubdred and twenty six poles to aStake in a glade thence N. Eighty two poles to a Stake and two black Jack pointers Thence East eighty four poles to a small white oak and chestnut pointer tyence South fifty poles to the Beginning

With the hereditaments and appurtenances To have an to hold the said tract or parcel of land with its appurtenances to the said Nathan Bartlett In witness whereof William Carroll, Govnor of the State of Tennessee, hath hereunto set his hand and causednthe Great S al of the State to be affixed at Murfreesborough on the Seventeenth day of November in the Year of Our Lord one thousand eight hundred and twenty five and of the Independance of United States the fiftieth

                                          By Governor
                                            Daniel Graham
                                            Secretary
                                    Wm Carroll

No 2886
Nathan Bartlett 50 acres
Overton County

Property of L. M. Bullington, Cookeville, Tenn, Putnam County.

Entry: John W. Simpson, Three hundred acres of Land in Jackson County on the Waters of Indian Creek (Caney Fork) Beginning on David McClinttooks South West corner running North to Drapers line West so far as to include three hundred acres by adjoining Holomansline, and the lines of two Entries of Huff and with Holomans line to the beginning for complainant.

July 22nd, 1821 $300. John W. Simpson

No 966   A Copy C. R. Scvanland, E. T. J. C.

No 966   John W. Simpson copy Entry   300 acres.

Property Of L. M. Bullington, Cookeville, Tenn Putnam Co.

Entry: No 3040, made in office White County, entered Nov, 18, 1847Taken of White County entered Nov, 1837, granted by the State, 9, 1830, unto Isaac A.Huddleston , containing 68 acres surveyed Nov, 24, 1838on Waters of Little Caney Fork, Beginning, Pointer, Charles Huddleston South W. corner of 100 acressurvey, running then E. to John Bullock corner, then S. to BullocksS. West Corner, East then S. to Lewis Huddleston corner, thenW, then North, with a tract 300 acre That Isaac L Huddleston now liveson them run in Davis Huddleston line of 86 acre tract.

    Test.   James K. Polk, Govner, of Tennessee.at Nashville,Tenn
                    Oct. 16, 1839.
                          By the Govner,
                          James K. Polk

Luke Lea, Secretary.

           Property of L. M. Bullington, Cookeville, Tenn, Putnam Co.

Deed: From David Huddleston to Isaac A. Huddleston, Jackson County, Oct, 17, 1850

    Consideration 106,00, District.No 10, 100 acres, Beginning on the Co line Countys of Jackson and White, running South to Thomas Hopkins North b line, West North then South.

                          Daivid Huddleston (x his mark)

Tests   J. L. Huddleston,   Russell Moore, Clerk, Putnam County Court
         John L. Huddleston
         Ack, Sept 25, 1854,

Recd for Reg. Oct, 5, 1854, In Book A Page 35

                William Baker,Reg.of Putnam County.

Reg. fee $1.00

State Tax 2 acres 15

           Property Of L. M. Bullington, Cookeville, Tenn. Putnam County

State Tennessee No 6931,Consideration one cent per acre paid in to office of the entry taker of Jackson County and entered May, 6, 1826, General Assembly of State passed on the 22 Nov.1823 and the acts Supplementalthereonto, by No934 Granyed by the State Tennessee to David Huddleston Land 100acres, Dec. 15,1826 on Falling Water, bounded, Beginningat a Hickory on the County line dividing the counties of White andJackson, running with lineSoutj. West, In Thomas Hopkins North boundry line West withHopkins line, then North then East, South to Beginning.
            In witness whereof William Carroll, Governor, of S. T.
      Sealed at Nashville, Tenn, Sept. 25, 1827.
                  By Gov. Wm. Carroll
Reg. of D. McGavoc   Daniel Graham, Secretary.
   D. R.
Recorded Dec. 18, 1827
I. J. Summer,D. R.
No 966,John W. Simpson.
copy of entry-300 acres

Property Of Virgil Denny, Buffalo Valley, Tenn.

The State of Tennessee No 7612
To all to whom these presents shall come, Greetings:
　　　Know ye that by virtue of certificate No 982 dated the 17th day of Aprile 1812 "esind" by the Register of West Tennessee to William P. Anderson and entered on the C day of May 1812 by No 8090.
There is granted bt the said State of Tennessee unto David Young assigne of the said William P. Adnrson a certain tract of land cantaining two and a half acres by survey bearing date the 21 day of July 1813 lying in White County in the first district on the Falling Water of Caney Fork and bounded as follows to wit: Beginning at a White Oaks atandin about five poles below said Young lower salt peter Cave formedly worked by him running thence North twenty one poles to a post on the side of a cleft thence West nineteen poles to a post and black gum chestnut & poplar pointers thence South crossing a hollow twenty one poles by two hickorys thence east nineteen poles to the Beginning including said Young Cave. With the Hereditoments & appartenances To have and to hold said tract or Parcel of Land with its appurtenances to the said David Young and his heirs forever
In witness whereof
　　　Willie Blunt Govnor of the State of Tennessee Hath hereonto set his hand and caused the great Seal of the State to be affixed at Nanhville on the Nineteenth day of Aug in the year of Our Lord one thousand eight hundred and fifteen and of the Independance of the United States the fortieth.
　　　　　　　　　By the Govnor
　　　　　　W. G. Blunt, Secretary　Willie Blont

David Young is entitled to the with in mentioned tract of land
　　　　　　　　D. M. Gavåck Reg West Tennessee

Recorded in the Reg Office of West Tennessee, Sept 13, 1815
　　　　　　　　DM Gavåck Reg.

No 7612 David Young
　2½ acres, White County.

Property of Virgil Denny, Buffalo Valley, Tenn.

State of Tennessee, Putnam County.
    Personally appeared before me County Court Josiah Cole as describing to the with in deed of conveyance who being first sworn depose and say that he was acquainted with the bargainors of the with in deed of conveyance and that they acknowledge the same in his presence to be their act and deed for the purpose and things therein contained.
    Witness my hand at office the 10th day of August A. D. 1857
        Russell Moore, Clerk

State of Tennessee, Russell Moore, Clerk of Putnam County Court John Jared as ascribing witness to the with in deed of conveyance who being first sworn depose and say that he was acquainted with the bargainors of the with due deeds of conveyance and that they acknowledge the same in his presence to be their act and deed for the purpose and things therein contained.
    Witness my hand at the office th 14th day of December 1857.
        Russell Moore, Clerk.

The following was written on the back of old deed)
    The Annex Deed of conveyance was filed in my office and noted for registration in Reception Book Pages 56&57 on the 2nd day of January 1858 at 3 o'clock P. M. and reg. in B. on Page 2, 13, 14i 15, 16, and 17
        William Baker, Register Putnam County.

Property of Virgil Denney Buffalo Valley, Tenn

Heirs of Mark Young, Doc. To Deed Distributive shares.
Clks. 50
State Tax 26.
Recorded on Page 147, Book A Putnam County, Tennessee,
     R. Moore Clerk.
Clerk fee and Tax 76
Reg. fee   1.62½
Maid to S. Anderson, State of Tennessee, Putnam County.
    To Moses Jared Esq. You are here by artherised and Empowered to the examination of Leaner McKee, polly Ballard and Ruth Helens the feñal covet Prevately and apart from her husband relation to her free execution of the with in or annexed Deed and the same to taken certify ender your hand and witness.
    Russell Moore, Clerk of the County Court, Putnam County at office the 15th day of Aprile A. D. 1857.
    Russell Moore, Clerk, Putnam County.

Property of Judge F, Harris, Cookeville, Tennessee

STATE OF TENNESSEE, PUTNAM COUNTY.

I, E. H. Stone, Clerk of the County Court, do hereby certify that proof under Oath has been made before me that J. C. Freeze falls within the provision of Section I, of an Act entitled "An Act to Limit the Elective Franchise" passed June 5th 1865, and is therefore a qualified voter of said County.

Given under my hand at office the 31 day of July, 1865.

E. H. Stone, Clerk.

C. N. O.   32

Dist. No 2

Records Owned by Mrs, JOhn Howard, 207, Locust St. Cookeville, Tenn.

Gentlemen and Commissionera the undersigned wish you to employ Ralph Scott to Te&
Teach the publick School at Nails School house We believe him to be competent as
to Scholarship and he can give a good reccomendation as a teacher July 16, 1848

No talking and laughin in time of School, no swaring, no climing cross no name
incleur no telling tales in School nor out of School. No nicknaming-you must not
go to no neighbors house at twelve oclock without make it none to me.delay no time
going nor coming from school noquarling nor fiting .

All that is sixteen years old will quit School or take the licking if they
brake the Rules.

(Contract for school teaching)

March 24th 1847

Mr. Monroe, Miller Brothers & Sisters,
Mr.& Mrs. Vandever request to your Company at the house on friday the 26th
of this Inst. to a quiltin & N. B. You must come without fail,
I am Respectfully
W? M?.Dawson

Mr. J. M. Miller
S Vally
Trd by Mr. Fergerson

Records Owned by Mrs. John Howard, Cookeville, Tenn (Con)

Montgomry County, (Va.) I do hereby certify that Robert Miller hath taken and subscribed the oath of affirmation of allegiance and fidelity, as directed by an act of General Affembly intituted An act to oblige the free male inhabitants of this Sftate above a cetain age to give affurance of allegiance to the fame and for other purposes, witness my hand seal this Death da of Sept 1777.

            Stephen Trigg (Seal)

State of Tennessee, Putnam County : To any Regular Ordained Minister of the Gospel having the care of Souls or to any Justice of the Peace in and for said County or to any Judge or Chacter of said state Bond and security having bin given according to Law you are here but given or authorized to solemnize the Rites of Matrimony between Lancaster Randolf and Rebecca Shirley of said county and join them together as Husband and wife in the Holy Wedlock given under my hand at office this 27 day of November A. D. 1854

            Russell Moore, Clerk
            Putnam County Court.
          by byrum C. Johnson,
            Depty

Lancaster Randolf
 us writ

Rebecca Shirley

          Tax Receipts

June 30th 1813, Recd of Samuel Miller one dollar Seventy five cts in full of all amount against him Recd by me John Cain for
         Samuel Harrison

Received this 28th Aprile 1817$ .15 cts from Samuel Miller foe direct tax upon the property of said Miller in the County of Overton, for 1816 under the act of Congress foe the 3rd collective district of Tennessee.
 Under the act of Congress for the 3rd Collective District of Tennesee.

         W. Brown, Dept
         Collector 3rd District Tennessee

Records Owned by Mrs John Howard, 207, Locust St, Cookeville, Tenn (Con)

Article made and Entered into We the Undersigned doth agree to imploy James M. Miller To Teach School at the Stamps School house forthe Term of two months said Miller doth agree to Teach the School to the best of his Skill and Judgment at Eighty Cents per Schollar per month We the undersigned doth agree to pay said Miller good Trade at the Market price such as young cattle or pork hogsdelivered on foot or corn paid at the experation of the School this the 30 day of Sept, 1850

James Whiteacer	Paid	1
Mary Netherton	"	2
Joseph Henry	"	2
Job M, Jackson	"	2
William Stamps	"	3
James Stamps	"	1
John Henry	"	1
Robert Roberts	"	1
Ligeard Henry	"	1
Thomas Hill	"	1

(This Record is 165 Years Old)

This are to Certify that Robert Miller and His wife and her from her Childhood up and him since he came amongst us the Both always Behaving them selves in a Christian manner and may be Remembered to any Christian society where God and his Providence shall order their lot Certified by us his day of May 15th 1771

    Cedar Bridge Congogation,   J. L. River
                                      James Gilmore
                                      JohnPage

Records Owned by Mrs. J_hn Howard, Cookeville Tenn (Con)

No. I22I7
Department of the Interior

War of I8I2   Survivors Pension

T. Certify That in Conformity with the Law of the United States approved February I4, I87I, Samuel Miller late a Lieutenant of Captain Jno. Millet's Company Tenn Militia is inscribed on the Pension List Roll of the Nashville Tenn Agency at the rate of eight dollars per month to commence on the fourteenth day of February one thousand eight hindred and seventy one No Sale transfer or mortgage of any description whatever of the whole or any part of the pension payable in virtue of this certificate is ofany lagal or binding force against either the pensioner or the United States.

Given at the Department of the Interior this 7th Day of February, one thousand eight hindred and seventy two
                   B. C. Cowen
                       Actg Secortary of the Pensenor

Examinined and Countersigned.
         J. W. Batton
         Commisiioners of Pensions

Payable quarterly on the 4th of September and 4th of December at Nashvile, Tenn
By William J. Stokes
  U. S. Pension Agt.
John Mayhew Clerk

Records owned by Mrs. John Howard,
207- Pocust St. Cookeville, Tenn.

State of Tennessee, Putnam County.

To any Ordained Minister of the Gospel having the care of Souls, or to any Justice of the Peace for said county, or to any Judge or Chancellor of said state
Bond and security having been given according to law youare hereby authorized to solemnize the Rites of Matrimony between John Randolf and Mary Randolph of said county and join them together as Husband and wife in Holy Wedlock.
    Given under my hand at office in Cookeville the IIth day of Dec. A. D. 1855.

                Russell Moore, Clerk
                Putnam County Court.

By virtue of the above License I have this day Solemnized the Rites of Matrimony between the parties therein named, in the presence of respectable witness.
    Given under my hand this the day 1855.

John M. Randolf
 To Marriage License
Mary Randolf
 IIth Dec. 1855

Records Owned by Mrs. John Howard, Cookeville, Tenn. (Com)

State of Tennessee, Putnam County

This indenture made and Entered into this 15ht day of November One Thousand and Eight hindred and forty four Between Noah Sherly of the one Calvin Eldridge of the other part both of county and State afore said his the Sd Noah Sherly for and in consideration of the sum of one hundred dollars inhand by the said Calvin Eldridge the recipt whereof is hereby firmly acknowleds hath granted bargained and sold and by these presents doth grant Bargained and sell alied convey and confirm unto the Sd Calvin Eldridge his heirs Executors Administrators or assigns and from all and every other person Claiming or to claim a tract or parcel of land containing fifty acres be the same more or less situated lying and being in the County of Putnam and State of Tennessee his Beginning on Samuel Johnson North Bounding line of his fifty acre survey on a poplar running thence North West to a Spotted Oak on the side of a ridge thence West to a Chestnut on yhe top of the Bench Thence meandering the top of the Bench to hutsons South line This Conditional line between the two tracts now owned by Calvin Eldridge thence to Hustons corner thence fourteen poles to Hustons Corner running West fourteen poles to a white oak and Sugar tree thence South one hundred and nineteen poles to a poplar and a chestnt on a hillside thence East to Samuel Johnstons corner of his fifty acre Survey passing same to Beginning with all the singular heredetiments and appertuances to have and to hold for the use and benefit of the Sd Calvin Eldridge signed and delivered in the presents of us

Attest--James W. Tenessee, Wm. Sparks, Noah Sherly X His mark

By virtue of part of Said warrent of Christiany Tally Enters 20 acres of land in our 3rd District and County of Overton on the Drye fork of obes river adjoining john Millers 50 acres Entry beginning at a black gum tree thence east 40 poles to a stake at the past of the bushey Mountain thence North 45 Deg. East with said Mountain for complement

December 7th 1809.
Christiany Tally
Locator

Christianys Tally's Location 20 acres.

Property of Judge B. C. Huddleston, Cookeville, Tenn, Putnam Co.

The State of Tennessee, No 10143,
To all to whom these Presents Shall come Greetings: Know ye that in considerstion of Military service performed by Benjamin C. Jeffries to the State of North Carolina Warrent No 4436 dated the 2nd day of Dec, 1796 and entered on the 15th day of November 1816 byNo 346 S, There is granted by said State of Tennessee unto Thomas Hopkins assignee of the heirs of the said Benjamin C Jeffries, a certain tract or parcel of Land containing Thirty two acres part of Said Warrent by survey leaving date the 13th day of May 1815 lying in White County in the third district on the waters of the Falling Waters & East of the Wagon Road leading from Sparta to William Jones Esq. and bounded as follows Towit: Beginning on two beeches near a marshy branch running thence South near the foot of the Mountain one hundred and two poles to a Beach & Dogwood, Thence West fifty poles to a white aok near a branch, Thence North one hundred and two poles to three blackoaks, Thence East including Welches improvements to the Beginning. With the hereditaments and appurtenances, To have and to hold the said tract or parcel of land with its appurtenances to the said Thomas Hopkins and his heirs forever in witness whereof Joseph McMinn, Gov. of the State of Tennessee hath hereunto set his hand and caused the Great Seal of the State to be affixed at Knoxville on the Eleventh day of June in the Year of Our Lord one thousand eight hundred and seventeen and of the Independenac of the United States for the forty First.

By the Governor.
Wm. Alexender Secretary.   Joseph McMinn.
Recorded in the Registers office of West Tennessee, Sept. 26th 1817
D. M. McGavock, Reg.

Property of Judge B. C. Huddleston, Cookeville, Tenn. Putnam Co.

State of Tennessee No 20516, To all to whom these Presents shall Come, Greetings: Know ye that virtue of a part of certificate No 2535 dated the 13th day of November 1816 ipued by register of West Tennessee to Robert Searcy for 320 acres and entered on the 21st day of March 1817 No 5369, There is granted by the State of Tennessee into Charles Huddleston assignee of the said Robert Searcy, a certain tract or parcel of land containing Twelve acres by survey leaving date of 22 day of October 1818 lying in the Third District in White County on the waters of the Falling Waters and bounded as follows towit: Beginning at the South east corner of Welches 32 acre survey running thence east twenty four poles to a stake and pointers on the side of the Mountain thence North along the same as a natural landing eighty poles to a pointers thence West striking said Huddlestons corner and with the same twenty four poles to Welches corner thence South along his line eighty poles to the Beginning. With the hereditaments and appurtenances to have and to hold the said tract or parcel of land with its appurtenances to the said Charles Huddleston and his heirs forever. In witness whereof William Carroll, Governor, of the State of Tennesseehath hereunto set his hand caused the Great Seal of the State to be affixed at Murfreesborough on the 25th day of September in the Year of Our Lord one thousand eight hundred and twenty three and of the Independance of the United States the forty eight.

Wm. Carroll. Gov.
Daniel Graham, Secretary

Property of Judge B. C. Huddleston, Cookeville, Tenn
Putnam County.

This Indenture made and entered into this fifth day of August in the Year of Our Lord one thousand Eight hundred and neneteen between Thomas Ingram heirs and legal representative of William Ingram, Decd. of the County of Hawkins and State of Tennessee by William Mitchell his attorney in fact of the one part and Charley Huddleston and John C. Huddleston of the county of White and State afore said of the other part, witnesseth that for and in consideration of the sume of two thousand dollars current money to him the said Thomas Ingran his legal representative of William Ingram Decd. in land paid by the said Charles Huddleston & John C. Huddleston the receipt whereof he doth hereby acknowledge and thereof doth elquith and power dischsrgethem the said Charles Huddleston and John C. Huddleston their heirs executors and administrators, Doth Grant bargans sell aline enfossed and confirmed unto them the said Charles Huddleston and John C. Huddleston, their heirs and assigns forever two certain tracts and parcel of land containing in all three hundred and forty acres lying and ening in the County of White and State of Tennessee to William Ingram by Grant No 13252 for 100 acres and Grant No 13253 for 200 a acres Granted to the heirs of William Ingram, Decd., both dated the 1st day of Apr. 1819, and bounded as follows Towit: Grant No 13252 Beginning at two small hickory the South West corner to Wolsey W. Pearces occupant survey running South and bounded forty poles to a stake thence East one hundred and sixty poles to a small white oak and water white oak on the South side of ridge, thence North one hundred and forty poles to a white walnut mulberry and elm and said Pearces South boundry, Thence West with Pearces line one hundred and sixty poles to the Beginning including part of the land originally surveys as an occupant right in the name of Joel Alexandria Grant No 13253 for 200 acres bounded as follows Towit: Beginning at a stake the south West Corner of William Ingram 140 acres boundry line thence East one hundred and sixty poles to a white oak and water white oak Wm. Ingram South East corner thence Sot South two hundred poles to a black oak & two white oaks, thence West one hundred and sixty poles to a stake a chestnut black oak & two post oak pointers near an at road, thence North two hundred poles to the Beginning including part of the land formerly surveyed as an occupant sight in the name of Joel Alexandria, Togather, with the hereditaments and appurtenances, To have and hold the above tracts or parcels of land to gather with the hereditaments and appurtenances thereunto or in any wise asscertaining to the only proper use of them the said Charles and Jno. C. Huddleston their heirs and assigns forever, and the said Thomas Ingram heir and legal representative of William Ingram Decd. for himself his heirs, Executors administrators and assigns the title interest claim and demand of in recd. to the above discribed tracts or parcel of land will warrent and forever defend unto them the said Charles Huddleston and John C. Huddleston their heirs, executors administrators and assigns against the right title claim interest or demand of all and all manner of person or persons claimimg or to claim the same or any part thereof, In Testimony whereof be the said Thomas Ingram by his attorney in fact William Mitchell hath hereunto set his hand and affixed his seal the day and year first above written signed, sealed and Acknowledged in presence of,

       A. R. Low
       Rashford Irwin (X his mark)
       William Mitchell, all yenfail for
       Thomas Ingram   atty in fact

State of Tennessee, October session, A. D. 1819, W. County
 The due execution of the foregoing Deed of Conveyance from Thomas Ingram to Charles Huddleston and John C. Huddleston was this day acknowledged in open court by William Mitchell attorney in fact for Thomas Ingram for the payment and things therein mentioned and ordered to be recorded let be Registered Given at office the 18th day of october, 1819.
       Jacob A Lane, Clerk (Seal)
       Putnam County Court by his Depty,
       A. R. Lane

Recd. the State Tenn,
Test of Conveyance,

State of Tennessee, White County, Thomas Barnes, Esq. comes before M. Samuel Johnson an acting Justice of the Peace qr. said county and made oath that sometime between the sixth & twentieth of June test that John Cleghorn and Charles Huddleston come before him and confess three judgments on three notes for eighty five dollars Eighty seven &½ per cts each in favor of William Hunter sew which notes a warrent was left by him the said Thomas Barnes in the hands of William Hows Esq. of Jackson County to render the judgment on each warrent which warrents was to have been transferred by the said Wm. Hows, Esq. to him the said Thomas Barnes on the day after residition of the said judgment which means was the said Thomas Barnes further deposeth & Layeth the reason why he got William Esq. to write the judgment for him was that he had been after medicine fer his son who was very sick at that time & the parties following him to act on the notes a day after they confessed judgment on the notes both parties agreed that he was in a hurry to get home that said William Hows should write the judgment agreed to the amount of the notes.

Sworn to & Subscribed to before me, Lamb Johnson, justice of the Peace.
January, 11, 1821

Thos. Barnes,
Affidvit-

Property of Judge B. C. Huddleston, Cookeville, Tenn. Putnam Co.

State of Tennessee, No 2039. To all to whom these presents shall come, Greetings-
Know ye that for and in consideration of sum of twelve and one half cents per acre paid into the office of the Entry Taker of Jackson County and entered on the 26th day of June 1824 pursuant to the provisions of an act of the General Assembly of said State passed on the 22nd day of November 1823, by No 144, there is granted by the State of Tenn. unto Charles Huddleston a certain tract or parcel of Land containing Fifty acres by survey bearing date the 2nd day of Aprile 1825, lying in the said county on the waters of the Falling Waters and bounded as follows, to-wit: Beginning at a black oak it being rhe South corner of said 20 acre tract then East with North boundry line of said tract twenty poles to a hickory in Thomas Barnes West boundry line thence North said Barnes line forty five poles to a post oak the south east corner of said Huddlestons 15 acre tract thence west with the south boundry line of said 15 acre tract twenty four poles to a stake and two chestnut pointers, thence North thirty six poles to a Spanish oak the Norty west corner of sd said Huddleston 15 acre tract, thence West twentyseven and a half poles to a hickory thence South one hundred and twenty one poles to a Spanish oak, thence east forty one and one half poles to the beginning. With the hereditaments and appurtenances to have and to hold the said tract or parcel of land with its appurtenances to the said Huddleston and his heirs forever. In witness whereof William Carroll, Governor of the State of Tennessee hath hereonto set his hand and caused the Great Seal of the United States to be affixed at Murfreesborough on the 13th day of August in the Year of Our Lord one thousand eight hundred and twenty five and the Independance of the United States the fiftieth

By the Governor, Wm. Carroll

Daniel Graham, Sec.
Recorded in the Registers office of West Tenn. Feb. 4th, 1826
H. W. McGavock. D. R.

Property of Judge B. C. Huddleston, Cookeville, Tenn Putnam Co.

State of Tennessee No 20511-To all to whom these presents shall come, Greeting:
Know ye that by virtue of part of Certificate No 943 dated the 2nd day of June 1815 ipued by the Register of East Tennessee to Nathaniel Taylor for 50 acres and entered on the 25th day of August 1815 by No 4114, There is granted by the State of Tenn, unto Charles Huddleston assignee of the said Nathaniel Taylor, a certain trat or parcel of land containing fifteen acres by survey leaving date the 17th day of February 1816 lying in the Third District in White County on the waters of Falling Waters and bounded as follows to wit: Beginning at a hickory and white oak on the We West boundry line of Thomas Barnes claim and near the foot of the Mountain running thence east sixty nine poles to a chestnut and postoak on said Barnes line thence North to the Beginning. With the hereditamenst and appurtenances to have and to hold the said tract or parcel of land with its Appurtenances to the said Charles Huddleston and his heirs forever, In witness whereof William Carrolle, Gov. of the State of Tennessee hath hereunto set his hand and caused the Great Seal of the State to be affixed at Murfreesborough on the 25th day of September in the Year of Our Lord one thousand eight hindred and twenty three and the Independance of the United States the forty eight.

By the Governor, William Carroll.
Danile Graham, Secretary.

Property of Judge B. C. Huddleston (Con)

45

State of Tennessee, White County, J. Turner Lane, Register of the County of White of aforesaid Do hereby certify that the within Deed of Conveyance together withithe testimonies thence endorsed was this 15th day of December, A. D. 1819 Registered in the register's office of said county fo White in Book F. and Page 374 given under my hand at office the date above written.

Test-
                                   Turner Lane, Register
  Thos. Ingram   To 340 acres in 2 tracts.
  Shas. & Thos. C. Huddleston

Property of Judge B. C. HUddleston, Cookeville, Tenn,

I, Charles Huddleston have this day barganer and sold and do hereby Transfer & convey to Jordan F. Huddleston his heirs& assigns forever for the consideration of Fifty Dollars to one in hand paid a certain Tract or Paecel ofland in the State of Tennessee, Putnam Co, District No1 containing by estimation Eighteen and a half of acres be the same more or less and bounded as follows, Beginning on a mountain oak the said Jordan F. Huddleston South East corner running South 40 poles to a stake &pointers the South East corner A 12 acres Grant No 20516 Granted to the said Charles Huddleston thence West 74 poles to a white oak near a small branch, thence North 40 poles to a stake & Dogwood pointerthe said Jordan F. Huddleston South E. corner, Thence East 74 poles to the beginning to have and to hold the same unto the saidJordan F, Huddleston his heirs & assigns forever I do covenant with the said Jordan F. Huddleston That I am Lawfully seized of said land have a goodright to convey it and thatthe same unemcumbered I dothen covenant and bind myself my heirs and Representatives to warrant and forever defendthis title to the said land and Every part thereof to the said Jordan F. Huddleston South East corner, Thence East 4 poles tothe beginning to have and to hold the same unto the said Jordan F. Huddleston, his heirs & assigns forever. I do covenent with the said Jordan F. Huddleston That I am Lawfully seized of said land have good right to convey it and That the same is unemcumbered I do for this covenant and bind myself, my heirs & representatives to warrent and foever defend land and every part there to the said Jordan F. Huddleston his heirs & assigns against the lawful claims of all persons whatsoever this 26th day of January, A. D. 1839.

                                                            Charles Huddleston (Seal)

Test-Russell Moore
    Joe Algood

State of Tennessee, Putnam County, Personally appeared before me Russell Moore, Clk. of Putnam County Court Charles Huddleston the within bargainer with whom I am personally acquainted and who acknowledge the due execution of the within deed of conveyance to be his act and deed for the purpose andthings therein contained is Recorded witnessed my hand at office the 26 day of January, 18 39

                                                            Russell Moore, Clerk

The written deed of conveyance was filed for Registration on the 26th day of Jan. 1139 & was noted on filation Book at pages 84& 85 at 4 p. m. I was registered on Book C. pages 181& 182

                                     S. W. Brown, Reg.

Charles Huddleston   To Deed 18½ acres
   Jordan F. Huddleston State Tax
     Clerk Fee 25
Reg.   Fee   1D5   Paid.

Property of Judge B. C. Huddleston, Cookeville, Tenn, Putnam County.

State of Tennessee No 7743-
To all to whom these presents shall come, Greetings, Know ye that by virtue of E Entry No 2517 made in the office of the Entry Takerof Jackson County and entered on the 4thday of December 1837 pursuant to the provisions of an act of General Assembly of said State passed on the 9th day of January1830, There is granted by the said State of Tennessee unto Chas. Huddleston a certain tract or parcel of Land containing Eighteen acres and Eighteen poles by survey bears date the 27th day of November1838 situated in said County Beginning at a small Spanish Oak and past Oak and Spanish Oak and past Oak pointer the South East corner of a fifty acre survey that the said Huddleston now lives on running thence Westwith the Sou South boundry lineof said survey forty and one half poles to two Spanish oaks the SouthWest corner of said fifty acres surveythence North with the West boundry line of said surveyonehundred and twenty one poles to a hickory which is now dead four dogwoods and black gum pointers the North West corner of said fifty acre survey, Thence West and xix and one half poles to a small hickory and hickory and dogwood pointers in theE. Boundry lineof an old survey Granted to Wm. Ingram thence South with the E. boundry line of thesame an hundred and sixty five poles to a white oak and pointers in the North boundryline of David Huddleston one hundred acre tract thence E. with the North boundry line of the same forty eight poles to a stake in the West boundry line of a thirty two acre tract,now belonging to the said Chas. Huddleston, thence North forty four poles. With the Hereditaments andappurtanances to have and to hold the said tract or parcelof land with its appurtenances to the said Chas. Huddleston and his heirs forever.

In witness where of James K. Polk, Gov. of the State of Tennessee has hereto set his hand and caused the Great Seal of the State to be affixed at Nashville on the 9th day of December 1839,C. 4th year of an Independance.

                                        By the Governor,
                                        James K/ Polk.

Jno. S. Young, Secretary.
Charles Huddleston is entitle to the within described tract of land
                                        Richard Nelson, Reg.of the Mountain Dis.

                                        By W. G. Sims D, register
Recorded in my office Book P. Page 325
                                        R. Nelson, Regst. of the Mountain Dist.

No 7743   Charles Huddleston, 18 acres and 18 poles, Jackson County.
Filed for registration in my office February 6th, 1855, at 10 o'clocka. m.
Registered in Book A-and Page 132-133&134
                         William Baker, Reg. for Putnam County

11 state-----$2\frac{3}{4}$

(From Collection of Mrs. B. C. Huddleston, Cookeville, Tenn. Putnam Co)

47

LIVINGSTON COUNTY MISSOURI,
JULY 14, 1845.

My Dear Father & Mother, Brothers & Sisters:

God bears me witness when I say that I know not how to begin to write to you, not-with-standing I am young yet I have wrote several letters, But this Cadmus, I was taught from my child-hood not when I say that thou wert a false prophet, yea, I say that htou wert a fool: If thou ever thought that thy flimsey invention though multiplied in to forty thousand ways, would be a full conductor to a Father & Mother of the feelings and emotions of an absent child, as this is worthless then I command the not but ask the to touch their hearts Almighty with the remembrance of by gonedays. Wake up; O, thou muse of other times and seasons, Bring flesh to some of their memory's the feelings of their own hearts, Almighty, with the remembrance of bygone days, Wake up O thou muse of other times and seasons, Bring flesh to some of hteir memory's the feelings of their own heart on the 12th of Aprile, 1810, and the first of Aprile 1812, that they may the better know the felings of their own child on the day of the first cause of this epistle the 11th of Aprile, 1845.

Mother, though the long lapse of thirty two years has passes I doubt not but you will recall your mother's valedictions on the 2th of Aprile 1812. Little did you then think you would see her no more on earth Hard sorrowful it is to part with friends, but it is harder still to part with her on whose bosom in helpless infancy we slept and from whose benevolent veins we draweth the first support of life. There is something in it which the painters brush has never touchd and the writers pen has never told, But it is so, From the mammoth to the mite, that can't be caught by microscopic eye neither and I loath to say it was so with me, For I know no man on earth ever loved his Father more than I love mine or more tnan I on every one of his brothers and Sisters wished a greater Blessing than on himself, Yet I say that it hurts me worse than all the rest to part with thee and though into an unutterably full and thankful heart I received al l their prayers and last words and remembered them well-yet thine I shall never forget. For oft that day as the roaring of the Stage wheels died away in echo on the destant hills, I could see thy venerable form drawn with the diseases and afflictions of the body and sorrows of mind, as thou raised thy withered hand and in agonizing prophetic tones that sounded like a death knell to my heart. The agonizing prophetic tones that sounded like a death knell to my heart, exclaimed I shall never no never, see my Child again.

O, my God, the agony of that moment, a prophecy concerning another one of thy children and now an unknown grave in a distant land interperts the prophecy Will mine be so Oh God, Thou knowest.

The sun was two hours high when we arrived at Carthage. The other Stage came not till dark and as the general confusion of the city and land laughs of the young men just returning from muster, did not corrospond with my feelings, I took a walk through the back streets and old lanes until I found myself upon the banks of the river. I satdown upon the green grass to my wonted employment a long and silent meditation, Up the river in full view was the confluence of the Caney Fork and Cumberland. I was looking at the immediate waters of my native land perhaps for the the last time and as I strained my eyes far up the clear blue waters of the former I imagined I could see its very fountains bursting out from beneath the mountain bas, I could see the sweetest of earths fountains where first I water uses knew, where oft in childhoods happy hours I slaked my burning thirst and cooled my heated brow. Then, too, I could see my noble old grand fathers where I have spent many happy hours in my childhood wandering its melancholy way around the deserted dwellings and lonesome orchard of thet once happy place, Neither did I ever look one that runs from beneath the grove where my own Father lived and where I had

(From Collection Of Mrs. B. C. Huddleston, Con.)

spent my later years.

Then, too, where the waters of the pleasant grove where from the score of saints ascended prayers for me when a disconsolated mourner, there is imagention I could see them all as on there gravelly beds they went gently murmering down, mingling joining in one as if to showpoor vain selfish hearted man, that united thet could carry their course even amid the mighty hills and barriers and that he himself, by devisions, wrangling and quarreling was proving the death of that heaven born truth, he trying to establish.

Many were the reflections I had at this place, Many the thoughts of days that are gone. Alas, gone forever. So great is the nature of the Soul that a volume is but a preface to what I thought and felt in that hour. Loud would I ask myself "If you be a land of such tall groves, sweet sorings and heaven inspieing breezes, Why do I have to leave thee? Why go from my father and Mother , Brothers and Sisters , Friends: Yea, all I have ever knew and all that was ever dear to me? Who have I murdered? Whose goods have I stolen? What great eveil have I done that I mustexile myself from them forever? Has slander with her hateful poisonous tongue tried to disgrace me with the family to whom I allow it an honor to belong? Do I go forth like Cain leaving my Father's family weeping more for my crimes than the loss of hteir Brother out of their circle? To none of these questions would my heart respond, Yea and I was lost as to what was the cause, Amid a thousand perplexing and unsatisfactory conjectures. "O thou, I exclaimed" who fixed the destiny ofman, who directeth the paths of hisfeet and pondereth all his goings Thou who firected with the samecare the fate of nations and heroes and causeth the blood in the veins of the fly, Tell me, Show me the cause Alas? I implore in vain,"I seem to be unobserved by God and all his creatures until evercome with anguish of Spirit my head insensibly sank upon my knees and I gave way to a relieving flood of tears, when I raised my eyes it was growing dusk, a blue mist was upon the waters, A spectre arosefrom the strem with seven large letters, his name, Written on his brow, O, could you have seenthat Spirit you would not blame me for writing a lengthly about him. His pale solem melancholy look; his tattered raiment, hisanxious deep gazing countenance. The haart of the affluent stoic though made of steel would have shed a tear over his forlorncondition. The dregs of disease were seated in his vitals whichtime and circumstances had changed into that most loathsome of all diseases, Dyspepsia. His cou tenance that was once happy and cheerful was notovercast with desponence and gloom and as I very anxiously gazed upon it my eye caught the letter on his brow; Hah "Poverty" I exclaimed and hevanished from my sight. The vision was of a moment and theinterpretation was of the same , and it is the Thou Unhappy fiend thatconducteth my hence Yea I see it, I feel it, I know it now. O, poverty; unfortunate, unhappy , unwelcome guest how many sweet daughters hast thou torn from a mothers heart and sent them into a land of strangers to fine a sustenance wherelieu they soon found an earlygrave? How many sons hastthou raised up and thrust out from their fathers to the utt ernost parts of the earth to make a fortune and a home and then threwpoor poor worm give up the ghost and die and know not wheather heleaves themt to a wise man or a fool. Yea, Time and Fate and circumstances has decreed it so fu from the foundation of the Earth Go to the Land of Nod and ask Cain and he will tell thee it was so with him and as thou returnest the Sons of Europe, Asia and Africa willc ry out unto thee. It was so with our Fathers "Yea the voice of Jacob hears witness to what I saw as he lay alone in the gloom of plains of Paden-Aran and it is answered by a sigh from the youthful Jacob aspensively he sat in the dark walls of Potiphars prison. Then, O, Thou director of all things as thou hast decreed it so with me I go resigned. I was stopped short in the midst of my meditations by the shrill sound of the drivers horn which told me the other stage had arrived. I arosefrom the ground. twas growing dark and pointing my hand up the astream exclaimed, "Tennessee; Land of my friends, Lands of my Fathers, Thou of only place I ever loved, thou only place I ever knew, Farewell, Blow on Heavenly breezes, Blow on and you tall nuciferous groves bend your giant heads and mingle yo youth linesome praise with theirs for ages yet to come,And you that first attracted my mindseyr , your crystal fountain of my Fathers Farewell- and should I ever

(From Collection of Mrs. B. C. Huddleston ConO)

taste thy cooling waters more continue to pore out thy jasper treasures, Flow a down the vale untill like thy formerowners and their children thou art scattered and lost in Times mightydispersion, And thou nearestone to the place of meditation like the old Spring of Castalia, may youpertify your attendants in rightousness, that as they meet from year to year to celebrate the works of the Lord they may continue tooffer up prayers for me for I am a mourner yet and will be to my grave For my heart is in the house of mourning but the heart d of the fool is in the house of mirth, (Ecc.7, 4) Come to me thou narrow hearted selfconceited sectarian and look at one who has the satisfying pleasure of feeling the same love for all the laborers in God's vine yard yes go the same Methodists, tho Indolent Denominations, I point the to them for the same purpose that Solomon pointed the sluggard to the ant , Thou Pleasant Grove Fountain Field Wood, and Friends, Farewell. And should I never again in body be with thee, oft in summer evenings twilight gray thou mayst see me in your mind eye as through your fileds I pass in the Golden Balloon Of Imagination, In a few Moments.

In a few moments we were sailing down the road towards old man dusk. We entered Nashville. We were up late that night. The next evening at business. Next morning at 8 O'clock when we got our matters finished, I went to the office to get Spartan's letter and drop Bro. Watson a line. The letter was not there although ithas since come by mail. I hurried back tomthe river, when I arrived the boat was unmoored. I sprang aboard and in twentyfour hours I was in Smithland. Here we waited twenty hours for a boat passing from Pittsburg to St. Louis and on Tuesday morning the 15th at sunrise we embarked on an Orleans boatb come from the South. As I stood here watching the slow blue waters of Ohio as they gently flow and poured into the Indians "Mad waters" and wasrapidly hurried off to the burning plains of the South. I could but exclaim with the Old Prophet I am a Hebrew and I fear the Lord , the God of Heaven, that made the sea and the dry land. At 2 o'clock a boat from Orleans stopped . We embarked and on Thursday morning the 17th we hove in sight of the glittering spires of St.Louis. There was near thirty boats anchored here and soon as we landed we hurried up the wharf watching the signsuntill we found that read Black Snake Hills, 4 o'clock this day". We went to the Captain made the arrangements, put our things aboard and having nine hours to stay we set out to search for Dorinda's grave. We went to the house where she died and consulted with Houston as the best means to proceed. He advised us to go to a place called Black Stables as the Sexton had lived there. We went there. They could tell us nothing of the sexton and his name was not on the Books. They directed us to the Catholic Cathedral Wentnthere and old Father Panco could'ntfind her name on his books. He directed us to the city Register. We went there and her name could not be found , not with standing there were numbers of graves in and around the place, and we knew not to which one to go. We determined to go no more of the register and we set out to hunt till we found it. Between 10 and 11 o'clock we found the grave yard. Although twas dark when he was there before, he knew the place and showed me whr where the carrage came in. There is about six acres enclosed, embracing two largesinks and a sharp ridge between, we followed the road around on the ridge till we came to the place where the hearse stopped.Now we knew we were in ten ft feet of her grave. Mother, shed not a tear when I tell you that though I was now so I could put my handon her grave(I wanted to have it walled in if it had taken mt lastgroat) but we could not tell which it was. We stayed there an hour or more, the sexton with us trying to ascertain but no purpose. I shall not attempt to say anything about my feeling as I turned and left the grave. Sleep on, My Sister, Sleep on. Though our bodies are close together theyknow it not our Spirits arecloser still and though thy wasted frame lies here

    Amid a land of Strangers
   Alone,unepitaphed, unshrouded, Unregistered, unknown,

FROM COLLECTION OF MRS. B. C. HUDDLESTON (CON)

If thy name is not registered here it is in Heaven,
By Angels hands
Whose pen is quill from his ethereal wing,
And his ink is liquid gold,
Whereby the Telescope of Faith I see thee now,
Looking on the family record
Anxiously waiting to see the only remaining
Two enrolled.
I could write a volum on this half would'nt then be told
But I leave it in the hands as the Poet did his case,
When he felt all and had no words to express it he said
" Come, thou expressive Silence, Tell the tale"

We left St. Louis at sunset Friday 18th and Tuesday night at dark the 22 we reached Brunswick and on the morning of the 23rd we struck into the Prairies I felt as the Israelites must have felt when they saw all the beauties of the Old Jewish Caanan. There was now befoer my mortal eyes a most pleasing prospect a more delightful view than I had ever pictured even in my Imagintion. For thirty miles, Yea farther then the eye could see twas an uninterrupted sea of waving grass without the entervention of a tree or shn shrub on Tuesday morning we reached my brother in laws and found them all well and getting on finely in the world. I reckon there was joy at our arrival. Many were the questions about you all and many the answers, forgetting the pwtty faults and turning them into graces.

In a day or two I went on to Ruben Perkins and nothing would do now but I must teach them a school. He had been looking for me out here for months and had determined that as soon as I came I should teach them a school. I told them that in ten days I was going on to Goshen and from there to PLatte and that I should not be here again for months.

Louisa would'nt listen to me talking of setting anywhere only close to he and we kept on till finally I told him if he would make me up a school if my breast would permit I would teach them a school for six months.

On the 11th day of May I went to Gishen. I found all well there, met my Aunt Nancy, Old man McClelland, Ruben and Maria a mile or two this side of Uncle Rhea's. Mother, My Aunt is the most hale healthy looking woman you eve saw. I rode with her that evening home and ask her the cause of such an uncommon change in her health and person she told me it was the air. She said when she first came here she thought she had never felt such a delightful breezein her life and she would go out in the yard to a flat rail she had and get on the top of the fence and let the wind blow on her for hours and this is what brought her to. It would take a fence indeed to hold her now So much for the breeze of Missouri. At two hours by sun we arrived at her house an excellent farm. They are getting rich. The children are all much improved. The next day the 12th we went to Brother John McClellcnds Iwish I had room to tell you something about how he is fixed. If you could see it you would not blame him for not wanting to go back to Tennessee to live.

Thursday the 13th I went to L--- to see old man Linsey and if I had been John it seemed they could not have been much better pleased to have me. I reached their house about 2 o'clock and stayed till 1o o'clock the next day. The old lady and me went ot the kitchen and talked a long time time I talked to her just as if she had been my own mother without any hems and haws about it. I told her it was the general impression in Tennessec

FROM COLLECTION OF MRS. B. C. HUDDLESTON (CON)

that they wanted to go back. How the boys had been talking of coming after them and that they had relenquished the idea for this reason., simply that I could find out as much as them and let them know. She was hurt at your havingfailed to move and more particularly at your not coming to look at the country. "Tell John, said she If he ever lives with me it will be here for I know I shall never get to Tennessee again" The next morning I left there and turned toward Goshen and dined with Kizzie Ray. You don't know how glad she was to see me. The day my cousin Susna and me went up to see Miranda. I had a fine time with them all, of which I will tell uoi more, Loga when I write to you for I am going to write to you and Amos and Dan and other of the neighbor boys that ought by all means be here. You know Logan? I did not expect to like this country but I say so far as I know now I am well pleased with it When I returned from Goshen Ruben Perkins had my school made mad up. Two months of the six are gone and I am clearing $1.04 per day. I have an excellent claim between brother Johns and my school house; at which work evenings and on Saturdays. I have another across the Creek with an excellent spring on it anda large shingle roof house which there seems to be no owner, though oneman claims it and says he will take ten dollars for his claim. I am going to buy it the first time I see him and then I wi will have an excellent place forsome of my friends. Mother, My school house is a large hewed log house with a excellent plank floor. It is our church. There was singing at it last Sunday was week and old Brother Thompson preached a sermon there yesterday, one today and will preach another this evening. The clerk of the Court is down and waiting for my letter to take to the office.

                        Farewell,
                  C. W. to R. F. and Margaret Cook.

Iwrote my letter a week ago and have waited a week to hear from Goshen. There are four coming down from there to go to school. I looked for them this evening, but can't wait for the news they bring. Aunt and Uncle Rhea was down a week ago, all was well and Bro John trying to make him a school. Don't know how it resulted.

    Don't fail to send my books by Jim Whitefield. All the friends send love to you, Betsy Perkins in particular.

(Calvin Whitley Cook was born Mar, 18, 1825, so was twenty years old when this letter was written. The date 1810 refers to the time of their , his gather and mother leaving Virginia to come to Tennessee.)

LETTER TO COL. SEBIRD RHEA FROM RICHARD C. M. COOK.
OENED BY MRS. B. C. HUDDLESTON? COOKEVILLE? TENN.

                                          Double Springs, June 8th,
                                          Jackson, County, Tenn.

Monday Morning, June 5th, 1848,
Dear Bro. & Sister-
             I received your favor of the 10th of Aprile By the Hand of Johns Louisa Perkins vivi at my house on the 15th of May with out any accident & all well, you may Judge, But we cannot express our joy- they found us all in usual helth and have visited many of their friends and old acquaintances and are gone to see Harriet. She was married last fall to Willaim Oscar Haws and lives near the white plains he is a young man of fine appearance & good sense & has a good start in the world Your sisters Byers & Family with other friends in general are well- I have had accounts from Brother John William Alexan and Elias this spring all well- Bro. John wrote that Sister Sallie Goodgains with several of her family was gone to Texas to live he persuaded her to continue with him but she chose to go with her children which was natural to expect. We shall seeher no more, though as a family we have been blest with general helth and has by the help of God Been permitted to continue almost unbroken to a good old age- though death has spared most of us, yet it has fell to my lot to pass through and other trying since somt time before Christmas last our Brother Jess a Cook was attacked with something like Tpphus fever and on the 8th day of January he departed this life and I buried him by the sister of our Father. He was willing to go, all is well I much Regretted to hear of Spartians affliction which had been of so long a continuance and of so serious a character though I still hope he may Recover as Bird C. Kinslow once lay near five months in a semlar condition & contrary to all Expectation finally recovered. I am much pleased to hear that your selves and your children are all doing well I should bemuch gratified were it in my power to see you all though I begin to Doubt ever havong that pleasure, as I find age advancing a pace and wi with it an increase of flesh and the loss of action, Incident to those who have past three score years. it is time to cast our eyes down toward the tomb instead of look to the world for its good or Hapiness our family are all gone and we are left alone thiugh blest with usual helth & plenty I find myself denied that Tranquility of mind I am antisipated after seeing all our children raised and Educated and able to provide for themselves. Yet I have as little cause of complaint as otherswho have been bereft of children in all ages of the world. My son Watson who is here doing well & has made a man Equal to my most sanguin wishes But our other two are gone & whereon to Organ & the other to the Mexican war perhaps to see them no more, which may heaven forbid, But we are human & hea our pray thiugh God is able to save that which seems to be lost I will therefoe hope We feel grateful for your kind attentions to our Request in Regard to your Enquery afterWhitley which I wish you to continue to do By every opertunity that you think you have any chance to hear from him and By way of Rewarding your faithful attentions to my Request I must inform you that I take the Earliest opertunity of informing youthat on last Sunday we had the Joy of Receiving a letter from him Bearing date the 23 Day of Dec. last he was in Organ, but Every sweet has its bitter, he informs that the Indians has broke out and killed and destroyed a Missionary Station in the Walla Walla Vally and he was on the poi of Statging as a volunteer against them there is four tribes that has beeen host and the Emigrants has sent Wm. Meeks to the City of Wazshington to obtain assist ance from the goverment though I am at a loss to see how troops can be got there in time to save the Colony. Mr. Meeks Brought the latter to St Joseph & then it was mailed I shall write in hopes of his Return soon from Washington & that he i

LETTER OWNED BY MRS. B. C. HUDDLESTON, (VDN)

will convey it on the City of organ ,Whitley is well pleased with the country and says if he lives he will Return in 1849. I have seen Meeks Journal in the papers and he states that they had had four engagements with the Indians before he got out of the Territory in all of whichthe whites had been Successful he left the army only four hindred strong on the 26th of January & the first Battle was fought on the 8th of the same month, two weeks after Whitleys letter was Rote I will also Inform you that the letter last Bolivor & Col. John Seartland Raised a voluntear company in going through and about the 17th Statted to Mexico Seartland command the company and Bolivor is Lieutenant, they landed at Venierys about the 20th of November and passed immediately on to the City of Mexico, where they have continued the most of the winter.

  Seartland was taken sick soon after they got there and the command Divolved on Bolivor Everlence I Received a letter from Seartland the other day, he informed me that he would join his company again in a Day or two. Bolivor haswrote many letters to us his health has been good and if peace is made Rite he will be home soon if he lives, if peace is not made he will not come till next Aprile.

  We were at preaching last Sunday at Masidonia on Cane Creek and there saw a great many of your old relatives & friends among them Wm P. Peak, A. Ditty, Campbolls cous Ellizon & all as far as I heard in usual health. Samuail Rays funeral was preached by William Townsdon and a great many people out, I wish you to never cease Riting to us as long as you can see to make a letter and now farewell.

    S. & Nancy Rhea-Richard F. C. M. Cook.

ENVELOPE-
  Double Springs, Tenn
  June 8th

    Col. Sebird Rhea
     Mercer County M. O.
      Princeton P. O.

Seal.

P. S.
I hear since this was wrote that sister Elizabeth got a fall from a horse Beast & is badly hurt in her hip so she cannot walk thiugh I have not seen her.

Land Grant, July, 20, 1837, Recorded in Book H. Page 406 407.
Land Office for the Mountain District of Tennessee, Town of Sparta, White Co. being entry No 777 in E. Takers Office Jackson County, Tenn. Dated Nov.14, 1831 by No 777, Jan, 9, 1830. Granted by the State of Tennessee unto Richard F. Cook, tract containing 500 acres, Oct. 21, 1836, on Cane Creek, Beginning at Joseph Ray's 100 acre South, to Samuel Maxwell, East of Bald Knob. The road leading from Gainesboro to Sparta, North then of the place called Pall Ridge.

    Test.   Newton Cannon, Gov. of Tennessee (Seal)

        At Nashville, Tenn, July, 20, 1837 and of the Independance of the United States the 62nd   by Gov. N. Cannon

Luke Lee (Seal)

Secretary of State.

Property Owned by O. D. Massa, Cookeville, Tenn.

State of Tennessee No 14542, Know ye that in consideration of Military Service performed by Daniel McDanile to the State of North Carolina Warrant 3086 dated the 5th day of Dec, 1785 for 640 acres and entered on the 30th day of December, 1812 by 9791 there is granted by the State of Tenesee unto John Massa assignee of the heirs of the said Daniel McDaniel, a certain tract or parcel of land containing 50 acres part of said warrant by survey bearing the date 20 day of September, 1814 lying in the firstdistrict of White County, on a branch of Glade Creek waters of the Falling Waters and bounded as follows to wit:Beginning at South West Corner of Henry Williams, running East then South by a small branch Then North to the beginning with the hereditaments and appurtenances to have and to hold the said tract or parcel of Landwith its appurtenances to the said JohnMassa and his heirsforever. In witness whereof Joseph McMinn, Governor of the State of Tennessee, have hereunto set his hand and caused the great seal of the State to be affixed at Murfreesborough 1820, Independance of the United States , the Forty Fourth.

By the Governor, Joseph McMinn

Daniel Graham, Sec.

Recorded in the Register's Office in Tennessee, Apr, 4, 1821

By Sterling H Lester, D. R.

State of Tennessee #14542
John Massa, 50 acres, White County.

Property of O. D. Massa, Cookeville, Tenn.

BOND: Knows all men by thispresent that I am held andfirmly bound unto Sarah Wallas in the primal sum of Two hundred Dollars being for value received of his I bound myself my heirs and assigns to her the said Sarah Walles his heirs and assigns.

The consideration of the above obligation is such that if the above bound Jacob Young Shall well and truly mark unto Sarah Walles, A good and Lawful rightn unto surtain Tract or Parcel of land beginning at the beginning corner of a seventy-acre tract ofland entered under warrant in the name of George Cullem now enters in the name of James Carr running North and then to a dry branch then down said branch through the lain between whar said Sarah Walles and Henry Carr now lives, Till it stakes Rock Spring Creek then up said Creel to the beginning then the above obligation to suposed to be Twenty three acres and one there be the same more or less to be void otherwise toremain in full fore andvirtue, as witness my hand and seal this day of July, 1834.

The Right to be made so soon as a survey and Grant may be obtained.

Jacob Young (Seal)

James Mc Kinly, (Seal)

For value received in full 2 asign over the within Bond toWade H Wallace, this 30th of Apr, 1836

Sarah Wallace (Her Mark)

H. L. McD"niel

Sarah Walles Bond on Jacob Young & M Kinley.

Property Of O. D. Massa, Cookeville, Tenn.

The State of Tennessee No 7032.

To all to whom these presents shall come Greeting:
Know ye, that by virtue of part of Certificate No 18b8, dated the 26thday of August 1814 ossind bythe Register of West Tennessee to Bennett Searcy and entered on the 27th day of August 1814 by No 13225, There is granted by the said State of Tennesseeunto James Townsend, assignee of the saidBennett Searcy,A certain tract or parcel of land centaining, One hundred and fifty acres by suevey bearing date the 12th day ofJanuary, 1815, lying in White County in the first District on Cane Creek of the Falling Water, adjoining a survey of Isaac Taylor, Jun.of four hundred and two acres on his South boundry Beginning in his line at a post in Cane Creek, Seventy poles of his beginning corner running South two hundred poles to two black oaks thence West one hundred and Sixteen poles to a Chestnut and hickory, thence North Striking the South East corner of Levi Sweats 100 acres survey at eight poles containing North with Sweats line and crossing Cane Creek the three times in all one hundred and eighteen poles to two post oaks, said Sweats North East corner thence West with another of his lines ten poles to a postoak thence Northeighty two poles to a hickory post oak and black oak thenceEast striking the before mentioned corner, of Isaac Taylor Junior, survey at eighty six poles and crossing Cane Creekseveral times, in all one hundred and twenty six poles to the Beginning, Encluding the farm and spring where Levi Sweats formerly lived,with the hereditaments and appurtenances, To have and to hold the said tract or parcel of land with its appurtenances to the said James Townsend and his heirs forever? In witness whereof Willie Blount, Govenor of the State of Tennessee hath hereunto set his hand and caused the Great Seal of the State to be affixed at Nashville on the twenty fourth day of May in the Year of Our Lord, One Thousand and eight hindred and fifteen and of the Independance of the United States the thirty ninth.

                  Willie Blount.

W. G. Blount,
  Secretary.

Early History Of Putnam County By W. S. McClain,
Cookeville, Tenn

Shopping ninety years ago from an old day book of sales at the White Plains General Store, the trading center for mant miles in every direction, we take the following items entered in the year 1838-1840.

Joseph Bartlett

    2¼ lbs coffee   .50¢
    2 Almanacks   .18

Robert Peek

    One fine comb   .12½

Ann Quarles

    One silk handkerchief   1.25
    One nut meg   .06

William Marchbanks

    2½ lbs lead   .31
    half dozen flints   .06

John Choat

    Half pound powder   .25
    2 lbs lead   .25
    3½ yds calico   .87½
    half oz. camphor   .10
    2 lbs sugar   .25

dudley Hudgens

    81 lbs nails   1.00

Benjamin Gerdenhire

    2 yds flannel   1.75
    2 " calico   .67
    ¼ yd Bobinette   .18¾
    ½ yd X-barred muslin   .37½
    1 tucking comb   .12½
    1 sett bridle leathers   1.00

Curtis terry

    One pair cotton cards   .75
    1 yd domestic   .37½
    One ribbon   .25
    One fur hat   4.00

John Barnes after purchasing powder, lead, sugar and coffee adds one History of United States. One letter writer, four primers and one Charlotte Temple.
  (Can any one shed any light on this last item?)

Copied from original account book of White Plains General Store, Book owned by W. S. McClain, Cookeville, Tenn, Putnam County.

COPY OF WILL
OWNED BY MRS. MOLLIE McKINLEY, CHESTNUT MOUND, TENN.

State of Tennessee, Febuary Session, Jackson County of the County Court, 1834.

I William Gailbreath Clerk of the Court of Pleas and Quarter Session for said County do certify that Alfred Vanherson and Simon Carlisle executors of the last will and testament of Robert McKinley deceased appeared in Court and were qualified as exicutors of said will and werepermitted to perform their duty as such without giving security according to said Wll in testimony where of I have set my hand and affixed the Seal of my office at office this 10, day of Febuary 1834

William Gailbreath, Clerk.

In the Name of God Amen I Robert McKinley of Jackson County andState of Tennessee being in sound mind and memory for whichI thank God and calling Mind the uncartainty of his mind and life and knowing that it is appointed once for all "men to die- and being desirous to dispose of such worldly substance asit hath pleased God to bless me with do hereby make ny last will and testament in name and from following, that is to say,

1st I desire that after my death I shall be decently bured andall my Just debts be paid out of the proceeds of my perishable property.

2nd-After the payment of my debts and furnel expences I Give to my loving wife, Sally McKinley all the houses plantations Lands and stack of every discription whereon I now live and have and my negro woman Priss and all her children during her natural life and should she have more stock of any kind then she may needshe shall be at liberty to give it to either of my th three sons herein after named by value as low so as to make them equal in all such property I give away, and at her death my wish and will is that my negro woman Priss shall be set free and that she Priss may live with either of my children that she may make choice of-

3rd My wish and will is that at the death of my wife that my son Mathew Mc Kinley shall have the tract of land and plantationwhereon I now live and no other part of my property from me.

4th-My wish and will is that my six negro children of Priss viz-Ned, Dick, Chind, Hanna, Lewis, & Milly be divided between my two sons James and joseph in this manna Towit I desire that my son James shall have the two first choice and my son Josiah the two next and the balance equally divided between them

5th- My wish and will is that shallthere be any more I wish it or them be equally divided between my three sons and my wish is that should Priss have a any children she is freed or after my death it or they shall also be slaves and equally divided among my three sons before mentioned as I do not wish for someof her children to be free and the ballance slaves.

6th- My will and request of my beloved children is that these negros here above mentioned shall be kept if possible in my family among my own children and never sold to strangers or any body else/

7th- My wish and will is that my house hold and kitchen furniture and farming utencels shall remin and belong to my wife during her natural life and at her death to be equally divided between my three sons by sale or otherwise as my Exicutors herein mentiomed may think proper.

McKINLEY WILL (CON)

And lasly I do hereby constitute and appoint my true and faithful friends Simin Carlisle and Alfred Vannerson Exicutors of this my last will and testament hereby working all other former will and testementw nby me here to fore made and my will and wish is that neither of these my exicutors shall be bounded to give security and that they do perform the dutiesherein requirred as soon as possableband without delay when my loving wife shall depart this l life In witness whereofI have set my hand and affixed my seal signed sealed published and   Robert McKinley
declared to be the lastwwill and testament of the above named Robert MCKinley In the presents of us who at his request and in his presence Have hereunto subscribed our names as witness to the same this the fifth day of June one thousand eight hundred and thirty.

Test-
   Simon Carlisle
   Alf Vannerson

State of Tennessee, Jackson County, Febuary Session 1834
There was the last within will and testament of Robert McKinley Deceased in Court for probate and Simon Carlisle and Alfred Vannerson subscribing witness to saidlast will and testament beingsworn to testify touching themaking signing and publishing said will deposed and saidthat the Robert McKinley signed said will in the presence and that at the time he signed it he was of sound mind and disposing memory and on motion it is ordered that said will be certified and recorded.

                       William Gailbreath
                       Clerk of Jackson County Court.

State of Tennessee, Jackson County, I William Gailbreath Clerk of the Court of Pleasant Quarter Session for said County of Jackson do certify that the above and foregoing is a true and pwefect Copy of last will and testament of Robert McKinley by Deceased takenfrom the original on file inmyoffice and also atrue and perfect copy of the entry of the probate od said last will and te testament taken from the record in my office, In Testimony Whereof I have here unto set my hand and affixed the seal of my office in Gainesboro this 10th day of Febuary 1834

                       William Gailbreath Clerk
A copy of the last will and testament of R. M. McKinley dec.
  Original Records Book C. pages 313 & 314 in my office
                     William Gailbreath Clk.)

RECORDS OF MRS. MOLLIE McKINLEY (CON)

State of Tennessee No 7273,
To all to whom these presents shall come, Greetings:
　　　Know ye that for and in consideration of the sum of one cent per acre paid into the office of the Entry Taker of Jackson County and entered on the 245h day of Febuary 1826 pursuant to the provisions of an Act of General Assembly od said state passed on the twenty second day of November, one thousand and eight hundred and twenty three and the act supplemented thereto by No 904, there is this day granted by the State of Tennessee unto Mathew McKinley a certain tract or parcel of Land Containing One hundred sixty two and one half acres by survey bearing date the Second day of May, 1826 lying in said County on the ridge dividing the waters of Indian Creek of Cumberland River and Rock Spring Creek of the Caney Fork and boundee as follows to wit: Beginning at two sugar trees on the North side of rhe Walron Road su south with point of ridge on the waters of said Indian Creek Running thence East two hindred and twenty eight poles to three lynns growing out of the same rout in a hollow the waters of said Indian Creek Thence South crossing the Walton Road at 34 poles inall one hundred and fourteen poles to a sugar tree and four Lynns growing out of the same woods West side of a hill the waters of Rock Springs valley thence Waest two hundred and twentyeight poles to a stake Thence Northcrossing said Road in all one hundred and fourteen poles to the Beginning Encluding said McKinleys improvement known by the name of Mount Richardson With the hereditaments and appurtenances, To have and to hold the said Tract or parcel of Land with its appurtenances, to the said Mathew McKinley andhis heirs forever Inwitness whereof Samuel Houston Governor of the State of Tennessee hath hereunto setbhis hand and caused the Great Seal of the State to be affixed at Nashville on the twelfth day of November in the Year of Our Lord oneThousand eight hindred and twenty seven and of the independance of the United States the fifty second
　　　　　　By the Governor, James Houston
　Danial Graham
　　Secretary.
Matthew McKinley is entitled to the within mentioned tract of Land
　　　　　　　　D. M. McGavock Register of
　　　　　　　　West Tennessee By
　　　　　　　　H. W. McGavock D. R.
Recorded in the Registers offive of West Tennessee in Book No 9
　　　　　　　　Stith Harrison D. R.
　　　No 7273 Matthew McKinley
　　　　162½ acres Jackson County

RECORDS OF MRS. MOLLIE McKINLEY (CON)

To Sarah Walles and her heirs and assigns and All mans of persons whatso ever In Testimony here unto have set my hand and seal this day and date above written

                 Jacob Young

Test-Simon Carlisle
  James McKinley

LAND GRANT

  State of Tennessee No 7183
To all to whom these presents shall come Greetings:
Know ye that by virtue of Entry No 1914 made in the office of the Entry Taker of Jackson County and entered on the 13 day of August 1832 pursuant to the provixions of an Act of General Assembly of S id State passed on the ninth day of January 1830 there is Granted by the Said State of Tennessee unto James McKinley certain tract or percel of Land containing one hundred acres by survey bearing date rhe 27th day of March 1838 lying in said County ont the waters of Indian Creek of Cumberland River Bounded as follows: Beginning at a poplar andchesthut Stump North East corner of a fifty acre Entry made inthe name of said McKinley nera the Walton Road Running thence West with said lineone hundred and sixty two poles to a stake thence North one hundred and sixty poles to a Stake the East sixty poles to a large Beech North West corner of a tract Granted Jordan Sullivan now belongs to McClellon Jones thence South with said tract crossing two branches in all ninety six poles to a forked Lynn on the North side of a hill corner of said tract thence East with said tract crossing two branches and a road from t the pond Spring passing beech corner of said tract at 94 poles in all one hundred and two poles to a stake on the west side of a hill thence South sixty four poles to the Beginning including the improvement purchased of George Blair with the hereditaments and appurtenances to have and to hold the said tract or parcel of land with its appurtenanc s tonthe said James McKinley and his heirs forever, In witness of Newton Cannon Govornor of the State of Tennossee has hereunto set his hand and caused the great Seal of the State to be affixed at Nashville on the 14th day of September 1839 and 64 year of our Independance

                 By the Govnor
                  James K. Polk
               Luke Lea
                 Secretary

No 1387 James McKinley
  vs
B. F. Brinley etal
Exhibit No 1 to
 Disposition of
R. B. McKinley

Filed May, 29, 1903, J. H. Watts Com.

RECORDS OF MRS. MOLLIE McKINLEY (CON)

      Know all men by these presents That I Martin Brown of the County of Jackson and State of Tennessee am hheld?) and firmly Bound unto James McKinley of the same County and State in the parcel sum of six hundred a dollars to which payment will and truly to be made and done I bine myself heirs executors and Administrators joinlty and severly firmly by these presents signed joinlty and severly firmly by these present signed with my name and sealed with my seal this 2nd day of Aprile in the Year of Our Lord 1830
      The condition of the obligation is such that whence the above Bounded Martin Brown hath this day bargained Sold and delivered unto said James McKinley the following tracts of Land To wit One hundred acres of land perchased by the said Brown of Hezakiah Brown and also one tract of fourteen acres purchased and one six acre tract perchased of said Hezakiah Brown also a tract of Onehundred which the said Martin Brown rendered at one cent per acre which is not yet surveyed and also One tract of fifty acres which was granted to the said Martin Brown by the State of Tenessee Under the act of General Assembly passed in 1823 commonly called the 12½ cts Law and also one tract offourteen acres which is of his own right to land that belonged to the estate of his father now Deceased Now Therefore Witnesseth That whereas the said Martin Brown holds a Bondon the said James McKinley fot three hindred dollars payable in the following manner towit One hundred dollars to be paid on or before the 20th day of Aprile 1831 One hundred dollars payable on or before the 20th day of Aprile 1832 and one hundred dollars payable on or before the 20th day of Aprile 1833 in consideration of the before mentioned and bargained premises now of the said Martin Brown shall well and truly make or cause to be made a General Warrented to the said James McKinley his heirs or assigns on or before the 20th day of Aprile 1831 Then this obligation to be i void else remain in full force and virtura

                                                                       Martin Brown   (SEAL)

Witness Geo Elgin
Robert McKinley

Martin Brown
   To   Bond
James McKinley

RECORDS OF MRS. MOLLIE McKINLEY (CON)

    Know all men by these present s that James McKinley of the County of Jackson and State of Tennessee am held and firmly bound unto Martin Brown of the Same County State in the Personal sum of Six hundred dollars to which payment well and truly to be made and done I bind my self my h heirs executors and Administrators Jpinlty and Severally firmly by them presents Sogned with my name and Sealed with my Seal this 20th day of April 1830

    This condition of the all above obligation is such that when as the ab above bounded I James McKinley hath this day purchased of Martin Brown several tracts of land whereon the said Martin now lives which land s are discrebed in a bond from said Martin Brown bearing date the same date of this, Now therefore Witnesseth that wherever the said Martin Brownm shalt mk make or cause to be made a General Warrantee deed or a good and sufficient title to the said James McKinley for the siad bargained p remises The said James McKinley bind himself to pay rhe said Martin Brown or his heirs three hundred dollars on the foll owing payments to wit One hundred dollars on or before the 20th day of Aprile in the year 1831 One hundred dollares on or before the 20th day of Aprile in the year of 1832 and also one hindred dollars on or before the 20th day of Aprile in the year 1833 Now if the said Brown sh shall make or cause to make a good and sufficient title for said lands and thes said McKinley Shall and trult make or cause to be made the three several payments of foresaid then this obligation to be void else remain in full forse and virtue

                                                                James McKinley (SEAL)

Witness Geo Elgin
   James McKinley
      To Bone $300
M. BROWN

RECORDS OF MRS. MOLLIE McKINLEY (CON)

Jackson County State of Tennessee 27th Aprile 1831
I do hereby certify that on the 17th day of March last I was on my way from Summer County in this State to Warren County in North Carolina and that I did on that day fall incompany with Mr. Johnson at a Mr. Bailleys in Smith County in Smith County and that we then traveled to gether that day and Staid that night at Mr. James McKinleys In Jackson County where we arrievd about night and found Mr. McKinley and Family from home-nevertheless we staid all night and was treated very well I slept in a little room to the right hand as you enter the Big or public room Mr. Johnson slept in the public room by the fire in the morning after Breakfast we paid our Bills to a little Boy Mr. McKinley's Son I suppose and was pursued our Journey on to gather as far as the forks of the Road where the Walton Road leaves the Sparta Road about ten miles I suppose there we parted and I had not heard from Mr. Johnson since till this evenong when I called at Mr. McKinleys on My return home and he Showed me an advertisement of Mr. Johnson Stating that he had loss some money and his pocket Book at Mr McKinleys on the night we staid there together now all this is entirely new to me. I never heard Mr. Johnson say a word about such a thing while I was with him-and as to any necessity of using any precaution while at Mr. McKinleys I must confess I saw no need or Cause of any apprehension. I further understand that Mr. Johnson stated that he did not know my name or who I was Now if this be fact it is wrong as he both knew my name where I live and where I was going and if any body wants to know I live in Summer County State of Tennessee Near Hendersonville and my name

             Edward Turner
Is Witness Henry W. Kirby, Alf Vannerson

RECORDS OF MRS. MOLLIE McKINLEY (CON)

Design No 38 L. B.
Pekin Putnam County Tennesse Oct. 9th 1873
I have this day bought of J. O. Pool and J. D. Clark marble Dealers No 725 West Jefferson St. Louisville, Ky. two set of "Italian Marble Grave Stone Head Stone Marble 3½ feet high 18 inch wide 2 inch thick foot stone one third as high and one thrid the width of Head Stone Bases for Head and foot Stone Inscribed as follows:

James McKinley Born June 5, 1894
Died Feb 5 1839

Eliza McKinley Born Feb 1, 1800
Died Mar, 22, 1871

to be delivered at Grandville on Cumberland River any time between the first of Feb and the last of March next for which I agree to pay $70.00 Dollars on Delivery

Now Putnam County Date Aug, 25, 1936

Know all men by these presents that I Samuel Wallace of Jacksoh Couny State of Tennessee Pentioner of the United States do hereby causeth and appoint James McKonley My True and Lawful attorney for me and in myName to Receve from the agent of the United States paying pensions in Nahsville State of Tennessee my pention from the 4th day of Seotember 1834 to the 4th of March 1835 witness my hand and seal this 8th April 1835

Samuel Wallace X his mark (SEAL)

Lewis Fletcher Ely his Arleage

State of Tennessee, Jackson County, Be it known that on the 8th day of Aprile 1835 the Subscriber a Justice of the peace in fore said County personally appeared Samuel Wallace above named and acknowledged The foregoing power of attorney to be his act and deed In Testimony whereof I have hereunto set my hand this day and year Test above mentioned

H. L. McDanial (SEAL)
Justice of the peace.

State of Tennessee, Jackson County Be it known that bon the 8th day of Aprile 1835 before the subscribed a justice of the peace in and for said County personally appeared James McKnley the attorney Name in the foregoing power of attorney and made Oath that the same was not givenhim by reason of any sale transfer and mortgage of pension therein another to be received by him sworn and Subscribed the day and year last mentioned

H. C. McDanial,   James McKnley
Justice of the Peace

RECORDS OF MRS. MOLLIE McKINLEY (CON)

State of Tennessee, Jackson County,
Be it knaoen that before me Henry L. McDaniel a Justice of the peace in and for the county aforesaid personally appeared Samuel Wallace and made oath in due form of Law that he is the identical Wallace named in Orignal certificate in his posession of which I certify the following is a true Copy.

War Department Revolutionary Claim
I certify that in Conformity with the Law of the United States of the 7th Jan 1832 Samuel Wallace of the State if Tennessee who was a private in the army of the Revolution is entitle to Eighty dollars per anam? during his natural life comencing on the 4th March 1831 and payable SemiAnnually on the 4th of March and 4th of September in every year.
Given at the War office of the United States this 19th day of March one thousand Eight hundred and Thirty

Lew Cass, Secretary of War

Examined and Countersign
J. L. Edwards Commission of Pensions
th t he is entitle to a pension of Eighty dollars per anum on account of service rendered the Unoted States during the Revolutionary War that he resides in Jackson County Tennessee and has resided there fot the space of Twenty six years past previous then he resided in Georgia Sworn and Subscribed before me this 8th day of Aprile 1835

H. L. McDanial
Samuel Wallace X His mark (SEAL)

State of Tennessee Jackson County, I Henry L. McDanial a magistrate in the county above named do hereby certify that I have the most Satisfactory Samuel Wallace who has this ady appear before me to take the oath of identity is the identical person named in the pension Certifcate which he has exhibited before me Number 20573 and bearing date at the war office the 19th day of March 1834 and signed by Law Cass Secretary of War given under my hand at Jackson County Tennessee on the 8th day of Aprile 1835

H. L. McDanial (SEAL)
Justice of the peace

State of Tennessee Jackson County, I John S. Turner Clerk of the County of Jackson hereby certify that Henry L. McDanial is a magistrate as above and that the foregoing Signature perporting to be his are genuine in testimony whereof I hereunto set My hand and affixed my Seal of Office this 11th day o of April 1835

J. S. Turner Clerk of
Jackson County Court

Samuel Wallace
J. S. Turner Clk of Jackson County Court

RECORDS OF MRS. MOLLIE mMcKINLEY (CON)

State of Tennesse No 2913
To all to whom these presents shall come Greeting:
Know ye That for and in consideration of the sum of twelve and one half cents per acre paid into the office of the Entry Taker of Overton County and entered on the day of 27th of October 1824 pursuant to the provisions of an Act of General Assembly of said State passed on the twenty second of November one thousand eight hundred and twenty three by No 391 There is Granted by the said State of Tennessee unto Henry McKinney a certain tract or parcel of Land containing Fifty Acres by survey bearing date the 23rd day of July 1825 lying in said county on the waters of Bear Creek and bounded as follows to wit: Beginning ata stake a post oak and small hickory Running South Eighty poles to a small black oak and Black Jack thence East one hundred poles crossing the rock Island road to a small Stake a small hickory and post oak Thence North Eighty poles crossing said road to two small Hickorys Thence West one hundred poles to the Beginning
With the hereditaments and appertenances To have and to hold the said tract or parcel of Land with its appertenances to the said Henry McKinney and his heirs forever. In witness whereof William Carroll Govnor of the State of Tennessee hath hereunto set his hand and caused the Great Seal of the State to be affixed at Murfreesborough on the 21st day of November in the Year of Our Lord one thousand eight hundred and twenty five and of the Independance of the United States the fiftieth
By the Govnor-Wm Carroll
Daniel Graham Secretary
Recorded in the Reg Office of West Tennessee 21st March 1826 C
H. W. McGavock D. R.
No 2913 Henry McKinney 50 acres Overton County
Henry McKinney is entitle to the within mentioned tract
D. McGavock Registered of
West Tennessee

State of Tennessee No 2913
To all to whom these presents shall come Greeting:
Know ye, That for and in consideration of the sum of Twelve and one cent per acre paid into the office of the Entry Taker of Overton County and entered on the 15 th day of Aprile 1824, pursuant ot the provisions of an Act of General Assembly of said State , passes on the twenty second day of November one thousand eight hundred and twenty three by No 36 there is granted by the said State of Tennessee unto Nathan Bartlett a certain tract or parcel of Land containingnsixty six acres of survey bearing date the 10th day of June1825 lying in said County on the waters of Bear Creek whereon Henry McKinney now lives and bounded as follows to wit: Beginning at a two postoaks Running South seventy four poles to two small blavck oaks and Hickory pointers Thence East one hundred and forty three poles to a small black oak at the foot of a mountain Thence North seventy four poles to a small hickory and post oak thence west one hundred and forty three poles to the Beginning with the hereditaments and appurtenances To havd and to hold the said tract or parcel of Landwith its appertenances to the said Nathan Bartlett In witness whereof William CarrollGovnor of the State of Tennessee heth hereunto set his hand and caused the Great Seal of the United States to be affixed at Murfreesborough on the 21st day of November in the Year of Our Lord one thousand eight hundred and twenty five and of the Independance of

RECORDS OF MRS. MOLLIE McKINLEY (CON)

the United States the fiftieth
      By the Govnor William Carroll
      Daniel Graham, Secretary
Nathan Bartlett is entitled to the within mentioned tract of land
        D. W. McGavock Register of West Tennessee
No 2918 Nathan Bartlett 66 acres Overton County
Recorded in the Registers office of West Tennessee 22nd March 182 C
        D. W. McGavock D. R

RECORDS OF MRS. MOLLIE McKINLEY (CON)

State of Tennessee No 6829
To all to whom these presents shall come Greetings: Know ye that for and in consideration of the sum of one Cent per acre paid into this office of the Entry Taker of Overton County and entered on the 9th day of January, 1826 pursuant to the provisions of an Act of the General Assembly of said State and passed on this 3 day of December 1825 by No 544 made in said office there is granted by the said Sate of Tennessee unto Henry McKinley a certain Tract or parcel of land containing Two hundred acres by survey bearing date the 16th day of May 1838 Lying ih said Countynof on the head waters of Bear Creek Beginning at a small hickory the Barrens on the North boundry line of 66 acres Tract whereon said McKinnley now lives Running North Seventy poles to a small hickory and post aok ThenceEast 60 poles to two small Hickorys at the foot of a mountain thence South with the same thirtybeight poles to a white oak and chestnut thence East with the same ten ements six poles to a black walnut and hickory South with the same 12 pales to a small hickory and black oak pointers Thence East One hundred and Eighty poles to a Spanish Oak and two chestnuts pointers Thence South one hundred and thirty and two thirds poles to a Stake thence East west two hundred and twenty poles to a stake thence North one hundred and nine poles binding on the East boundry line of said 66 acres Tract to a Small hickory and post oak and pointers the North East corner of the same West with North boundry of the same forty poles to the Beginning with the hereditaments and appurtenences to have and to hold ths aid Tract or parcel of land with its appurtenences to the said Henry McKinloy and his heirs forever.

In witness whereof Newton Cannon Govnor of the State of Tennessee has hereunto set his hand and caused the Great Seal of the State to be affixed at Nashville on the 2nd day of May 1839 and 63 Year of our Independance

      By the Govnor, N. Cannon
      Luke Lea
       Secretary

Reg. in the office Book M. Page 97
      R. Nelson Reg, Mountain District
Henry McKinley is entitled to the within described Land
      R. Nelson, Reg.

No 6827
Henry McKinley 200 acres

RECORDS OF MRS. MOLLIE McKINLEY (CON)

The State of Tennessee No 7591
To all to whom these presents shall come Greetings:
Know ye that by virtue of part of Certificaye No 1591 dated the 9th day of September 1813 issued by the Register of West Tennessee to Robert Searly and entered on the 17th day of September 1813 by No 11438 There os granted by ths said State of Tennesse Unto Eake Brown assignee of the said Robert Searly a certain tract or parcel of Land cantaining four teen acres by survey bearingdate the 30th day of Aprile 1814 Lying in Jackson County in the first District on a branch of Indian Creek of Cumberland River and bounded as follows to wit Beginning at a branch Standig three poles West of the North East corner of said Brown survey of fourteen acres on said branch running North forty eight poles to a Spanish oak and Small white oak thence West forty seven poles passing the South East corner of said Browns survey of six acres at fifteen poles and with said line to a stake in a filed thence South forty eight poles to a sugar tree thence East forty seven poles to a forty eight poles to a sugar tree thence East firty seven poles to the Beginning. With the heredotaments and appurtenancs to have and to hold the said tract or parcel of land with its appurtenencest to the said Eake Brown andhis heirs forever in witness whereof Willie Blount Govner of the State of Tennessee hath hereunto set his hand nand caused the grear seal of the State to be affixed at Nashville on the Seventeenth day of Aug in the Year fo Our Lord one thousand Eight hundfed and fifteen and of the Independance of the United States the Fortieth

                  Willie Blount
                  By the Govnor

W. T. Blount
   Secretary
Received in the Registers office of West Tennessee Sept 11th 1815
                  D. M. McGavock Reg

No 7591 Eale Brown
  14 acres
  Jackson County.

    State of Tennessee No 7187
To all to whom these shall come Greetings:
Know ye that by virtue o f Entry No 2499 Made in the office of the Entry Taker of Jackson County and entered on the 22nd day ofMarch 1837 pursuant to the provisions of an act of the General Assembly of said state passes on th the ninth day of January '1830 there is warrented by the said state of Tenn essee unto James McKinley a certain tract or parcel of land containing Twenty five acres by survey beaing date the 30 day of March 1838 lying in said County on the South sideof Cumberland River on the waters of Indian Creek Beginning at a Beeahhand Elm on the South side of Indian Creek corner of a tract Ganted to Isaac Walton Running thence West with said tract twenty poles to a Stake thence East 20 poles to a Stake in the West boundryl line of Matthew Cowins tract thence North with said line two hundred poles to the Beginnijg including the improvement bought of Henry B. Clark bt said McKinley
No 7181 James McKinley 25 acres Jackson County
 Recorded in my office Book L. Page 152
                R. Nelson, Register of the Mountain District

RECORDS OF MRS. MOLLIE McKINLEY (CON)

The State of Tennessee No 7592-
To all to whom these presents Shall come Greetings:
Know ye that by virtue of part of cretificates No 472 dated the first day of January 1811 obtained from the commisiioner of West Tennessee by Ann Robertson Elizabeth Robertson Christopher Robertson and Mary Robertson and entered on the 11th day of January 1812 by No 7432 There is granted by the said state of Tennessee unto Zake Brown assignee of said Ann Robertson Jas Robertson Elizabeth Robertson Christopher Robertson Elijah Robertson and Mary Robertson a certain tract or parcel of land containing fourteen acres by survey baring date the 30th day of Aprile 1814 lying in Jackson County in the first district on a branch of Indian Creek of Cumberland river and boundes as follows to wit-Beginning at a branch marked E. B. about ten poles East of said branch and thirty poles above an improvement made by Meshack Hanbery runs thence West forty poles crossing said branch to a sugar tree thence South fifty six poles to a sugar tree thence East forty poles to a lynn and two sugar trees Saplings on the bank of a branch thence North fifty six poles to the Beginning Including the improvements where said Brown now lives. With the hereditaments and appurtenances to have and to hold the said tract or parcel of land with its appurtenances to the said Eake Brown and his heirs forever in witness where of Willie Blount Govnor of the State of Tennessee hath sey his hand and caused the great Seal of the State to be affixed at Nashville on the Seventeenth day of August in the Year of Our Lord one thousand Eight hundred and fifteen and of the Independance of the United States the fortieth
              By the Govnor,
                Willie Blount

William Blunte
    Secretary
No 7592 Zake Brown 14 acres Sept 11, 1815 Jackson County
Recorded in the Register's office of West Tennessee B.
Eake Brown is entitled to the within mentioned tract of land
            D.-M. McGavock Register,
            West Tennessee.

RECORDS OWNED BY MRS. MOLLIE MCKINLEY, CHESTNUT, MOUND, TENN.

State of Tennessee No 702,
To all to whom these presents shall greetings:
Know ye, that for and in consideration of the sum of twelve and one halfa cents per acre Paid into the office of the Entry Taker of Jackson County a end entered on the 5 day of the July 1823 pursuant to the provisions of an
Act of the General Assembly of said state, passed on the 22nd day of November 1823 by No 305,
There is granted by the State of Tennessee unto Andrew Ferrell a certain tract or parcel of Land containing fifty acres by survey bearing date the 18th of November, 1824 laying in said county on a branch of Indian Creek on South side of Cumberland river and bounded as follows: Beginning at an elm in the West bound thirty poles North of the beginning corner of said Ferrell 98 acre tract Running thence S. on a one hundred and twenty five poles to stake in Robert McKinley's field twenty five poles to a stake in Robert McKinley's field thence West Sixty four poles to a tract thence North one hundred and twenty five poles to an elm thence East sixtyfour poles to the beginning.

With the hereditaments and appurtenences To have and to hold the said Tract or parcel of Land with its appurtenances, to the said Andrew Ferrell and his heirs forever In Witness whereof William Carroll, Govnor of the stat of Tennessee, hath hereunto set his hand and caused the Great Seal to be affixed at Murfreesboro on the 7th day of January, In the Year of Our Lord one thousand eight hundred and twenty five and of the Independance of the United States the forty-ninth.

       By the Govnor
       Daniel Graham
          Secretary
       Wm. Carroll
Recorded in the Registers office of West Tennessee May, 28, 1825
       W. K. McGavock
        D. Reg.

No 702

  Andrew Ferrell
  50 acre
  Jackson County.

RECORDS OF MRS. MOLLIE McKINLEY (CON)

State of Tennessee No 727
To all to whom these presents shall come, greetings:

    Know yea, That for and in consideration of the sum of twelve and one cents per acre paid into the office of the Entry Taker of Jackson County and entered on the 25th day of June 1824 pursuant to the provision of an Act of General Assembly of said State passed on the 22 day of Nov. 1823 by No 130, There is granted unto Martin Brown a ceratin tract or parcel of Land containong fifty acres by survey date the 1st day of July 1824 lying in Said county on the waters of Indian Creek on the South Side of Cumberland River and bounded as follows to wit Beginning at a small beach on the West side of a hill thence West fifty poles to a stake in the east boundry line of Eake Brown 14 acre tract thence South with line thirty six poles to his South East corner thence West with his lune passing his corner in all sixty thence West with his line passing his corner in all sixty poles to a Stake rhence South fifty four poles three and thence four poles to a stake thence east one hundred and twelve poles to s stake thence North ninty & three fourth of a pole to the Beginning, With the hereditamenets and appurtenances To haveand to hold the said Tract or parcel of Land with ist appurtenences to the said Martin Brown ad his heirs forever, In witness William Carroll Govnor of the State of Tennessee hath hereunto set his hand andcaused the GreatSeal of the State to be affixed at Murfreesborough on the 11 day of January in the Year of Our Lord one thousand and eight hundred and twenty five and of the Independance of the United States for the forty ninthBy the Gonvor

                                      Daneil Graham
                                          Secretary
                                      Wm. Carroll

No 727
    Martin Brown 50 acres Jackson County
    Recorded in the Registers office of West Tennessee May 30th 1825
            M. Gavock, D. Regt

    Know all men by these presents(?) are held & privy reviel unto Jane Wallas Penal sum of six hundred & Twenty four dollars the consider of this obligation is such that the said shall make or cause to be made by way of general Transaction deed on the 20 day of January 1844 to Jane Jane Wallas a certain tract or parcel land containing seventy four acres lying in the State of Tennessee and County of Putnam on the waters of Indian Creek of Cumberland River and bounded as follows Beginning at a Lynn on the road the North East Corner of Lot No 5 surveying thence North sixty thee poles to a beech standing near the Road thence North seventy four and a half degrees thence one hundred and Thirty four poles to a sugar tree on the top of the rodge thence South thirty degrees thence runningthe ridge sixty eught poles to a small Beech a hickory & maple pointers thence South with the ridge twenty four poles to a stake in the N. Boundry line of Sam Young fifty trail thence East with Sam Young fifty acre tract thence East with said Youngs line thirty poles to a sugar tree the N. corner of Lot No 5 thence East fifty poles to a sugar tree in the North boundry line of Lot No 5 thence

RECORDS OF MRS. MOLLIE McKINLEY (CON)

South survey six degrees East Eighty eight poles to the Beginning
There this obligation to the round or thence to the main in full form
in Law & equally in witness where here set my seal affixed my seal this
26 day of December 1843 in pen of therein Sarah McKinley
         Witness Robert G. Hufey (SEAL)
Test-John Kovirs   Elijah McKinley (X his mark)
 Fichecher
 S. M. McK^lnley P. G. & Hayhs
  To Bond J. Wallam

State of Tennssee No 740
To all to whom these presents shall come Greetings:
  Know yea that for and in consideration of the sum of one cent per
acre paid in the office of the Entry Taker of Jackson County and enter
thereon the 13th day of January 1826 pursuant to the provisions of an Act
of the General Assembly of sid State passed on the 3rd day of December
One thiysand ight hindred and twenty five by No 750 there is Granted by
the said State of Tennessee unto Hezakiah Brown a certain tract or parcel
of land lying containing two hundred acres by survey bearing date th
14th day of Dec. 1826 Lyingnin said County ont ehwaters of the Indian
Creek of Cumberland River and Bounded as follows Beginning ata Beech
Maple and sugar tree on the South side of a hill near the head fo a Small
branch that runs through his field and not far abpve a Spring running tha e
North One hundred and twenty six and one half poles to a Beech and dogwood
in the South boundry line of Gifion Browns fifty acre tract Thence East
with his line crossing a branch at fifty two poles ian all fifty two pole
in all two bundred and fifty two poles to a lage chestnut and two m ples
on the top of a high ridge Thence South one hundred and twenty six and one
half poles to a Dogwood and two populars sapling on the point of a ridge
not far above Jordan Sullivans fence thence West twohundred and fifty three
poles to the Beginning. With the hereditaments and appurtenances To have
and to hold the said Tract or parcel of land with appurtenances to the said
Hezakiah Brwon and his heirs forever In iwtness whereof Sam Houston Govnor
of the State of Tennessee hath hereunto set his hand and caused the great
S al of the State to be affixed at Nashville on the 14th day of August in
teh Year of Our Lord One thousand Eight hundred and twenty eight and of
the Independance of the United States th e Fifty third
       By the Govnor _James_ Houston
Daniel Graham
 Secretary
Hezakiah Brown is entitle to the within described Land R. Nelson Register
of the Miountain District Recorded in my office In Book 13 page 172
         R. Nelson
        Reg of the Mountain District
No 740 Hezakiah Brown 200 acres Jackson County
Isd 14 Aug 1828

McKinley Records (Con)

Know all men by these presents that I Andrew Ferrell, of Jckson County and state of Tennessee of some title and firmly bounded in the sum of Three hundred dollars unto Robert Moore or heirs and each other and administrators or assigns for each payment will and truly be made and Bind myself my exicutors administrators jointly and severly formerly by this presents sealed with my seal and dated the 20th of Feb. 1836 the conditions of above obligation is such that if the above bounded Andrew Ferrell or his airs Exicutors administrators make over all his rite and title unto sexenty five acres of land lying in the County of Jackson and on the waters of Indian Creek and beginning on a large chestnut and two mapleson the top of a rddge it being the North East corner of said tract of Land running thence west to a stake on the top of a ridge North East corner of a tract of Land sold by Hezekiah Brown to Marlin Brown thence South corner with said Marlin Brown line meandering to said ridge to a stake on the South Boundryline thence East on said line seventy poles to a stake James McKinley South East corner on a twenty five acre tract thence North with said McKinley line sixtu four poles to a stake thence east with McKonley line sixty four poles to a stake in the last Boundry line thence with said line to the Beginning unto RobertbMoore his airs administrators thence the above obligation to be voyd other virtue in law in witness untill I have set my hand and seal this day and date above written

                 Andrew Ferrell (SEAL)

bind sealed and Delivered in presents of Jefferson Ferrell
Asign the with Bond to James McKinley Jacob Young for value received of them as witness my hand and seal this the 13th of March 1837

                 Robert Moore (SEAL)

and Ferrell to Bond to Robert Moore

RECORDS OF MRS. MOLLIE McKINLEY (CON)

This Indenture made this 23rd day of July in the Year of Our Lord One thousand and Eight hundred and thirty Between Hezekiah Brown of the County of Jackson and State of Tennessee of the one part and William Collins of the same county andState of the other part witness with That said Hezakiah Brown aforesaid and cohsideration of the sum of Seven dollars and fifty cents in handpaid the receipt whereof is hereby acknowledged hath Given Granted bargain Sell amd deliver unto the Said William Collins a certain tract place or parcel of Land Situated lying and being in the County of Jackson of said on the waters of Indian Creek it being a part of the State of Tennessee to the Hezakiah Brown by Bearingdate the 14th day of August in the year 1828 and nembered 740 and Beginning on a Large Chestnut and two Maples on the top of a Ridge it being the North east corner of said tract of Land Running tnence Westvtoa stake on the top of a ridge the North east corner of a tract of Land sold by said Hezakiah Brown toMartin Brown thence to Southern Corner with said Martin Browns line meadows the Said Ridge to s stake in the South Boundry line thenceeast on south line to sixty poles to s take James McKinley South east corner of a twenty five acre tract purchased of the said Hezakiah Brown thence North with said McKinley line sixty four poles to a stake his north esat corner thence east with said McKinley Boundry line sixty four poles to a stake in the east boundry line of the original survey thence North with said line to Beginning containing by Estimayion Seventy five acres be the same now or less togetharwith the Hereditaments and appurtenances to him the sia d William Collins his heirs and assigns forever and the said Hezakiah Brown for himself & his heirs doth hereby covenent and agree to ans with the said William Collins that he will forvevr warrant and defend the title of the above bargained premises to him he said William Collins his heirs and assigns forever from the lawful claim of any person or persons whatsoever InTestimony whereof the said Hezakiah Brown hath hereunto set his hand Seal the day and date first hand Seal the date first above written

James McKnley Hezakiah Brown
(SEAL)

Gro Elgin

Hezakiah Brown
To Deed 75 acres
William Collins

RECORDS OWNED BY MRS. MOLLIE MCKINLEY, CHESTNUT MOUND, TENN

This Indenture made this 21st day of July in the Year of Our Lord one thousand Eight dundred and thirty Between Hezekiah Brown of the County of Jackson and State of Tennessee of the one part and James McKinley of the State and county aforesaid of the other part witnesseth That the said Hezekih Brown for and in considerationof the sum of One hundred dollars to him an Land paid by the said McKinley the receipt whereof is hereby acknowledged hath given granted bargained and sold and delivered and by these prosents doth give Grant bargained sold and delivered to the said James McKinley his heirs and assigns a certain price parcel or tract of land situated lying and being in the County of Jackson of said on the waters of Indian Creek Beginning on a Dogwood and Two poplar Sapling Running thence North Sixty four poles to a stake thence West sixty three poles to a steak thence South sixty four poles to a steak thence East to the Beginning continuing twenty five acres it being the South East corner of the tract of Land of Two hundred acres granted by the State of Tennessee tonthe said Hezekiah Brown by protest Bearing datedate the First day of August, 1828 and Numbered 740 which said tract includes a part of the plantation that George Blair formerly owned Togather with the Heroditaments and appurtenancesthereunto belonging to him the said James McKinley and hisheirs and assigns forever and said Hezekiah Brown for himself and his heirs doth hereby covenant and agree toand with said James McKinley that he will forever warrant and defend the title of th above premises from the lawful c claim or claims of all persons what so ever lawfully claiming the same to be the said James McKinley his heirs and assigns forever In Testimony where of the said Hezekiah Brown Hath hw re unto set his hand and Seal the day a and date tfirst above written

Witnesses present
The words " a part of" Intered before assigned

          Hezekiah Brown (SEAL)

      William Collins X his mark
      Geo. Elgin

Hezekiah Brown
 Deed 25 acres
James McKinley

This endenture made and entered into this The twentieth day of November one thousand Eight hundre and thirty five Between JacobYoung of the one part and Sarha Wallas all of the County of Jackson and State of Tennesee Witnesses that the said Jacob Younghath bargained and sold and by these presents do the bargain and sell To said Sarah Wallas a surtain Tract or parcel of land lying and being in Jackson County on th South bank of Rock Spring Beginning at the corner of seventy acre Tract Entered in name of George Cullom Beginning on an ash and oak thence West To the first dry branch and thence down the meadowsbof said ranch a long a Lain deviding between Sarah Wallas and Henry Carr thence up said Rock Springs To the Beginningsupposed to be Ywenty three acres and one third be the same mote or less which trail of land I do warrent and defend from me my Heirs and assigns,

RECORDS OF MRS. MOLLIE MCKINLEY (CON)

State of Tennessee, No 1498
To all to whom these Presents shall Come, Greetings :
Know ye, that for and in consideration of the sum of one cent pwer acse paid into the office of the Entry Taker of Jackson County and entered on the 13th day of January 1826 pursuant to the provisions of anAct of the General Assembly of said TState passed on the day fo December one thousand and eight hindred and twenty five No 758 there is granted by the State of Tennessee unto Thomas Gillehan a certain tract or parcel of land containing Fufty acres by survey bearing date the Fourteenth day of December 1826 lying in said County on Young's fork of Indian Creek South side of Cumberland River and boundes as follows Beginning at a sugar tree in the South boundryl line of his one hundred acre tract on the point of a ridge not far from his house and about sixty four poles East of his South West corner Running thence South soxty poles to an elm in the North boundry line of Gideon Brown 50 acre Tract Thenec East with his line twelve poles to his North east corner a beech Thence South with his line twenty two poles to a hickory Thence east seventy two ploes to a hickory a sugar tree in the West boundry line of Robert McKinley 50 acre T act thence West passing his North west corner at thirty pole in all one hundred and five and one half poles to two suger trees Thence West fiftybeight poles to a sugar tree in the East boundry line of said William Tract of one hundred acre Thence South with his line twenty three and one half poles to a suger tree his corner Thence West with his line twenty six poles to the beginning, With the Hereditaments amd appurtenances To have and to hold the said tract or parcel of land with its appurtenences tot ehs aid Thomas Gillehan and his heirs forever, In witness where of WilliamCarroll Governor of the State of Tennessee has hereunto set his hand and caused the great seal of theState to be affixed At Nashville on the 14th day of November intthe Year of Our Lord one thousand eight hundred and twenty nine and of the Independance of the United States the fifty fourth

By GovernorWm. Carroll
Daniel Graham Secretary

No 1498
Thomas Gillehan Fify acres Jackson County
Recorded in my office Book C page 331

R. N. NELSON Register of the Mountain District

PROPERTY OF MRS. DAVE HIGH, COOKEVILLE, TENN.

DEED.

Tis indenture made this 10th day of Dec., the Year of our Lord One thousand eight hundred and twenty six, Between James Ray of the County of Jackson and the State of Tennessee of the one part and John Ditty of the County of White, and State foresaid of the other part witnesseth, that the said James Ray, hath for the consideration of the sum of one hundred and sevwnty dollars to him in hand paid the receipt whereof is hereby acknoeledged and there witg satisfied and content, hatn this day bargained and conveyed unto the said John Ditty his heirs and assigns forever a certain tract or pareel of land containing by estimation one hundred acres, the same more or less, lying and being on the County of Jackson and State afores and on the waters of Cane Creek, it being the place whereon the said Ray now lives, butted and bounded as follows, viz; Beginning at a Spanish oak it being the North west corner of sd. tract runnung then South, one hundred and eighty eight poles ro a Steak h thence West Eighty six poles to the beginning, To have and to hold the above described land and bargained premices with all the propertyemeluments and appurtenances thereunto belonging or in any wise appertainigg to the land I hereby bind myself and my heirs and executors to warrent and forever defend the right of said land from all and every person or persons claiming or to claim the sam or any part thereof. In witness I have here unto set my hand and affirmed my seal this day and date above written in presence of us,

James Ray (X his mark)

Test
W? M. Peak, Wm. I. Ray   A C td, 19th Nov, 1839

State of Tennessee, Registered Office, Feb, 10, 1840, Jackson County,
I, Saml. E. Hare, Reg. of said County do hereby certify that the within and foregoing deed of conveyance from James Ray to John Ditty to Gather with the d clerk, certificates is all duly Reg. in my Office Book E & R 435 & 426.
Sam E. Hare, Reg. Jackson Co.

State of Tennessee, Jackson County, Personally appeared before me John T. Turner, clerk of the county court of Jackson, I am Ray the bargner or with whom I am personally acquainted and who acknowledges this the granted within and for the purpose herein contained, witness my hand at office, 19th Nov, 1839
J. S. Turner Clk.

DEED.

This Indenture made this 15th day of Dec, One Thousand Eight Hundred and twenty six, Between George Carson, of the city of Baltimore and State of Maryland by his Attorneys in fact Nehemiah Carsons of the County of Butler and State of Kentucky of the part, and James and Matthew McKinley of the county of Jackson and State of Tennessee of the other part, witnessed that the said George Carson by his Attorney Nehemiah Carson for and in consideration of the sum of Five hundred dollars in hand paid the receipt whereof is hereby acknowledged hath granted, Bargained and sold unto the said James & Matthew McKinley a certain tract or parcel of Land containing Fifty acres lying and being in the said county of Jackson on the Walton Road including the plantation and possession known by the name of Roulstons Stand or Mount Richardson agreeable to the Entry made fot the same bounded as follows, viz; Beginning a a Sugartree running Eighty nine polea to a Beech thence S. eighty nine poles to a Line thence W. eighty nine poles to a stake thence N. eighty nine poles

DEED (CON)

to the Beginning. Also one other tract or parcel of Land int eh County and State aforesaid containing Twenty acres Biunded as followsto wit: Beginning at a sugar tree on the Ridge near where the path leading from Shadwick Bridges intersects theWalton Road running thence N. forty poles to an elm & sugar twie thence W. eight poles to a Dogwood & Ash, thence S. forty poles to a Beech & Dogwood thence E. eighty poles to the Beginning. To have and to hold that abound described Tracts and Bargained premices unto the said James & Mwtthews McKinley three heirs and assigns forever and he the said George Carson by his Attorney in fact Nehemiah Carson, does for himself his heirs and assigns forever warrent and defend the right and title claim and interest of the said pri mices to the only proper use and behalf of the said James & Matthews McKinley their heirs and assigns forever In witness whereof the said George Carson by h his Attorney in fact Nehemiah Carson hath hereunto set his hand affixed his seal the day and date above written .

Nathen Carson, Attr in fact
for ex Carson (Seal)

Sghned, sealed and Ack in presence of
   Rich M Cornwell
   James Carson
   John Pacse

At a County Court Began and held at the Court house in the Morgantownon Monday 12, day of Feb. 1827 the forgoing Indenture of Bargain estate from Nehemiah Carson all in part for George Carson to James & Matthews McKinley was inopen court proven to eb the act of sd. Carson, Testimony whereof I have here unto set my hand at office the seal of said County Court, Feb. 12, 1827.and in the 35year, commondcults.

R. O. E. Morrison, Clerk,
State of Kentucky, Butler County.

McKinley To Amonet, Fixed near 1888.

Property - Mrs. Davey Nichols, Ensor, Tenn
and Mrs. Dave High, Cookeville, Tenn

The State of Tennessee,
    To all to whom these presents shall come, Greeting.
  Know ye that in consideration of Entry No. 1652, made in the office of the Entry Taken of Jackson County and Entered on the 16th day of Feb, 1830 pursuant to the provisions of an cat of the General Assembly of said State passed on the (th day of January, 1830, There is granted by the said State of Tennessee unto William Brown a certain tract or parcel of land containing fifty acres by survey bearing date the 27th day of April 1833 lying in Jackson County on the waters of Martins Creek, Beginning at a Beech North of Peter Crooms Improvement
  running North sixty four poles to two Beeches and a WhiteOak, thence East one hundred and twenty five poles to a Chestnut and Black gum, Thence South sixty four poles to a Hickory and a Chestnut Oak on a ridge, Thence West one hundred and twenty five poles to the Beginning, including John Morgan Sugar Camp with the hereditanrents and appurtendances, To have and to hold the said tract or parcel of landwith the hereditaments and appurtenances, To have and to hold the said tract or parcel of landwith its appurtenances to the said William Brown and his heirs forever
    In witness whereof Neil S. Brown, Govner of the said State of Tennessee hath hereunto set his hand and caused the great Seal of the State to be affixed at Nashville on the 25th day of Aug in the year of Our Lord One thousand and eight hundred and forty nine and of the Independance of the United States the Seventy Fourth Year,
                                  W. B. A. Ramsey, Secretary.

I, M. F. O'Conner Register of the Mountain District do hereby certify that the abo above is a true and perfect transcript of grant No. 10176 for so acres Granted to William Brown as appears on record in my office in the Book W. Page 694.
    Given under my hand at office the 23rd day of April A. D. 1870
                        M. F. O'Conner Reg. Of the Mountain Dis.

Copy of Grant No. 10176
William Brown
    50 acres
Jackson County.

Property Mrs. Dave Nichols, Ensor, Tenn also
Mrs. Dave High, Cookeville, Tenn.

We, William Jared and Matthew Jared have this day bargained and sold and do hereby transfer and convey to Malinda Jared and his heirs foeever for the consideration o of ten dollars to us paid a tract of land in the State of Tennessee, Jackson County and laying on the waters of Indian Creek of Caney Fork containing by estimation thirty acres be the same more or less and bounded as follows, beginning where the East boundry line of a forty five acre tract granted to William Jared Dec, II crossed the North fork of said Indian Creek running thence Eastward with the South bank of said Creek to the mouth of a branch running into the South side of said Creek thence South Easterdly with said branch to where the first left hand fork of s said branch thence Eastwardly to the east boundry line of a 75 acre tract granted to William Jared thence North to the North East cormer of said 75 acre tract thence West to the North Bank of said Creek thence Westwardly with the North fork o of said Creek to the beginning to have and hold the same to the said Malinda Jared her heirs and assigns forever.

    We do covenant and bind ourselves and heirs I representatives to warrent and defend the title of the said land to Malinda Jared her heirs and assigns forever against every claim to be made by ourselvesor any persons claiming through or under us, but no farther this IIth day of Nov. 1839-Signed and delivered in the presence of

                      William Jared(Seal)
                      Mat. R. Jared   (Seal)

William R. Vance

Lawrence Byrne Jared, Nov, IIth, 1839.

   State of Tennessee, Jackson County
    Personally appeared before me John S. Tiuner, Clerk of the County Court of County of Jackson, Tennessee, Byrne a subscribing witness tot he within deed who being first sworn depose and say he is acquainted with William Jared and Martha R. Jared the bargainors and that he saw them sign and heard them acknowl- edge the execution of the same to be their act and deed for the purpose herein con& tained and upon the day it bears date witness my hand at office this I9th daoy of Nov. 1839,
                      J. S. Turner, Clerk.

State of Tennessee, Jackson County,
    Personally appeared before me Alex Montgomery Clerk of the County Court of Jackson County, William R. Vance a subscribing witness to the within deed named and who being first sworn depose and say that he is acquainted with William Jared a and Mat. R. Jared the bargainors and that they acknowledge the same in his presence to be their act and deed upon the day it bears date witness my hand at office this Ioth day of Nov. 1840
                      Alex Montgomery, Clerk

Property - Mrs Davey Nichols, Ensor, Tenn
also   Mrs. Dave High, Cookeville, Tenn.   Putnam County.

State of Tennessee, Putnam County.

To Jas. W. McDaniel, Esq.
You are hereby authorized and Empowered to take the examination of Mary A. Boyd the fenne covet Privately and apart from her Husband and relative of her free execution of the within or annexed deed and the same so taken certify under Putnam County Court at office the 14, day of Aug, A. D. 1857.
      Russell Moore, Clerk

State of Tennessee, Putnam County
  Mary A. Boyd, (Fern Cobet) Having personally appeared before me and having by virtue of the authoritys ma vested Examined the said Mary A. Boyd feth covet Privately and apart from her said husband, J. W. Boyd, and she having caknowledged the due Execution of the within or annexed deed freely, voluntarily and without compulsion, constraint or coercian by her said Husband, the same as therefore certified witness my hand and seal this day 15, of Aug, A. D. 1857.
      J. W. McDaniel

State of Tennessee, Putnam County.
  Personally appeared before me, Russell Moore, Clerk of Putnam County Court, Alexander Boyd and Jas. W. McDaniel subscribing witnesses to the within foregoing deed of conveyance, who being first sworn depose and say that they are acquainted with the bargainors and that they acknowledged the same in their presence to be their act and deed for the purposes and things therein contained which is Recorded witness my hand at office the 29th day Of Dec, A. D. 1858.
      Russell Moore, Clerk.
      J. W. McDaniel. J. P.
      for certificate pReg. fee 1.60

State Tax 28½
Clerk fee 75
certified

    Head Quarters, Unitef States Forces,
      Provost Marshal's Office,
       Nashville, Tenn, Aug, 6, 1864.

I, certify That Betsy Ann Nichols of Putnam County, Tennessee, has this ady sworn to and subscribed the Oath Of Amnesty as prescribed in the proclamation of the President of the United States of the 8th day of December, 1863.
    James S. Boyd,
     Provost Marshal
     Capt and Asst.

Mrs. Davey Nichols original owner of records,

Records owned by Mrs. J. P. Nichols (Con)
Baxter, Tenn   R. F. D.   I

July, 17, 1854

Cumberland Mountain White County, Tenn
Dera Neese
I received a few lines from you a fewdays ago which gave me great satisfaction to here from you all once more as it has bin a long time since I hard from any of you your letter found me in as good health as could be expected from my age
You wrote that you would come out this fall and seeme I want you to do so wothout fail health is Very good on the Mountain at present and I think if you will come you will want to stay all the time give my respects to all of the connection and tell them that some of them might come and see me I hope ypu will not forget your promise so I will close. when you write direct your letters to ClaysVille White County Tenn

Bashaba Mires
To Malinda Jared

To
  Miss Malinda Jared
      Byrne Po
      Jackson Co
      Tenn

COPIED FROM AN OLD SCHOOL LEDGER IN POSSESSION OF, MRS. DAVE HIGH,
COOKEVILLE, TENN. OCT. 1857.

I. Boyd, Jef Boyd, I. Hawes, J. Jared, J. Ament, J. Holliday, W. Ensor, T. Holliday, T. Smith, D, Malone, W. Leftwich, G. Maddux, Arichet, Baker, R. E. Fain, C. Raulston, S. R. Jared, J. Garland, J. James, M. Harvey.
The free School in the 11th District, Putnam County Taught at Pleasant Grove camp Ground closed it Session Nov, 13th 1857. Session three months. Branches taught During the Session Spelling, Reading, Arithmetic & English Grammer. Average attendance of Students 29½. Price for teaching $20 per month. Amount expended $60, $56 of the Free School fune, $4.00 from subscription.
J. Jared.

John Boyd, John Ament, John Hawes S. R. Jared L. J. Boyd, Vance Malone, Woodson Yates, David Nichols, George Maddux, William Leftwich, James Carland, William Johnson, R. E. Fain, E. Dunnivan, Dow Yates, John Jared, I. Boyd, I Ament, J. Hawes, S. R. Jared, L. J. Boyd, G. Malone, W. Yates, D. Nichols, G. Maddux, W. Leftwich, J. Carlen, W. Johnson, R. E. FAin, E. Dunnivan, J. Jared, A. K. Kerr, Dow Yates, J. Evans.

January, 1858.

John Boyd, John Ament, John Hawes, S. R. Jared, T. J. Boyd, G. Malone, W. Yates, D. Nichols, G. Maddux, W. Leftwich, J. Carland, W. Johnson, R. E. FAin, C. Dunnivan, J. Jared, A. F. Kerr, Dow Yates, J. Evans, J. Boyd, J. Ament, S. A. Jared T. J. Boyd, Y. Malone, W. Yates, J. Evans, J. Ament.
The School at Pleasant Grove camp Ground closed Feb, 5th, 1858. Session 2 months. Branches taught during the session, Spelling, reading, writing, Geography, Arithmetic & English Grammner, Average daily attendance of Students 24. Price for teaching $100 per Scholar for each month. Whole amount for the session $49.75 State of Tennessee, Putnam county, District, No 11, This Feb. 5th, 1858.

July L859.

J. Plunket, V. R. Scott, C. F. Butler, C. F. Burton, G. Evans, J, Evans, J. Denny, G. J? Maddux, C. R. Ford, J. Herbert, W. Stokes, R. W. McDowell, J. A. Huddleston, J. Pulliam, J. Fletcher, E. Evans, J, Newmand, M. Apple, O. Apple, A. Burton, E. Benson,

Aug. 1859

J. Plunket, R. Scott, C. F. Burton, G. Evans, J. Evans, J. Denny, G. J. Maddux, C. L. Ford, J. Herbert, W. Stokes, R. W. McDowell, J. A. Huddlest on, J. Pullum, J. Fletcher, E. Evans, J. Newman, M. Apple, O. Apple, A. Burton, E. Benson, A. Matthews, B. Scudder, S. Benson, W. Johnson, J. Jared,

Sept. 1859

J. Plunket, R. Scott, C. F. Burton, T. Evans, J. Evans, J. Denny, J. G. Maddux, C. R. Ford, J. Herbert, W. Stokes, R. W. McDowell, J. T Huddleston, J. Pulium, J. Fletcher, E. Evans, J. Newman, M. Apple, O. Apple, A. Burton, E. Benson, Buffalo Valley, A. Matthews, B, Scudder, S. Benson, W. Johnson, J. Jared, H. Whitehead,

Oct, 1859

J. Plunket, C. F. Burton, T. Evans, J. Evans, T. J. Maddux, J. Newman, S. E. H Huddleston, S. J. Denny, A. Burton, M. Scudder, R. Scott, J. Pullum,

Nov. 1859

J. Plunket, C. F. Burton, E. J. Newman, T. J. Maddux, J. Evans, T. Evans, J. Denny, J. E. Huddleston, J. Pullum, M. Scudder, A. Burton,
The free School closed at Rockey Springs, Nov, 16th, 1859. Session four month Branches taught during the School, Geography, reading, writing, Orthography, Arithmetic, English Grammer. Average daily attendance of Students 24, Price for teaching $25.00 per month, amount of public Money expenses $100,00, Dis,11, Putnam county, Tenn,
John Jared,

OLD SCHOOL LEDGER (CON)

J. Y. McKee, S. Maddux, W. Camard, L. Leftwich, J. H. Young, J. Jared, S. Cameson, E, Cornwell G. Austin, H. Maddux, E. Dunnivan, V. Spery, L. Young, H. Oaks Jo. Ballard, W. Gleaves C. Young, F. Berk, E. Parched, D. Souger, Jon. Overall, J. Maxwell, C. Rogers, A. R. Lowe, A. Cameron, Fox, R. Young, J. McKee S. Maddux J. H. Young, G. H. Maddux, S. Cameron, E. Cornwell, G. Austin, Prichet,

September.

J. Crowell, J. Maddux, C. Fox, J. G. McKee, S. Maddux, W. Chanard, J. H. Young J. Jared, S. Cameron. E. Dunnivan, V. Spivey, L. Young, A. R. Lane, H. Oaks, W1 Gleaves. D. Sawyer, L. Leftwich, Robert Young, David Cornwell, J. G. McKee, D. Maddux, S. H. Maddux, J. Jared, G. Austin, E. Dunnivan. F. Berk, J. Ballard Marley Young,

October.

J. G. McKee, S. H. Maddux, W. Chanard, J. Jared, E, Dunnivan, V. Spivy. S. Cameron, J. Ballared, H. R. Lowe, J. H. Young, S. H. Maddux, L. Leftwich, V. Spivy W. Chanard, E. Dunnivan.

November.

J. G. McKee, J. H. Maddux, S. Maddux, W. Chanard, J. Jared, E. Dunnivan, J. Ballard, W. Leftwich, Marley Young, John Jared,

December.

F. Berk, G. Austin, J. G. McKee, S. H. maddux, S. Maddux, John Jones, E. Dunnivan, L. Leftwich, Marley Young,

The Common School at Wesleys Chapel District No Eleven closed its Session, Dec. 1860 Session five months, Branches taught during the School, Reading, Writing, Geography, Arithmetic and English Grammer. Average Daily attendance of Students . Price for teaching $25.00 per month , Amount of public money expences$ 100 District No 11, Putnam County, Tenn,

John Jared.

J. W. McDowell, J. Jared, D. Nichols, L. Gentry, J. E. Young, P. Young, E. J. Boyd, B. B. Jared, C. Reeves, I. Boyd, P. McCallahan, V. Spivy, J. Maxwell. R. Jentry, W. Jentry, A. Ballard, F. Austin, C. Brasel, J. H. Cullom, Marley Young, J. W. McDanial, J. Jared, D, Nichols, S. Gentry, J. H. Young, P, Young, E. J. Boyd, B. B. Jared, C. Rogers, A. Boyd, P. McCullough, V. Spivy, J. Maxwell, W. Gentry, C. Grace, Silas. Gentry, J. H. Young, C. Brasel, Dallas Byrne P. McCallahan, B. B. Jared,

The Common School on Indian Creek closed its Session Sept. 5th 1862. Session two and a half momths. Branches taught during sesion , Reading, Writing, Geography, Arithmetic and English Grammer. Average Daily attendance of Students Prices for teaching $25.00 per month, District No 11 Putnam County.

PROPERTY OF BOB PEARSON

This Indenture made this fifth day of March, one thousand eight hundred and thirty two By and Between John Ramsey of the State of Tennessee and County of Jackson of the oned part and William Shelton of the State and County aforesaid of the other part witnessed that for an in consideration of the sum of one hundred and fifty dollars to me in hand paid By the said William Shelton- the Receipt whereof is thereby acknowledged and therewith satisfied and content I have this day Bargined and sold and conveyed unto the Said William Shelton a certain tract or parcel of Land containing fifty acres by survey Be the same above or less- Situated lying and being in the County aforesaid & on the Waters of Blackburns fork of Roarong River Butted and Bounded as follows - Viz- Beginning at a post oak running South one hundred and Twenty five poles to a post oak and hickory thence North one hundred and Twenty five poles to a post oak thence East twenty four poles to the beginning encluding the sd. Remsey Dwelling house and the place foremely occupied by Randolph Ramsey with a part of the Said Ramsey Improvment- with the hereditions and assetainances to have and to hold the said tract or parcel of Land and above Described premises with its assertainces to the said William Shelton and his heirs for ever- I hereby Bind myself my heirs and Executors Jointly and severally to warrant & forever defend the same from all amd every person blaming the I am from all and Every person blaming the I am on any part thereof in witness whereof I have here unto set my hand this day and date above written in presence of us the Two Subscribing,   His mark/ John Ramsey(Seal)
Test- Thomas Nicholas, John Nicholas.

State of Tennessee, Jackson County, Pearsonally appeared before John S. Turner Clerk of the Court Pleas and Quarter sessions for said County John Nicholas subscribing witness to the within deed who being first sworn despose and say that he is acquainted with John Remsey the Bargonar and that he acknowledged the mentiined of the same in his presance at be his act and Deed for the purpose therein contained upon the Day it Bears date Witness my hand at office this 15th-1834,December J.S.Turner(clk)
John Ramsey, Deed to William Shelton, 50 acres Registered in Book D.
Page 531- Registration 1,2½
State of Tennessee, Jackson County, August session 1835, Deed of Conveyance from John Ramsey to William Shelton Deed of conveyance for fifty acres of land lying in Jackson County was intered in Court and the exeCution thereof fully proven by the Oath of Thomas Nicholas and the same is or deced to be certified for Registration. J.S.Turner- Clk.

State of Tennessee, Jackson County, Registers office, September 15, 1835. I Leroy B. Little Register of said County do hereby certify that the within foregoing deed to gather with eht several Certificates is duly Registered in my office Book D. page 531. LeRoy B. Little Register of Jackson County.

Dec 14th 1827, No. 6919.
The State of Tennessee, To whom these Presents Shall Come-- Greeting- Know Ye, that in consideration of the sum of one per cent an paid into the office of the Entry taken of Jackson County and entered on the 1th day of January 1826 presentment to the provision and act of the General Assembly of said State: passed on the Twenty second day of November one Thousabd eight hundred and twenty three and the acts empannelled thereunto by no. 698, This is granted by the Said State of Tennessee unto Arnol Fisk.

BOB PEARSONS RECORDS CONTINUED

A certain Tract or parcel of Land containing One hundred acres by survey hearing date the 10th day of November 1826 lying in said County and bounded as follows to wit: Beginning at the center of what is called Moses Fisk Turnpike road in the North boundry line of a three hundred and twenty one tract entered in the name of Sarah Perry Fisk running thence East fifty poles to two black jacks Thence were crossing said tract at 74 poles in all one hundred poles to a black jack, thence South one hundred and sixty poles to a black Jack, thence East fifty poles to the beginning.

With the hereditamants and appurtances to Have and to Hold the said Tract or Parcel of Land, with its appurtances to the said Amul Fisk and his Heirs forever.

In witness whereof Wm. McCarroll, Governor of the State of Tennessee hath hereunto set his hand and caused the Great Seal of the State to be affixed at Nashville, on the 24th day of Sept. in the yeat of our Lord one thousand eight hundred and Twenty, sworn and of independence of the United States the fifty second, BY THE GOVERNOR. Daniel Graham, Secretary
Registered Office Nashville Feb. 14th 1854. The within a true Copy from the Record of my office Record in Book No. 8, witness my hand at office Moses M. Swan (Reg) Middle Tenn.
Copy of Grant No. 6919 Jackson County 100 acres Omel Fisk.

State of Tennessee No. 22434- To all to whom these presents shall come Greeting: Know Ye that By Virtue of part og certificate No.571 dated the 23 day of July 1812 passed by the commissioners for West Tennessee to Narcissa Hays for 27 acres and entered on the 9th day of November 1814 by No.3386
A Certaint tract or parcel of Land containing Ten acres by survey bearing date the 14th day of April 1815 lying in the Third District in Jackson County on the waters of Roaring river and bounded as follows to wit: Beginning at a black jack and post oak about 65 yds North east of the spring by the said Phillips running South about 60 poles to a stake and two black jack pointers thence West fifty p. thence sixty eight and a third poles ti a spanish oak thence East to a Chestnut tree thence thirty poles to the beginning including the place of the said Phil lives.
With the hereditamants and apputances to have and to hold said tract or parcel of Land with its appurtances to the Said Phillips and his heirs forever in witness whereof William Carroll, Governor of Tennessee hath hereunto sset his hand and caused the Great Seal of the State to be affixed at Murfreesborough, on the 8th day of September in the year of our Lord one thousand eight hundred and twenty four and of the Independence of the United State the forty-nine, By the Governor, Daniel Graham Secretery Recorded in the Registers office of West Tenn. Oct. 26, 1824.
Wm. Garock Register of West Tennessee By Alex Mc Garock DK.

DeKalb Co. Mo. Dec 27 1860
Mr. Joe Pearson- Dear Sir your letter containing a check for $1400.00 has been reced & you can retain this as a receipt for the same A.H.Owens Susan S. Owen, You remember in your letter that when I acknowled the receipt of the check you would write and inform me all about my claims aganist the Estate of Isacc Clark deced, If there is any more comming to me except the above receipted you will please forward & forthwith as the times are distressingly close as it regard money - we are as a general thing in

a state almost bording on distress. we have had foar bad crop years in
seccession but the last was almost a complete failure- the present is
bad enough but we dread to think of the future almost everything of the Stock
kind have been sold out of the country and the counrty wi l have nothing
to sell The next year- This with the great Political troubles does make
the prospect of the future gloomy beyoun description- We here are for
the Union provided we can keep togather on Hohorable terms If the
threving Northers States will surrender up our Negros they have stolen
and attend to their own bususness and let us attend to ours we are for
the Union but if the law undermining and Ungodly acts of Robery as'd
Kep up we choose honorable recession to cowardly Submission, You know
how it is with rusty form about writting, I have no legal excuse but
will ask you to forgive the seemingly negligance for my long silence,
As it Regards the health of the Country it is good All your friends
are well & all join me in sending our best wishes to you and all enquir-
ing friends, We will be pleased to have a letter from you or any other
friends in the Land of Old Tennessee, Respectfully Your brother &
Sister A.H.Owen, Susan S.Owen.

      ENVELOPE;
Postmark.
Cameron Mo.
Dec. 27,

          Mr. Joseph Pearson
          Putnam County
          Cookeville, post off.
          Tenn.

PROPERTY OWNED BY BOB PEARSON HILLHAM ROAD COOKEVILLE TENN.

This indenture made the 31st day of January in the year of our Lord 1831
By and between John Petress of the County of Overton in State of Tennessee
of the one part & Thomas Shoat of the County of Jackson and State afore
said of the other part witness that the said John Patross for and in
consideration of the sum of sixty Dollars to heir in hand paid by the said
Thomas Shoat the Recept of the same is here by fully acknowledged hath
and by their presents doth give grant bargin sell alien enfe off. convey
& confirm into the said Thomas Shoat and his heir Executiors admistrtators
a certain tract or parcel of land lying and being in the County of Jackson
State of Tennessee on the waters of Blackburns Creek aprat of the Roaring
River and bounded as follows to wit beginning at a chestnut twelve poles
North of a blacj oak and post oak marked as Pointers South of a pabh leading
from Phillips Pys to James Terrys running thence South one hundred and twenty
fice poles to a black jacj thence wesr sixty four poles tia Hickory thence
East sixty four Poles to two Hickorys thence East sixty four poles to the
beginning containing fifty acres be the same more or less it being a tract
of land Granted by the State of Tennessee unto the said John Patress by
Grant No 3968 Dated 11th day of September 1826 the said John Patress for
his self and his heirs Executors and adminstrators that the before Recited
land and bargained Premises that he will warrant and forever defedn free
from all persons or manner of persons what sosver claiming the same or any

Part thereof but to the only proper use of Heirs the said Thomas Shoat ans his Heirs for ever in witness where of the said John Patross hath Here on to set his Hand and affix his Seal the Day and year first Written in the Presents of Test- John Oliver William R. Savage, John Patross (Seal) John Patross Deed to Thomas Shoat 50 acres Land.

RECORDSOWED BY BOB PEARSON HILLHAM ROAD COOKEVILLE TENN. R#1.

The State of Tennessee No.11688- To all to whom these shall come--- Gerrting Know Ye, That by virtue of entry No.46 Made in the office of the Entry Taker of Putnam County and entered on the 3rd day of September 1855, pursuant to the provisions of an act of the General Assembly said State passed on the 9th day of Januarym 1830. There is Granted by the said State of Tennessee unto Joseph Pearson, a certain tract or parcel of land containing Eighteen Acres by survey, bearing date the Sixth day of June 1856, lying in the said county of Putnam on the water of Blackburns Fork beginning on a Post Oak and Post Oak and black Jack pointers convey of a one hundred acres track belonning to said Pearson Running West Eighteen poles to a Stake on the time of a Three hundred and twenty acres tract that said Pearson lives on now with the East boundry line of the same one hundred and sixty poles to two post okes and pointers cover of the same on the west side of the Road leading from White Plains to Terrys East crossing said road at two poles crossing the Cookeville Read at Eighteen poles to a Black Jack on the East side of the Road covers to the one hundred acre tract. South with the West boundry line of said one hundred acre tract one hundred and sixty poles to the beginning. with the hereditamants and appurtances to have and to hold the said Tract or parcel of land with its appurtances to the said Joseph Pearson and his heirs forever.
In witness whereof Andrew Johnson, Governor of the State of Tennessee, h hath hereunto set his Hand and caused the Great Seal of the Sate to be affixed at Nashville, one the 10th day of July in the year of our Lord One thousand Eight Hundred and fifty six. and of the independence ofthe United States the Eightyth Year, By the Gevernor Andrew Johnson L.M.Burford Secetary.
Joseph Pearson is entitled to the within described Tract of Land John T. Day Register of the mountain district Recorded on the Registers office for the mountain District on Book No 10 Page 751, John T. Day Register of the Mountain District.
Grant No.11688 Joseph Pearson 18 acres Putnam County 1st July, 1856

State of Tennessee No. 1842.
To all to whom these presents shall come--Greeting: Know Ye that for and in consideration of the sum of one cent per acre, paid into the office of the Entry Taker of Jackson Countym and entered on the 9th day of January 1826, pursuant to the provisions of an act of the General assembly of said State, passed on the third day of December one thousand eight hundred and twenty five by No. 715 there is granted by thhe said State of Tennessee unto Thomas M.Ñolas--A certain tract or parcel of land containing one hundred acres by survey beraing date the 16th day of Feburary 1829 lying in said county on the waters of Blackburns fork of Roaring "iver and bounded as follows. Beginning at a Black Oak North of a field occupied by Isaac Richmonds, Running North one hundred and sixty

poles to a small post oak and Hickory Thence west one hundred poles to two dogwoods in the part boundry line of James Terry's 640 acres Tract, Thence South with said line one hundred and sixty poles to two small chestnuts Thence East one hundred poles to the Beginning including Austin Shoats improvments. With the hereditamants and appertances. To have and to hold the said tract or parcel of land with its appertances to the said Thomas Nicholas, and his heirs forever, in witness where of William Carroll, Governor of the State of Tennessee, has hereunto set his hand and caused the great seal of the state to be affixed at Nashville on the 9th day of August in the year of Our Lord One thousand eight hundred and thirty and of the Inde pendance of the United States the fifty fifty, By the Gevernor Wm. Carroll Daniel Gooham Secretaty, Thomas Nicholas is entitled to the within described land R. Nelson Register of Mountain District. Recorded in my office Book C. page 533 R. Nelson Register of the mountain District.
No. 1842 Thomas Nicholas 100 acres Jackson County.

State of Tennessee NO. 4279 - To all to Whom these Presents shall come Greeting: Know you that by virtue of entry N537 made in the office of the entry taker of Jackson County and entered on the 8th day of January 1830 pursuant to the provisions of an act of the General Assembly of said State passed on the 3rd day of December 1825. there os Granted by the said State of Tennessee unto William Shelton assigned of John Ramsey a certain tract or parcel of land containing three hundred acres by survey bearing date the 2day of March 1832 lying in said County on the waters of Blackburns fork of Roaring River Beginning at a black oak Wesr of improvements n now occupied by Randoph Ramsey running East Two Hundred and two poles to a Black Oak and post oak on the Old Collins River tract: Thence North passing the South west Corner of Jess KeyKendall's fifty acre tract at fifty eight poles in all with said line One hundred and fifty poles to a Hickory the North West corner of said tract, Thence East with the North boundry line of said tract thirty nine poles to two blackjacks and a hickory in said line, thence North one hundred and fifty two and one foutth poles to two small post oaks thence west with the South boundry line of John Petross fifty acre tract passing his South West corner at Ninty eight poles in all one hundred and twenty four poles to a black oak, in the East boubdry line of Jess Kuykendall one hundred acre tract, Thence South with said line twenty six and one fourth poles to a chestnut the South East corner of said tract thence West Eighteen poles to a post oak in said corner of Thomas Nicholas North East corner of his one hundred acres, Thence South with the Easr boundry line of said tract one hundred and sixty poles to a black oak the South East corner of said tract, Thence West with the South boundry line of said tract one hundred poles to a chestnut tree the South West corner of said tract, Thence South one hundred and sixteen poles to the beginning.
With the hereditamants and appurtances, to have and to hold the said tract or parcel of land with its appurtances to the said William Shelton and his heirs forever. In witness whereof Newtan Cannon, Governor of the State of Tennessee has here unto set his hand and caused the great seal of the State to be affixed at Nashville on the 22n d of January 1836 and Year of our Independence By the Gevernor N. Cannon Luke Lee Secetary.
William Shelton is entitled to the within described land T.R.Nelson Register of the mountain District.
No. 4379 William Shelton assignee of John Ramsey 300 acres Jackson County To be left at Major Richard F. Cook's in Jackson County with request for him to have it delivered to the owner - Register.

PROPERTY OWNED BY BOB PEARSON   HILLHAM ROAD   COOKEVILLE TENN.

State of Tennessee No 800- To all to whom these presents shall come Greeting, Know ye that for and in consideration for the sum of one cent per acre paid into the office of the Entry Taker of Jackson County and entered on the 8th day of Feburary 1826, pursuant to the provisions of one act of the General assembly of said State passed on the third day of December one thousand Eight hundred and twenty-five by No 874 then Geanted by the said State of Tennessee unto Mathew Kuykendall a certain tract or parcel of land containing fifty acres by survey bearing date the 8th day of May 1827 lying in said County on the Waters of Thomas Nicholas Mill Creek and bounded as follows Beginning at a hickory thence West Eighty nine poles to a post oak- thence North ninty poles to two hickories, Thence East Eighty nine poles to the beginning with the hereditaments and appurtendances to have and to hold the said Tract or parcel of land withits appurtendances to the said Matthew Keykendall and his heirs forever, In witness whereof Sam Huston Gevernor of the State of Tennessee hath hereunto set his hacd and caused the Great Seal of the State to be affixed at Nashville on the 10th day of the Independence of the United States the fifty third, By the Gevernor Sam Huston, Daniel Graham Secretary, Matthew Kuykendall 50 acres Jackson County Recorded in mu office Book B page 232 R. Nelson Register of the Mountain District.

State of Tennessee Jackson County- This day came John Dowell before me John Terry a Jistice of the peace for said County & made oath in due form of law that a certain note of hand Executed from Joseph Pearson to him for one hundred and six dollars Sometime in December 1851 is lost or unintentionally mislaid or the possessions of the same has been filoniously obtained by Irme Pearson & that he has not sold Bartered transfered assigned or acnveyed by him self or by any Person for him said note, This 16th day of November 1853. Sworned to & subscribed before me the date above John Terry J.P. John Dowell .

State of Tennessee, No 3670- To all to whom these presents shall come Greeting: Know Ye that by virtue of Entry No 1666 made in this office of the enrty taker of Jackson County and entered on the 30th day of December 1830 pursuant to the provisions of act of the General Assembly of said State passed on the 9th day of January 1830 thence Granted by the said State of Tennessee unto Thomas Choate a certain tract or parcel of land containing fifty acres by survey bearing date the 2e day of march 1830 lying in the Said County on the Waters of Blackburns fork of Roaring River Beginning at a small Black Oak the South East corner of said Choates original fifty acre tract running East with John Raineys North boundry line of his three hundred acre tract passing his North east corner at thirty two poles in all sixty four poles to three black jacks, thence thence North one hundred and twenty five poles to three chestnuts, thence West sixty four poles to a chestnut the North East corner of said original fifty acres tract thence South one hundred and twenty five poles to the beginning. With the hereditaments and appurtnedances to have and to hold the said tract or parcel of land with its appurendances to the said Thomas Choate and his heirs forever. In witness whereof William Carroll Gevernor of the State of Tennessee had hereunto set his hand and caused the Great Seal of the State to be affixed at Nashville on the 3rd day of February 1835 and 59 years. By the Gevernor Wm Carroll, F.G.Keith Secretary. Recorded in my office Book E. page 409 M. Nelson Register of the mountain District.
No.3670 Thomas Choate 50 acres Jackson County, Thomas Choate is intitled to the within discribed land R. Nelson Register of the mountain District.

BOB PEARSON'S RECORDS CONTINUED

This Indenture made this third day of January in the year of Our Lord Eighteen hundred and thirty four Between Mathew Kuykendall of the County of Jackson and state of Tennessee of the one part and William Shelton of the State and County aforesaid of the other Part witness that for an inconsideration of the sum of forty dollars to him in hand Paid by said Shelton the Receipt whereof is hereby acknowledged hath this Shelton a certain tract or parcel of land situated as follows Viz) lying and being in the said County of Jackson and state aforesaid on the waters of Thomas Nicholas mill creek supposed to be the Waters of Bear Creek and bounded as follows. Beginning at a Hickory running south ninty poles to a hickory thence West Eighty poles to two hickories thence East eighty nine poles to the beginning with the hereditaments and appurtendances to have and to hold the said tract or parcel of land with the appertances to the said William Shelton and his heirs forever and containing in all fifty acres and do bind myself my heirs Executors Adminstrators to warrant and forever defend from me and my heirs in witness whereof I have here unto set my hand and seal this day and date first above mentioned. Matthew Kuykendall (S$_e$al) Peter K$_u$ykendall Curtis Terry,

State of Tennessee, Jackson County. Pearsonally appeared before me William Scanland clerk of the Court of Pleas & Quartly session for said claim by Matthew Kuykendall and acknowledged that he executed the within Deed of conveyance for the purposes therein contained. witness my hand at office this 10th Nov. 1834, William Scanland(Clk).

This Indenture made this Day of January in the year of Our Lord Eighteen & Thirty four between Mathew Kuykendall of the one Part and William Shelton of the other Part.

State of Tennessee, Jackson County, Registers office Jan. 21, 1835
I Leroy B. Settle Register of said County of Jackson do hereby Certify that the within & foregoing deed of Conveyance together with the Clerks Certificate is duly registered in my office Book D. & page 517.
Le Roy B. Settle Register of Jackson County.

State of Tennessee - No 3968   To all to whom these presents shall come------Greeting: Know Ye, That for and in consideration of the sum of Twelve and one half cents per acre paid into the office of the ^{E}ntry Taker of Jackson County and entered on the Twelth day of July, 1842 pursuant to the provisions of all Act of the General Assembly of said State passed on the 22 day of November one thousand eight hundred and twenty three by No 399. There id granted by the said State of Tennessee unto John Patross a certain Tract or Parcel of Land containing fifty Acres by survey bearing date the 30th day of Aughst 1825 lying in said County on the waters of Blackburns fork of Roaring River and bounded as follows to wit: Beginning at a Chestnut twelve poles North of a black oak and post oak marked as pointers South of a path leading from Phillips Phys to James Terry's Running thence South one hundred and twenty five poles to a Black Jack thence West Sixty four poles to a hickory, Thence North one hundred and twenty five poles to two hickories thence East Sixty four poles to the beginning including the house and improvements last occupied by Mathew Patross.

With the hereditaments and appertenances To have and to Hold the said
Tract or Parcel of Land with its appertenances to the said John Patross
and his heirs forever. In witness whereof William Carroll Gevernor
of the State of Tennessee hath hereunto set his hand and caused the great
Seal of the State to be affixed at Nashville on the Eleventh day of
September- In the year of our Lord One t ousand eight hundred and twenty
six and of the Independence of the United States the fifty first.
By the Governor Wm. Carroll, Daniel Graham Sectrary.
Recorded in the Registers office of West Tennessee Febryary 28" Stith
Harrison DK. John Patross is entitled to the within mentioned tract
of land T.M.Garack D. Register of West Tennessee.
No. 3968 John Patross 50 acres Jackson County.

Know all men by these presents that I Thomas Choate have this day bargained
and sold and do hereby transfer and convey to Joseph Pearson and his
heirs for ever for the consideration of Thirty five Dollars to me paid
two tracts of Land in the State of Tennessee, Putnam County and district
No 3 on the waters of Blackburns fork containing by estimantion one
hundred acres be the same more ot less and bounded as follows;
1st Tract Beginning at a chestnut twelve poles north of a Black oak& post
oak marked as pointers South of a path leading from Phillips Phy to Jmaes
Terry 's running thence South one hundred and t wenty five poles to a ___
Black Jack thence North one hundred and twenty five poles to two hickories
thence East Sixty four poles to the beginning containing fifty acres by G rant
No. 3968 Dated 11th day of September 1826.
2nd Tract Begining at a small Oak the South East corner of said Choate
original fifty acre tract running East with John Ramseys North boundry
line of his three hundred acre tract passing his North east corner at thirty
two poles in all sixty four poles to three Black Jacks thence North one
Hundred and twenty five poles to three chestnuts thence West sixty four
poles to a chestnut the North East corner of said original fifty acres
tract thence South one hundred and twenty five poles to the beginning
containing fifty acres by Grant 180 3670 Dated 3rd day of February 1825
To have and to hold the same ti the said Joseph Pearson his heirs and assign
foe ever do convenant withthe said Pearson that I am lawfully stixed of
said land have a good rite to convey it and that the same is incumbered, I
do further convenant and bind myself my heirs and Representaves to warrant
and forever defend the title to the said land and every part thereof th the
said Pearson his heirs and assigns aganist the lawful claims of all persons
whatever This 25th day of February 1843, Thomas Choate.
Attest J.M.Goodbar J.L.H.Huddleston.
Thomas Choate to Deed Joseph Pearson 100 acres.

PERSONAL LETTER;

Joseph Pearson, Sir late last evening I understood that Isaac Buck was
going to start to Nashville I wish to send by him for some books for the use
of my office as this county have hereto fore been in dispute- The County
Court Authorized me to get Books and they would then pay me* I wish to get
$25.00 and if I can get the same or less amount please send me a few lines,
by the bearer of this and I will be at your house- and give note & security
if you want security and pay the same Back at the time the other note is due
with 12½ cts Interest thereon I would have to come this morning more than a
man came to my house late last Evening and is wanting some buisness done
in the office, Yours in haste W.H.Carr

I Joseph Pearson bind myself to pay Josiah Phy the sum of Six hundred
Dollars the consideration of this obligation in such that whereas the said
Josiah Phy has this day purchased of me for Three hundred Dollars on the
following payments to wit: one hundred Dollars to be paid the first day
of June 1853 and one hyndred the first day of June 1854 and the 3rd hundred
the first day of June 1855 For which his notes under seal have this day
him executed to me barring interest from the dates Five tracts of land
in Jackson County in District No.10 State of Tennessee Bounded as follows
Begin ing by estimanton fifty acres Beginning at a post oak marked with
H.T. Running west one hundred poles to a small Hickory, Thence South Eighty
poles to a small Hickory & Black oak, Thence East one hundred poles to a
stake in the Barnes, Thence North Eighty Poles to the Beginning including
Sume Springs about 17 a½ miles from Phillip Phy as staked in location
The second tract containing by estimantion fifty acres beginning at a
Hickory twenty five poles East of Nicholas North West corner of his orifinal
survey running North one hundred poles to a black oak thence East eighty
poles to a black walnut, Thence South one hundred poles to a stake in said
Nicholas North boundry line of said fifty acre survey Thence West Eighty
poles to the beginning the 3rd tract containing fifty avtes beginning at a
Hickory the North West corner of the said Nicholas Fifty Acre tract running
North Forty Poles to the two Hickories, Thence West Eighty Poles to A post
oak & Hickorys in the North boundre line of said fifty acre tract, Thence
North with said line sixty Poles to the begining Also one other tract containing fifty eight & half acres lying near the said discribed tracts od land.
conveyed by Thomas Choate to William Carr Also o ne other tract containing
twelve acres more or less lying adjoining the last mentioned tract of land
Now if I shall makek or cause to be made to the said Josiah Phy his heirs
or assigns a good and sufficient title in fee simple with general warrantly
to said tracts of land on the making of the last payment. Then this obligation to be void, this 1st day of June 1852. Joseph Pearson (Seal)
Attest John Terry Wm. A. Terry,

This indenture made this sixth day of January one thousabd Eight Hundred
and Thirty eight between Thomas Nicholas of White County and State of Tenn
essee of tje one part and Nathan W. Wallace of the County and State aforesaid
of the other part witness that whereas the said Nicholas hath Bargained
and solf unto the saod Wallace a certain tract or parcel of la nd containing
one hundred acres being the same more or less lying in Jackson County
on the waters og Blackburns fork of Roaring River and bounded as Follows;
Beginning at a Black oak North of a fiekd occupied by Isaac Richard running
North one hundred and sixty poles to a small post oak and hickory thence west
one hundred poles to two Dogwoods in the east Boundry line of James Terry
six hundred and Forty acre tract thence South with said line one hundred
and sixty poles to two small chestnuts thence east one hundred poles to the
Beginning with the hereditaments and appertentnaces to have and to hold
the aforesaid tract or parcel of land free from any claims either by me
or my heris forever in Testimony where the said Nicholas hath hereunto
set his hand and seal the date first above mentioned, Thomas Nicholas (Seal
Attest John Welch Hugh G. Huddleston
Thomas Nicholas Deed to Mathew H. Wallace 100 acres.

State of Arkansas , Carroll County, Sept 13th A.D. 1854.
Dear Mother, Brother & Sister, It is in and through the kind mercies of
an all wise Creator that we are in Tolerable Health that is they are all
well Except Bad Colds with out it is myself I am not well altogether

PERSONAL LETTER CONTINUED

I am teaching school at this time But we hape and pray that these few lines will find you all well at there arrival we have nothing very strange to ritbe to you only I received your letter on yesterday
which give us great Satisfaction to hear that you was all well and I was truly glad tb hear that Mother was living with you we have been looking with longing anixety for the news which have just arrived Our calculation is to come as soon as posable that sion & myself) If no providen trial him derence one or both of us will be there as soon as possible that is this fall and we are comming to fetch mother home with hs and to see Justice nowhere without any regard to Tom old Jake or any whom may consider themselves conserned on the stipe Tribe wee want mother to be in rediness atall times to come with us know knowing how soon wee will bee there I .F.Carter want you I Pearson to get the Best counsel for me conserning Polly the Negro & mothers dowery in that land in White County and wee will sell it cheap for the cash when wee come I know old Jake sold it But no title has never went from me yet, I have written to Wm B. Cumming of VanBuren County concerning the matter and I am looking for an answer Every dau I think I will straten them when I come we do not want to get into deficulties with Old Kake But so far as Tom if conserned wee do not ax him any favors whatever he is no Body and all who know him knows that, we will come in a two horse waggon and wee want mother to be certain and get ready and stay Reddy untill wee come wee will be there Isaac Clark your nephew will start to that Counrty in a few days John A. Anderson will come with us so he says give our best love to all friends wee will Bring our Letter to a close By Subscribing our names as your Friends till Doeth may God Bless you all. Wm. F.C. Carter & Sion .W"ife,J. Pearson & wife),
Rebecca Stipe Joseph Pearson & Wife. From Berryville Ark. Sept 20 To Joseph Pearson White Plains P.O. Putnam County Tenn.

I Elijah Car have this day bargained and sold and do herebe transfer and convey to Joseph Pearson and his heirs forever for the consideration of Three hundred and forty Dollars to me paid four tracts of land in the State of Tennessee Putnam County and District Nolst. containing by estimation Two hundred and eight and one half acres. First tract containing fifty eight and one half acres Beginning at a Post Oak and white oak & Pointer the North West corner of John B. Mc Carmacks four hundred acres survey & in the East boundry line of First entry on the North side if the Walton Roade of three hundred and twenty acres running thence North with said East boundry line fifty one poles to a chestmut and white oak & pointers the North East corner of said three hundred and twenty acres survey thence West thirty poles to a posteak and Pointers the North boundey line of said three hundred & twenty acre survey, Thence North with the East boundry line if Fisk's second Three hundred and twenty acre survey fifty eig t poles to a Readoak and Pointers in said Easr boundry line, Thende Easr supposed to be with or neat James Peaks line Eighty Poles to a Red oak and Hickory & Poihters at Murpheys West boundry line eighty six poles to a postoak amd Read oak & Pointers tje South West corner of said Murpheys Survey boundry line of said survey one hundred and eighty nine Poles to a stake & Pointers Thence South twenty three Poles to the North boundry line of aforesaid four hundred acre survey Thence West with the North boundry line of the aforesaid four hundred acre survey to the beginning fifty acre tract containing afifty acres. Beginning at a Postoak Marked J.L. Running West one hundred Poles to a

small Hickory and Blackoak , Thence East one hundred Poles to a stake, Thence
North Eighty Poles to the beginning Third tract containing fifty acres Beginning at a Hickory running North one hundred Poles to a stake in the North
boundry line of the first Discribed fifty acres tract, Thence West Eighty
Poles to the beginning, Fourth tract comtaining fifty acres Beginning at a
Hickory the South West corner of the first mentioned fifty acre tract running
North forty Poles to two Hickorues, Thence West Eighty Poles to a Post
oak & Hickories, Thence South one hundred Poles to two Hickorises & Postoak in the west boubdry line on the first mentioned fifty acre tract
Thence North with said line sixty Poles to the beginning. To have and to
hold the same to the said Joseph Pearson his heirs and assigns forever
I do convanant with the saod Joseph Pearson that D am lawfully seixed of
said land have a good right to convey it and that the same as-unincumbered
I do further convenant and bind myself my heirs and Representatives to
warrant and forever defend the title to the said land and every part there
of th the said Joseph Pearson his heirs and assigns agaiist the lawful
claime of all Pearso whatever This 11th day of April 1855.
Entered and delivered in our presents, This 11th day Apr. 1855,
Isaac Buck, J.M.Douglass,
State of Tennessee, Puntm County, Pearsonally appeared before me Russell
Moore Clerk of Putnam Court & Elijah Car the within bargained with
whom I am personally acquainted and who acknowledged the deed Executioner
of the within Deed of conveyance to be his act and Deed for the purpose
and things therein contained witnessed my hand at office the 1ath day of
April 1855, Russell Moore clerk, This deed was filed in my office and
dated for Registration the 24th Dec, 1857 at 7½ O'Clock P.M. in Reception
Book on pagees 54& 55 registered in Book B. on pg. 291& 92.
William Baker(Reg) of Putnam County.
Elijah Car Deed to Joseph Pearson 208½ Acres, State Tax 30 clerks fee 25.
ackn. Apr. 11th 1855, Recorded on page 142 Book A. Putnam County Tenn.
R. Moore Clk. Reg. Fee $1.75 From N,J,Pearson.

I mathew H. Wallace of Jackson County and State of Tennessee have this day
bargained and do hereby transfer and convey to Joseph Pearson of the
County and State aforesaid his heirs and assigns forever the consideration
of the sum of four hindred dollars to me paid three certain tracts or parcels
of land in the State of Tennessee Jackson County district No 10 the first coon-
taining by estimation one hundred and eighty nine acres be the same more or
less all said three tracts are situated on the waters of Roaring river on
Blackburns fork of roaring river the said first tract covers a fifty acte
survey which was granted to William Shelton assign of John Ramsey and from
said Ramsey by Grant No.4379 and from said Ramsey to the said William Shelton
the saod first tract bounded as follows Beginning at a hickory two hic ories
and chestnuts Pointers it being the beginning corner of a fifty nine acre
survey more or less conveyed to the said William Shelton to Thomas Choate
running thence, East Seventy degrees South one hundred thirty two poles to a
small Hickory & small post oak a chestnut & hickory pointers in the easr boundry
line of the original tract, thence South forty two poles to two black Jacks
and a hickory the North easr corner of Jess Kuykendall fifty acres tract, thence
West thirty nine poles to a hickory the North West corner of said Tract thence
South one hundred and thirty fore poles to a black Jack and three black Jacks
and one postoak pointers thence West fifty nine degrees North one hundred and
forty poles to a post oak & three postoaks pointers thence North twebty five
degrees West twenty two poles to a stake and four red oaks pointers in the South
boundry line of a one hundred acres tracr that I the so Mathew H. Wallace now
lives on thence Eastwardly four poles to a black oak the South East corner of
said tract thence North West to the East boundry line of said tract one hundred

and thirty poles to a post oak in said line the North east corner of
said one hundred acre tract thence East eighteen poles to a chestnut
the South east corner of said tract thence to the Beginningm the other
secind tract s pposed to be on the waters of Bear Creek & bounded as follows
Beginning at a Hickory running themce South ninty poles to a hickory thence
West Eighty nine poles to a post oak thence North ninty poles to two hickories
thence east eighty nine poles to the beginning containing fifty acres
which was conveyed from Jess Kuykundall dec'd to the said William Shelton
by deed of conveyance from Jess Kuykendall dated the 3rd of January 1834,
the third tract or parcel of land was granted by the State of Tennessee to
Thomas Nicholas by Grant No.1842 thence from saod Nicholas to ne the said
Matthew H. Wallace by a deed of conveyance dated the sixth day of January
1838 and bounded as follows to wit: Beginning at a black oak, North of a
field oxxupped by Isaac Richards running North one hundred & sixty poles
to a S,all post oak and hickory thence West one hundred pokes to two
dogwoods in the east boundry line of James Terry 640 tract , thence south
with sd line one hundred and sixty poles to two small chestnuts thence
East one hundred poles to the Beginning, containing one hundred acres including Austin Choate improvements to have and to hold the aforesaid land
to the said Joseph Pearson his heirs and assigns forever I do covenant
with the saod Joseph Pearson that I am lawfully seized of saif land, have
a good right to convey it- and that the same is unincumbered- I do further
convenant and bi d myself my heirs and representaves aho warrant and forever
defend tha title to the said land and every part thereof to the said
Joseph Pearson his heirs and assigns forever aganist the lawful claims of
all persons whatsoever Executed and delivered in the presence of John B.
Pointer, April 6, 1841, Anderson Cole, Mathew H. Wallace (Seal)
State of Tennessee Registeres office Sept 9th, Jackson Co. I Joshua R.
Stone Register of said county herebe certify that the within & foregoing
deed of conveyance from Mathew H. Wallace to Joseph Pearson together with the
clerks certification is duly Registered in my office Book E.& page 109&110
Joshua R. Stone Register of Jackson County.
Mathew H. Wallace Deed 330 acres To Joseph Pearson bargainors Sale.
Register fee $1.50

This Indentyre made and entered into this 30th day of May 1842, between
John Anderson of County od White and State of Tennessee of the one part
and William U. Sims of the County and State aforesaid of the other part in
trust for the benefir of my securities in the debted herein after mentioned
witnesseth that whereas the said John Anderson is justly endebted to Rebecca
Anderson in the Sum of $40. due by note dated 29 Apr. 1835 and akso
indebted to the said Rebecca in the sum of Ten Dollars per anum as an
amnity during her hational life as set fourth in a covenant between the
Heirs if James Anderson a nd Deed which instrument is registered in the
Registers office of White County on the 28th Oct. 1835 in Book J. page
222 & of which now due and unpaid and where as I amd justly liable and
responsibke to James Anderson for $700.00 which is payable in the Branch
Bank of Tennessee at Sparta dated 19th may 1842 and due 6 months after
said note os endorsed by Preston Anderson, James Scott and John Anderson
, this note was na e for my exculsive use and benefit And whereas I am
justly endebted to Jo Pearson in the Sum of $435.40 due 6th February 1841
in which James Anderson is my Security - and whereas I am justly indebted

to the representative of George Griffireth estate in the Sum of Eighty Dollar
due 5th March 1840, in which James Anderson is my Security and whence I am
justly indebted to the Guardian to the minor heirs of William Roberts Deed
in the Sim of $15.00 dated some time in the year of 1842 in which Daniel
Sandy is my security: none of which debts have yet been suid on- And whereas
I am justly indebted to William Hill Guardian in the sum of $72.16 dated 30 Dec.
1839 in which Preston Anderson my Security on which suit ins noe commended also
one other note to Isaac Taylor for $200. due some time in 1835 or 1846 in which
Warren and Debrell are my securities which is also sued on Also injudgment of
Lewis Bohannon agansit mysely andDibrell my security on a note foe $100 in
silver beofre John Pennington Wsqr amd stayed ny James Anderson also a Judgement
of W. Hills and aganist my self James Anderson security for avout $100. beofre
Robert H.M.Manns Esqr. stayed by Jo Herd- and also oneother Judgment in forever
of William B. Hall aganist myself for $50. Dollars before John Pennington
Esqr. stayed by Solomn Wilhite.   And whereas the said John Anderson being will
ing and desirous to some payment of all osaid debts and mentioned securities
in this several liabilities- now for the purpose aforesaid the said John Ander
on makes this transfer To wit. For that portion of debts upon thisch no suit
has yet been commanded he doth granted bargained and sold and transfered to the
said W.G. Sims his Ensor. Admr. in trust the following described real and personal property To.wit. One tract of land containing 12¾ acres held by De'sd
from James Anderson and dated 11th May 1829bRegistered in Registers office
on 22 Apr. 1835, in Book J. page 201, of Said County. Also one other tract
of land containing 120 acres held by Deed from John McAwly dated 18th 1831
and Registered 29 January 1833 in Book H, Page 381 also one other land
containing 160 acres held by Deed from Joe Dennison dated 6th Sept. 1833
Registered 6th Sept. 1833 in Book H, page 503 Refered to said Registration
willifully slow. also all my ho se hold and Kitchen furnityre and framing
tools such as are not ecempt from Execution- and also my Negro slave man
named Peter a slave for life and the siaid John Anderson does hereby
convey unto William G, Sims Trustee aforestis the following described
prpperty real and personal for the use and benefit of those debts before
mentioned exclusive which have been and upon To wit: One Tract og Land
hold by deed from Jess Bullock and wife and James Howard containing 114
acres Registered 28 Nov. 1838 in Book & page 145 Also one other Tract of 338
acres hold by deed from William Howard Registered 28 Oct 1834 in Book
J. Page 97 also one other tract 100 acres hold by deed from William Parker
dated 11th Dec. 1829 which Deed of registered also one half of a Tract
of Land lying on the main Caney Fork whereon Jacob Anderson Jr. now lives
conveyed by said Jacob Anderson Jr. by Deed to said Josiah Anderson by Deed
which Deed id Registered in the Registers office of said County , Also
2 stills and thirty Still Tubes now in the possession of Jacon Anderson Jr.
also six head of horses 2 yolk of oxen and one ox wagon, 10 heads of cattle
40 head of Hogs 7 sheep and one Negro woman named Vice a slave for live-
all of which property the saod John Anderson herebe conveys said Sims for
the purpose aforesaid and herebe warrants and binds himself to defend the
title thereof now this is the understanding that if the said John Anderson
shall will and truly pay ot cause to be paid all andevery of said debts
and judgments and shall save all his securities herein beofre mentioned
harmless and face from all less damages, then this Indenture to be null
and void and the right to said property shall revest him the said John
Andersonhis Heirs & . And in the mentioned said property both/and/ real
and personal shall remain in rhe ahnds of said John Anderson subject to the
provision of this Indenture, But shoule the said John Anderson fail to pay
or cause to be paif the baofre described debts and Judgments and should

he suffers an execution or executions to be run aganist any one or more
of all of said securities for the collections of said debts and judgments
shall be the duty of said Trustee to take posession of so much of said
property as situated for each particular character of debts herein provided as in his Judgement will be sufficient to Satisfy the particular debt
or debts that mey be then pressing of those herein contained and surrender
on the same into the hands of such officer or officers as may have the
collection of said debts or judgments that said officer may kame his
levy and sell same ordering to law andisolassreepecta each of the two
classes of debts herein describing to wit those that are sued and those
that are sued appropariting the proprrty to each class in the manner here
in particularly described But should the said Anderson require the said
Trustee to sell amd dispose herein he shall pursue the alw governing
Executiors sales and is execution except us to the land and regards thing
are required to be sold at the court house door in Sparta after giving 20
days public notice, This deed is not intended to debur said Anderson the
priviledge of selli g any of the above described property himself provided
he sells the same for sash price with the consent of the Trustee and shall
aos9 pay the proceeds thereof to that particular class of debts herein
mantioned- should the note of James Anderson of 700 payable Bank be renewed
agreeable to the rules and regulations of said Bank said note shall through
all its different renewals and it is hereby declared to have and to hold
a contranious line on said property- untill John Anderson shall have fully
dischared and paid off the same- should said Trustee be called upon to
sell said property agreeable to this deed he shall be allowed a fair com-
penseiob for his trouble, and if a surplus should remain in his hands he shall
pay the same to the said John Anderson his heirs and Ect., And the said
William G. Sims agrees to execute this Trustee- Witness our hands and seals
this date 1st above written, Sighnd, John Anderson ack. 30 May 1842
W.G.Sims (Seal) ack. 31, 1842.
State of Tennessee, White County- Pearsonally appeared before me Nicholas
Oldham, Clerk of White County Court John Anderson William G. Sims
Subscribers to the acked. Deed with whom I am personally acquainted and
who both acknowledged the due execution of the within Deed for the purpose
therein contained which is Recorded Witness my hand at office the 31st May
1842, Signed Test N. Oldham Clerk of the White County Court.
State of Tennessee, White County, I hereve certify that the amount Deed from
John Anderson to William G. Sims was filed and dated in R ceprion Book N.1
page 3 1st of June 1842 at ½ past 9 O clock A.M. (and) rigistered in my
office 2nd June 1842 in book N. pages 44& 45 an 46. Given at office same day
Test Oldham Deputy of R Smith Register of White County, Copy of Exhibit
A. Test R S. Rhea C.A.M. By W.E. Nelson D.C.
John Anderson Trust Deed To W.G. Sims

I curtis Terry of Jackson County and State of Tennessee and Distrive No.10
have this day bargained and sold and do herebe transfer and conveyed to
Joseph Pearson of the County State and Bistrict of foresaid fir the consideration of the Forty Dollars to me paif the receipt acknowledged a certain tract
or parcel of land in the county state and district aforesaid it being
a part of a survey Granted to William Ramsey by Grant No.335of containing
by estimation one thousand acres be the same more or less one Bounded as
Follows Beginning at a stake in the West fork of Bear Creek glade in the
west Boundry line of a three hundred and ten Acres survey Entered by Fisk
thence west 126 and one half poles to a Black Jack & pointers, Thence S
one hundred & twenty six and one halfpoles to a small Hickory, Thence

East one hundred twanty six and one hald poles to a stake in the west
Boundry line of Fisk said survey Thence North with said west Boundry line
one hundred and tewnty six & one half poles to the Beginning to have & to
hold the same to the said Joseph Pearson his heirs & assigns forever & do
covenant with the said Joseph Pearson that I am alwfully seized of said
land have a good tight to convey it & that the same in unincumbe ed I do
further bind my self my heirs & assignd, To warrant and defend the title
to the said land and convey part thereof said Joseph Pearson to his herir
& assigns forever aganist the lawful claims of all Persons what so ever
in witness whereof I the said Curtis Terry have here unto set my hand
and seal this twenty six day of November 1845. Executed & delivered in our
presents Thomas Cates, Ninson M. Terry, Curtis Terry (Seal)
State of Tennessee Pearsonally appered before me Sampson W. Cassetty clerk
of Jackson County Court Curtis Terry the bargainor to the written and fore
going deed with whom I am personally acquainted and who acknowledged the
same to be this act and deed for the purposes therein expresed witnessed my
hand at office this 6th day o f March 1848. S.W.Cassetty(Clk) March.
State of Tennessee Jackson Co. Refistered of Jackson County do hereby
certify that the with in deed from Curtis Terry to Joseph Pearson to gether
with the clerks entrys Registeres in my office in Book G. Page 426,
John M. Gipson Reg. of Jackson County.

State of Tennessee Jackson County, Pearsonally appeared before me Sampson
W. Cassetty clerk of Jackson County Court, John Harris the barginar of the
withim deed with who I am personally acquainted who being duly sworn
acknowledged the within deed to be his act and deed for the purposes therein
contained witness my hand at office this 26th day of January 1853,
S.W.Cassetty Clk.

State of Tennessee Jackson County, Registers office thus 3rd day of
Oct. 1853 at 2 Oclock P.M. I John M. Gipson di herebe certify that the
within Deed from John Harris to John M. Carlton together with the clerks
certificate thereto is duly Registered in my office in Registers Books
Page 125& 126 John M. Gipson.

This Indenture made and entered into April 28th 1849 Sold and confirmed
by me John Harris of the county of Jackson and State of Tennessee to
John H. Carlton of the countya nd State aforesaid Sixty acres of land
for the sum of one hundred dollars in hand paid lying in sd county on
the water of Bear Creek beginning at a Black oak the south East corner
of Absolom Williamd curvey then South seven poles to a stake the Southwest corner of Charles Phillips formily Noah Kuykendall survey thencw
East seventeen poles to a stake the northwest corner of a survey
in the name of Jeremiah Travis thence south with sd, Travis line one
hundred and nine poles to a Blakk oak & pointers thence west forty
six poles to a hickory on Joseph Pearson line thence north with sd.
Pearsons line twenty eight poles to a forked chestnur thence west with
sd. Pearsons notth boundry line sixty four poles to a chestnyt thence
north Eighty seven poles to a sassafras thenve East one hundred poles
to the Beginning and ilthe said John Harris for myself my heris Executors
and adminstrators according to the true intent and plain meaning if the
best form o deed of conveyance that one or ever shall be found and forever
defend and forever defend the said land with all the right liberties
and advantages their unto belonging to the sd. John W. Carlton his heirs
and assigns clear of all claims what soever in witness hearof I set my hand
and seal the day and date above written, signed sealed and delivered in
presence of us Attest Joseph Johnson Absolom Willims, John Harris (seal)

PROPERTY OWNED BY BOB PEARSON HILLHAM ROAD COOKEVILLE TENN.

Sparta March 18th 1855

Mr I pearson Dear Sir: Accordin to my promise when I left you I send these lines to inform you that I am well & in good spirits my suit in Court in en-emded & the dession is as follows I get pally & a thousand dollars in money to be paid to me in four months every thing connected with suit was all in my favor the sale that they made was made void Tom witnesses was as good for me as him he did not succeed to his montön at all, I am now at John Youngs in Sparta I shall be at your house in a month or two & then I can tell you what has happened since I saw you last. give my love to all the family Children & all yours & C.

Rebecca Stipes.

Envelope.

Postmark, Sparta, Tenn

Joseph Peæson
White Plains,
(in haste) Putnam Co. Tenn.

ACCOUNT WITH JOSEPH PEARSON THE YEAR 1853 AND 1854 AND 1855

Martin Laycock det to Joseph Pearson to 80 ppounds of beef	$2.50
to 13¼ pounds of bacon	1.35
to 35 pounds of beef	.97¼
to 12 pounds of bacon	1.20
to 2 bushels potatoes	1.00
to 65 pounds of beef	2.07
Received three hundred binds of fodder	9.09
	2.25
Received three hundred binds of fodder	3.00
Received nine Churns at 40 cts per churn	3.60
	8.85
And I paid him one dollar and	.24
fifty cts for the churn	1.50
	$1.74

The balance due me Joseph Pearson to thirty pounds and half of baken.

	$3.05
Received 4 churns	4.79
	1.60
Boutum 7 Cheres	.87

	2.47

	#2.32

WAR RECORD OF R. G. SMITH.
PROPERTY OF AUSTIN W. SMITH, COOKEVILLE, TENN.

The following is a very limited record of the Confederate Army service of R. G. Smith, written by himself sixty one years after the close of the war and in the eighty- eighth year of his life.

When the war between the North and the South came up in 1861, I was twenty two years old, and on May 16th of that year I was sworn into the Army of Tennessee. I had previously enlisted in the first company of volunteers raised in Cannon County, Tennessee, and commanded by Capt. M. R. Rushing. Th There were two other companies raised about the same time, one of which was commanded by H. J. St. John, and the other by Capt. Granville Wood, all of Cannon County.

These companies were sent to Camp Trousdale in Sumner County near the Kentucky line and were made a part of the 18th Tennessee Regiment which was organized there. It was composed of ten companies; three from Cannon County, two from Rutherford County, one from Wilson County, one from Cheatham County one from Coffee County, and two others from somewhere up the Cumberland Rive I think.

The first Colonel of the regiment was J. B. Palmer of Murfreesboro., Tennessee. The lieutenant-colonel was a man named Carden who lived in Coffee County and the Major's name was Davis.

There were a number of regiments formed at Camp Trousdale. To the best of ,y recollection they were as follows: the 7ht regiment commanded by Col Robert Hatton, the 8th regiment whose commander I can't recall, the 14th Col. Forbs, the 20th. Col Joel Battle. All were state troops at that time and were place along the northern border of Tennessee on all the main thorough fares leading into Kentucky, from Cumberland Gap to the Mississippi River.

All the Regiments mentioned were sent to other places except the ighttteenh which remained at Camp Trousdale until September. About this time all Tennesse troops were transferred from the state service to the Confederate State's service, Tennessee having seceded from the Union and joined the Confederacy.

We were sent now into Kentucky and occupied Bowling Green. At this place was collected a great army which encamped from September, 1861 to the last of January, 1862. At this latter date. some 8000 troops including the 18th regiment to which I belonged were sent to Fort Donalson. I was left behind on account of sivkness. In fact, I had already received a furlough to go hom in order to recuperate. Just as my time expired, I received the news that th the whole army at Ft. Donalson had been captured, also that Gen A. S. Johnen son , commander of the army at Bowling Green , had removed to Murfreesboro, Tennessee. At htis place I attached myself to the 23rd regiment, joining a company made up of my old neighbors and friends, principally whom I had known from childhood. I remained with this company until the end of the war.

Gen. U. S. Grant, who commanded the Federal Army at Ft. Donalson, was now transporting his troops by water up the Tennessee River and landing them at Pittsburg Landing not far from the Mississippi line, and almost in Johnsons rear. This move of Grants caused Johnson to evacuate Tennessee and transfer his army to Corinth, Mississippi. This was in March. 1862.

The Captain under whom I was now serving was M. M. Brien, a very prominent young lawyer of Woodbury, Tennessee. He had the best disciplined company that I have ever seen. He was never harsh nor unkind to his men, but he was very positive in his orders and they obeyed him to the letter of the law.

WAR RECORD OF R. G. SMITH, (CON)

We now started on the long march to Corinth, Mississippi, from Murfreesboro through Shelbyville and Fayetteville to Huntsville, Alabama. We marched through rain and mud, waded creeks and rivers waist deep. After resting two days at Huntsville, we boarded a freight train and crossing the Tennessee river at Decatur, mAlabama, we soon reached Corinth, Miss. Here we remained about two weeks. Trains from every direction were coming in every day loaded with troops, until there was assembled the finest army that I hd ever seen at that time. Here we were wrmed with brand new Endfield rifles brought from England on a vessel which had run the blockade.

I will digress here to mention the names of several soldiers who like myself had belonged to Captain Rushing's Company, and were not captured at Ft. Donelson. These men were: J. C. New, John R. Rushing, Becton Carnes, Je Ham and James Peyron. These, with M. L. Hollis who had lately come from Akkansas and was a first cousin to the writer, were members of Brien's Company. We were in Cleburne's Brigade which was composed of the following regiments and their commanders: The 2nd Tennessee, Col Bate, the 23rd Tennessee, Col. Neal, 24th Tennessee, Col. Wilson, the 35th Tennessee, Col. Hill, and the 2nd Arkansas, and the 6th Mississippi.

On the third day of April, I think it was, the whole army was sent in mOtiom headed towards Pittsburg Landing going in divisions on different roads. When night came we went into camp a few miles from Corinth. An orderwasvread to us in which Gen Johnston explained his reason for the move. He saidthe eyes of the whole Confederacy were turned toward us with great expectations.

The next day we marched to within about three miles of the enemy's camp. Ours was the leading brigade on the road. There was a small company of cavalry in front of us which came in contact with a small troop of Federal cavalry and we could hear the report of the guns. Our regiment quickly formed across the road and waited for for our little squad of cavalry to fall back behind our line thus driving the enemy with in reach. There was the pounding of horses hoofs, then over a rise came our men in fulltil with the Federals in close persuit. Through our line they came, a Yankee Major and men close behind. "Fire", came the order and it seemed that every gun answered the. Te He rolled from his horse in one direction, the animal going in another. This was the first Yankee soldier, except a few prisoners, that I had ever seen.

We remained at this place all night sleeping on the soggy ground. Wewere within three miles of Grant's great army. Early in the morning we weremarched out in the direction of his encampment. Our route lead us through adensely wooded country. Soon we heardthe bugles and drums of the enemy. Our brigd was placed in a suitable position and all troops coming in, were formed in line with us.

The generals had intended to make the attack that day, which was Saturday but owing to the rain and mud, many of the troops were miles behind. It took all that day to get them into position.

As our regiment was first in line, I had the pleasure of seeing all the army file past and take their places in line-a grand sight. These men came from the best families in the South-fine blooded specimen, but they had never been under fire and knew nothing of the advantage of position inorder to protect themselves from under fire. They were to get their first lesson. By Sunday morning, the great army of Tennessee was in line of battle, fronting ht e mighty army commanded by Gen. Grant. Orders to go forward were given early and then the extreme right wing was engaged with the Federals in the great struggle. Immediately the whole line plunged forward and the two long lines were gripped in deadly combat.

WAR RECORD OF R. G. SMITH, (CON)

I wish that I had the ability to describe what I saw and heard during this battle, I am unequal to the task and will have to simply relate a few things concerning the company to which I belonged. However I willsay that the booming of a hundred cannon, the screaming and exploding of shells. the incessant rattle of musketry, and the hissing of minnie balls made a noise that seemed to threaten universal destruction. If it had been as fatal a sit seemed to to our unaccustomed ears, there would have been no one left to tell the tale

We drove the Federal army back about two miles, almost to the river, afte an all day fight. We hoped to capture the whole army but Gen. A. S. Johnston killed and Beauregard was put in command. He ordered the pursuit stopped until morning, although it was known that a Federal army under Gen. Buell was marching through from Nashville to re-inforce Grant. It arrived during the night and took position in front of our line-fresh army of 30,000 troops. They proved tooo strong for our tired soldiers and after another day of hard fighting we had to give up the field and move back to Corinth. Our company lost more men in this battle than in any other during the whole war. Among those killed was my cousin M. L. Hollis, who was struck down on the field just as the fighting began. I did not see him fall but saw his dead body as he had fallen.

In the beginning, Ishould have explained that our regiment had but one field officer, the lieutenant-colone, whose name was Neal. He was to act asa full colonel and Capt. Brien of our company was appointed, temporairrily lieutenant-colonel. A Captain Moore was appointed Major. In the first days fight Neal was severely wounded and Moore was killed, thus leaving our captain to command the regiment throughout the remainder of the battle. This he did gallantly, but after the retreat to Corinth, he became too despondent over the loss of his men that he resigned and left us, althiughhe cpuld easily been elected colonel of the regiment. Seven of our company were killed outright and twenty wounded, some of them very seriously. Wewere about sixty strong at the beginning of the battle, so this was a large per cent.

A short time after this, our regiment was re-organized and our company was consolidated with Captain Low's company from Rutherford County, Tennesse All our original company's officers resigned and left us and we had to elect a new staff. Our new captain was W. A. Ott; first lieutenant, J. C. New; second lieutenant, J. A. Patrick; third lieutenant, J. M. Witherspoon, orderly, sergeant, John Murphy.

The Federal army now advanced to Corinth and formed their line in front of us. Day after day we expected to engage in battle, but to our great surprise, after a week or more, Gen. Beauregard withdrew his army from Corinth to Tupelo, Mississippi, about the first of June, 1862. Here we remained until the last of July when Gen Braxton Bragg took command.

Our regiment was made a part of Gen. Bushrod Johnston's Brigade. This brigade was composed of the following regiments: the seventeenth, the twenty third. the twenty fifth, the sixty third, and the fifth Confederate, a regiment of Irishmen. These regiments remained together until the end of the war

We now started on the long raid into Kentucky. Our brigade was in Gen. Buckner's division and Gen. Hardee's corp. We were sent by rail to Mobile, Alabama, then on a vessel up Alabama River to Montgomery, the nce by rail again to Atlanta, Georgia, and on to Chattanooga.

I forgot to mention the new officers of our regiment and will have to digress again to name them. Neal, though absent, had been made colonel, R.H Keeble was lieutenant-coloneal and Horace Ready, Major. Thelast two mentioned were Murfreesboro men.

WAR RECORD OF R. G. SMITH, (CON)

Taking up the description of our line of march again at Chattanooga where I left off, I continue my story of Braggs raid into Kentucky. From Chattanooga we crossed the mountain and passed through the town of Spencer Sparta, and Cookeville, Tenn, thence to Glasgow, Kentucky. From there we went to Mumfordville where we captured 4,500 Federal prisoners without the loss od a man. Marching om toward Louisville, we were suddenly turned toward Bardstown, Kentucky, and encamping there remained for several days. Gen. Buell was in our rear bringing his army from Nashville. When we turned east he passed on to Louisville where he was heavily re-inforced. Heturned backd and pursued us to Perryville where he made a stand and gave battle. We drov them from the field and they troubled us no further. Ourcompany lost men in this fight, among the rest our orderly sergeant. Capt. Ott was seriously wounded and fell into the hands of the enemy. We turned sough and came outh through Cumberland Gap to Knoxville, Tennessee, where we remained a few days While here there was an election to fill the place of orderly sergeant and I was chosen and held the place until the end of the war. This was in October, 1862.

From here we fell back to Chattanooga, then over the mountain again to Shelbyville and on up to College Grove in Williamson County. I don't remember how long we remained at each of these places, but we were in Murfree boro by the end of December. When we arrived at this place, we found two armies drawn up in line of battle facing each other. Gen Rosencrantz, who now commanded the Federal Army had advanced upon Gen Bragg.

On December 31st, the left wing of the Confederate Army, in which our brigade was placed, was hurled against the federal right and they were driven back about two miles. The next day there was no regular battle, but plenty of skirmishing and cannonading. This was Jan. 1, 1863. The next dy day our right wing made a desperate assault on their left, but failed to drive themback. Our commander, Gen. J. C. Breckenridge, reported that he ld lost1700 men in short time.

During the night Braggs army fell back to Shelbyville and Tullahoma. Our dompany did not lose heavily-only one killed and severalwounded.We camped at these two places for four months, then moved down around Wartrace and stayed there until the first of July. Then Rosencrantz advanced from Murfresboro and began pressing us.We held them in check several days and then started back across the mountains to Chattanooga. We reached there July 10h and remained until September.

The Federals had followed us, crossed the Tennessee river below Chattanooga and were moving south through Will's Valley to gain the roar of our army. This move compelled us to fall back toward Dalton Georgia. Here we were being re-inforced by Gen. Longstreet's corp from the Army of Virginia we turned west, crossed Chicamauga River and faced the mighty Federal force on the field of Chitamauga. In the great battle that followed, our comapany had one man killed and quite a numbrer wounded. Of htese one was numbered among my best friends, J. J. Davis. Hesuffered a severe wound in the head d and was thought for a time to be killed. He was carried to a hospital where he soon recovered and came back to us in about two months.

We remained in front of Chattanooga till about the middle of November, when the division to which our brigade belonged was sent to re-inforce Gen. Longstreets army in East Tennessee, sent htere to drive the Federals under Gen. Burnsides out of the state. Burnsides had statted from Knoxville to re-inforce the Federals at Chattanooga, was met by Longstreet and driven back to Knoxville, Tennessee.

WAR RECORD OF R. G. SMITH (CON)

Our Tennessee Brigade and Gen. Gracie's Alabama brigade constituted what was afterwards known as Johnson's Division. Now we bade farewell to the great army of Tenneassee and started on the terrible East Tennessee campaign right in the beginning of the winter of 1863-64. When we reached Knoxville, Longstreet had Burnside's army surrounded in the city hoping to starve them out and force them to surrender, but after we left Chattanooga, Grant attacked Bragg and drove him South to Dalton, Georgia. This gave Gen

Grant a chance to send Gen Sherman with a strong force to relieve Burnsides

As Sherman neared Knoxville, Longstreet undertook to force Burnsides to surrender by capturing one of his main forts. I think where were three brigades selected to storm Ft. Sanders, our being one of them. The attempt was made but it was a failure. The Confederate loss was considerable, but our brigade fortunately suffered but little. The night the siege of Knoxville was raised we passed on into upper East Tennessee. The Fedarals followed at some distance and at a little place called Bean's Station, weturned upon them and drove them back. This was a considerable fight, butour loss was not great. I don't know their loss, but they followed us nofurther. This was some time in December, 1863.

We were moved from place to place, staying some time at Dandrige, then at Morristown where we remained a month, perhaps. This was one of the coldest winters I have wver experienced. The mountains were covered with snow all the time and in the valleys the ground was frozen so hard that traveling was difficult. We had frequent skirmishes with Yankee Cavalry, but these did not amount to much.

We reached Bristol about the first of April, 1864, and remained until May when we were marched to Abingdon, Virginia. At htis place we took cars and reached Richmond May, 5, 1864. We were a rough, miserable looking set of men. While in East Tennesseewe were cut off from the outside world, all railroad bridges having been destroyed. We lived on what we could pick up
 from the surrounding country. We suffered for both food and clothing. Someof the men were barefooted. The merchants of Richmons seeing our condition, came with armsful of shoes and gave each needy man a pair. Soon after this we drew clothing from the War Department and were were fixed up very well.

At this time Gen Grant was in charge of the Federal army in Virginia, and he and Gen Lee were making the long desperate struggle above Richmond. Longstreet's corp had preceded us from East Tennessee and was with Lee's army. We expected to be sent there, but also instead we were sent down the James River to Chaffin's Farm on May 6th. We did not know there any Yankees near us, so went into camp expecting to get agood nights rest, but just after dark we were surprised/aroused by the beating of the long roll and hurried across the river on a pontoon bridge from the north to the south side of the river. After crossing, we struck the pike leading from Richmond to Petersburg and headed toward the latter place. We traveled a few miles and then camped till morning. When daylight came to our great surprise, we found ourselves facing a Dederal army. Gen. B. F. Butler had landed on the south side of the river a few miles from Petersburg and it was this force that we were now facing. We soon got into a fight with them at a station on the railriad leading from Petersburg to Richmond called Port Mellthall Junction.

WAR RECORD OF J. G. SMITH, (CON)

We were in a shallow cut of the railroad which served us for a breastwork. Here, when the cannonading was at its worst a shell exploded a few feet above my head and a fragnent cut through the crown of my hat and gashed my head. I was knocked unconscious and put out of business for three weeks. This was my first blood that I had shed since I had enlisted. I was sent to the hospital at Petersburg.

The fighting continued for several days and the wounded were being brought in every day. The surgeons were kept busy dressing wounds and amputating limb While I was here our brigade fought a hard battle at Drury's Bluff about half way between Petersburg and Richmond. The Confederates won in this fight. This was th only time I was ever absent, when our brigade went into a fight.

I rejoined my campany at htis place where we were under continual shellfire from gunboats till the fifteenth of June. The shelling did us smalll damage but was very annoying.

About this time Lee and Grant reached James River about twenty milesbelow Richmond and G$_r$ant began putting his whole army across. Lee had tomove up the river several miles to a pontoon bridge in order to cross, sothe front guard of Grant's army reashed the vicinity of Petersburg two days before Lee arrived with his forces. On the fifteenth we were hurried to the defense of Peters burg. That day we met the advance guard of Grant's army about six miles east of town. It was after night and we slept on the ground in line of battle. The enemy in our immediate front was commanded by Gen Hancock. When we awoke in the morning we found ourselves in fullview of the enemy. They seemed to b resting quietly and showed no signs of advancing. We went to work cutting a ditch for our protection. We weren on an elevation upon which stood a dwelling house, known I htink as the Webb House. The position of my company lay through the garedn belonging to this place. By noon we had our ditch finished and were prepared for what we knew was coming. About one o'clock there was aga great commotionamong the enemy. They began forming line to advance and came marching over the open space between our lines. About half way came within range of our guns and every man in our brigade rose at the command and poured such a deadly volley of musketry and artillery into their ranks that they begane panig striken and fell back in confusion leaving the ground strewn with their slain. They soon rallied and came again with the same results. T$_h$is was repeated foyr or times that afternoon and they were driven bcak every time. Night came but the fighting continued all night long.

At the foot of a hill in front of us there was some low ground which they reached and occupied during the night. This proved to be a heavy forcefor just at daybreak they rushed upon us in such overwhelming numbers that we were forced to give up our position and fall back a short distance. In this awful struggle I lost two of my best freindx, Alf Wimberly and Albert Justice both of whom were captured and sent to a northern prison. This was June", 17, 1864.

We now took another position still in sight of the enemy. They now massed a b strong force and began to advance towaßd us, but we were prepared for we had been re-inforced with another brigade and a battery of artillery. When they got within range the infantry and artilleryb turned loose such a tremendous volley of fifàballs and grapshot that the enemy again turned and fled in wild confusion leaving their dead and wounded behind. During the remainder of the day they contented themselves with throwing shells and skirmishing with our lines.

WAR RECORD OF R. G. SMITH, (CON)

When night came again we fell back to our main line of works, and our regiment occupied the very fort that was afterward blown skyward. The next morning, the enemy were at us again with a vengeance determined to capture this main line before Gen. Lee could come to our aid. They threw one heavy force after another against us during the day, but were repulsed each time. This was June 18th and just as night fell again Gen. Lee's army began to arrive and take their places in line of battle. When morning dawned everything along that great line was as still as a country Sabbath day. The enemy knew that htey were again facing the great army of Northern Virginia. The calm did not last long, but instead of attacking they began shelling us furiously, in fact did not cease for many months for we remained here until July, 25th. During this time it was currently reported that the enemy were tunneling under pur position and we expected to be blown to atoms at any time But, fortunately for us, we were sent from this place to the north isde of James River about fifteen miles below Richmond. I htink that the troops who took our place in that fort were from South Carolina. It was only three or four days after we left that it was blown up and every man in it killed. While we stayed thereour loss was considerable. Col. Keeble of Murfreesboro, was killed and also Col. Fulton of Fayetteville. Our company lost only one man, but several wounded.

There was small force of Federals on the north side of the river and our little brigade was sent to hold them back. I can't describe in detail what we had to undergo while on this side of the river. We were inder fire nearly all the time from the last of July until November, when we were sent back to the ditches in front of Petersburg. There were sometiems on one part of the line then on the other, helping to hold it during the long, cold winter of 1864-65. The shelling and sharp-shooting went on day and night snd it was easy for us to see that our lines were being gradually depleted without hope of being recruited. We knew that Gen. Grant's army was beingre-inforced steadily untilhe had all the men he needed. I became convinced during the winter that our cause was hopeless. On April, 2, 1865, the enemy moved against our line with an overwhelming force, broke it, and statted our army towards its doom at Appomatox. During this days great struggle against such heavy oddsi,I like several others was forced to surrender. This ended my career as a fighting soldier. About one hindred men from our brigade were captured and sent on cars down to City Point at the mouth of James River. There they were placed aboard a steam vessel and sent up Chesapeake Bay to Point Lookout, Maryland. This prison was located on a little neck of land wh where the Potomac Riverenters the bay. We were kept there until June 22. We were captured on Sunday, April 2, and the next Sunday Gen. Lee surrendered his army to Gen Grant with the atipulation that his men were to be paroled and sent home. We prisoners did not hear of the surrender until Monday morning. We knew that htis ended the war and wondered when we would be released from prison.

On April 15th, when we awoke in the morning, we noticed that all the flag had been lowered to half-mast. We knew that something very serious had happened,.but could not learn what until the newsboys brought in the papers and we read of the assasination of President Lincoln.

Our prospects were very gloomy and it seemed, after this, that all the prison officials tried to take out their spite on us. Rations had been very meager all the time, but now it seemed that we were to be starved to death for we suffered the very worst pangs of hinger. Many of the prisoners sickened and and there were deaths daily.

WAR RECORD OF R. G. SMITH, (CON)

I had been in very good health for the last three years of the war, but hehe in htis foul place my haelth began to fail and if I'd had to temain there all summer I doubt if I could have survived it. The members of my company who were still with me were: M. C. Neely, A. J. Jernihan, Bill McCullough, Catsby Edmonson, and J. A. Mitchell, whose sister I afterwards married. Bill McCullough died before we were released from prison.

About the first of June, the officials began releasing a few men at a tin time and on June 19th they called for the Tennessenas to report at the Provost Marshall's office. We understood and obeyed with alacrity. After being paroled, we were sent out of the main prison to an enclosure where there were no guards. We ramained there that night and till late the next afternoon, when we were told to report to the wharf where we found a steamboat waiting. We boarde tgis vessel and bade farewell to that prison forever. There are many places that I saw during the war that I would like to visit again, but I shall neber wish to see Point Lookout any more while I live.

A whiel after night, the boat statted up the Potomac River. It had on board a regiment of Indiana soldiers who had been discharged from the army and were on their way home. They were very kind to us, in fact I have never seen or met a soldier who had faced us in line of battle that was not kind and treated me with respect. We traveled all night and reached Washington City about seven o'clock next morning, Here we had the problem of getting transportation to Nashville, Tenn. I really suspect that we were the toughest lookingspecimens that ever struck the NationalnCapitol. We were directed to a certain place and when we got there we were sent to a second and thenb to a third and so on until we finally found the right place and bought our tickets to Nashville.

Late that afternoon we were alloed to board a train and statted home. We traveled through Pennsylvania, Ohio, Indiana and Kentucky. Whenever we stopped on that long journey the citizens treated ua with scorn and contempt until we reached Louisville, Kentucky. Then we felt that we had arrived amog our own people. We reached htere before noon and found that we had to wait over until seven o'clock in the m̶o̶r̶n̶i̶n̶g̶ evening before we could get a train to Nashville. While we waited the ladies of the citybrought us baskets of provisions and I can tell you we had a picnic. It was the first food we had tated for two years that was fir to eat.

We left Louisville at seven o'clokck in the evening and rolled into Nashville between eight and nine oC8clock next morn ng. There they issued us al tickets to Chattanooga. Med Neely, J. A. M'tchell, Jim Colemand and I got of at Murfreesboro and walked home to Woodbury, Tennessee, about twenty miles.

After a rest I went to work to repair the great damages that had been doae us by the war. There was not a horse left on myfather's farm and very little of anything else.

Tennessee's government had been re-organized with M. G. Brownlow as Governor. The Legislature had passed a law disfranchising the Confederate soldiers and all sympathizers and enfranchised all the negroes. These p̶e̶r̶s̶o̶n̶s̶ negroes and some white scalawags had full control of the state. I was dis-

WAR RECORD OF R. G. SMITH, (CON)

disfranchised about four years. In 1867 the Ku Klux Klan put a quietus on the negor and in 1869 there was a reaction in the state and every man became a voter. From that time for many years the Confederates had control.

I want to relate a little of my family history before I close this story. My grandmother on the maternal side was living during the war and had eleven grandsons to enlist. Only five of them lived through it. One, only was killed in battle. M. L. Hollis at Shiloh. James Hollis and Will Hollis, John Smith, my brother, and Andy Doak died of sickness. Will George was captured at Ft. Donalson and carried to a prison in Illinois. He and a boy named Wilcher escaped and Wilcher got home but Will George was never heard of again. This is a mystery that could not be explained. One Hollis, two Covingtons, tow Doaks and myself lived through.

On my father's side, I had a cousin named Goss, who lost an arm at the battle of Shiloh. I am the only one of them all that is still living.

A large majority of the soldiers of Tennessee were young men unmarried, but they did not remain so long. They were the best in society and genarally married into the finest families of the stste. On the twelfth of December I married a)1867, I married a little rosy-cheeked girl named Myra Mitchell and she is still with me. She was twenty two years old at that time and now she is eighty. Nearly all of our old friends have passed away. Of the two companies of soldiers with whom I served I know of only two who are t still living.

This writing is a very limited and imperfect record ofs a soldier in the Confederate Army. Had I written it sixty years ago while everything was fresh in my mind, I think I could have done much better. I want to say in conclusion that with all the hardships and terrible privations that I underwent, I never regretted the course I took. I tried to do my duty to my country to the best of my ability and have no apologies to make

I don't know that this littl e sketch will ever be worth anything to anybody, nut I thought that my descendents might some day like to read it. I have written it at the suggestion of my son, Austin W. Smith. I am sorry that I could not write a better one but I have done the best I could at thi late day.

(My father died May, 23, 1929 at the age of 90 years, 4 months and 4 days)

Austin W. Smith.

Austin W. Smith furnished this copy of his fathers war record .
Mr. Smith (Austin W. Smith) was for many years Dean of the Tennessee Polytechnic Instituta, Cookeville, Tenn.

CONFEDERATE VETERAN TELLS OF
EXPERIENCE IN FEDERAL PRISON.
BY R. G. SMITH.

RECORDS OWNED BY AUSTIN W. SMITH, COOKEVILLE, TENN

On April 2, 1865, General Lee's thin line of defense around Petersburg, Va., was broken and many of his men were captured by the Federals. I was serving in the 23rd Tennessee regiment and with others of this same regiment, was seized and taken to City Point, near the mouth of the James river. Here we were herded on a steamboat and carried up the Chesapeake Bay to the mouth of the Potomac river. We were landed on the Maryland side and conducted by our guards to a place called Point Lookout prison. This was located on a point of land lying between the river and the bay, and consisted of a ten-foot board fence which enclosed several acres of ground. Tents were spread in regular order within, the only building consisting of a long, ramshackle, frame dining hall.

Six men were placed in each tent with blankets and knapsacks for bedding This was spread on the bare, sandy earth, which was our floor.

Once a day, a fourth of a loaf of bread was given to each prisoner at his tent door. At the dining hall, he was allowed to get a tin cup of pork v or mutton. These three articles of diet did not vary while we were at this prison. Run-down and half starved as the prisoners were, scurvy set in and a squad of men was kept busy digging graves just outside the enclosure every day. Acres were covered with graves of former prisoners.

Near the top of the high board fence, a plank walk was built, around this paraded the insolent negro troops of a crack New York regiment. Their treatment of the Confederate Prisoners, solely at their mercy, was unbearable If a light was struck in a tent at night, a bullet came crashing through. No one was allowed to stick his head out at night for any reason.

A sick soldier who was suffering from extreme thirst crept out to a well near his tent. "Halt", came a gruff command from a burly negro. The man pleaded pitifully, explaining that he was almost dying for water. "Damn, you" came the answer, "I told you to go back" Instantly a report of a pistol shocked the listeners. The bullet missed its target but killed a sleeping man in a tent near by.

After this, complaints poured in upon the provost-marshall, who was not a bad man, Soon after the negro troops were removed and white soldiers, trid on the battle field, were put on guard. These troops treated us very kindly.

Gradually we were emboldened to approach some of them to ask small favors. One day I noticed a sentinal guarding some supplies near the fence. I cautiously approached the "dead line" between us, not knowing what reception I would get. "Would you like to buy a watch?" I asked guardedly. He answered briskly, "Yes, sir, have you one to sell?" I studied my reply. "I know a fellow who has one to sell". "Go and tell him to come out here and I'll buy his watch he said in a hearty voice. I still fely my way. " I don't know whether he'll come or not, He amy be afraid you'll take his watch from him" I said. "I'm not that kind of a mann," he said decidedly. "I'd rather give give him a watch than take one from him " "Well, I'm the man who owns the watch", I said, and handed it over the "dead line"
He gave it a critical glance and said, This ia a $15 watch, but the crystal is broken I'll give you $14 for it "This was far more than I had hoped to get and you may be sure I grabbed those greenbacks.

CONFEDERATE VETERAN TELLS OF EXPERIENCE IN FEDERAL PRISON (CON)

I sold two more watches for my comrades that day at good prices. I'd luckily approached the man who dealt in second-hand watshhes.

There was a sutler's shop with all minds of supplies in one corner of the enclosure. With greenback money a man could but almost anyhting he needed. That $14 did me mors good than any money I have ever owned, as it just about saved my life.

I shall never forget the morning after the assassination of President Lincoln. When we awoke every flag around the enclosure was flying at half mast. Our negro guards, who were still there at that time, were more surly and insolent than usual. We crowded around the bulletin board where all instructions and any news that the authorities wanted us to know were written Any disaster like Lee's durrender was sure to be posted there. This time the bulletin board was bare. Not until the newsboys began crying the black-bordered papers around, did we know what had happened. A good natured wag remarked " Oh, I see why the niggers are so thick around us this morning. We're in mourning",

About the middle of June, A Tennessee soldier, named Scruggs, had a happy thought. This was to send a petition to President Johnson for our release. To the best of my recollection it was very diplomatic and read something like this:

Point Lookout Prison, Md.

To the President of the U.;S:

The signers of this petition are all Tennessesns and have always been friends to you in your numerous campaigns back in th e old state. We know that the war is over, and remembering the leniency that has hitherto characterized your publiclife, we are confident that you will intercede fot us and have us released from this prison.

Signed

A few days after this was mailed, all the names of the signers appeared on thebulletin board with the instructions that we report to the provost-marshall. We lost no time ingetting to his office, as we guessed the reason for the call. Other soldiers had been called previously and sent home. Provost-marshall Grady was a very agreeable man in all our contacts with him. We were required to take the oath of allegiance and then received our parole papers.

The next evening er were placed on another steamboat and carried to Washington City. Her, after some trouble in finding the headquarters for transportation, we finally foundthe place and received our tickets, and boarded the next train out for Nashvillo, Tenn.

On the way we did not see a friendly face, being cursed and abused at many places, until we reached Louisville, Ky. Here ladies met us with large hamper baskets of provisions and we were royally welvcomed. We were back in Dixie Land.

A WAR TIME DRESS
BY MRS MYRA ANNE SMITH, MOTHER OF AUSTIN WHEELER SMITH.
PROPERTY OF AUSTIN WHEELER SMITH, COOKEVILLE, TENN

Since there are few oldtimers, now living, who had the experience of making a wartime homespun dress, I thought it might be of interest to the younger generation of girls, who but a dress ready to wear, to hear the story of the long, tedious and laborious process by which we war time girls made our year's supply of homespun dresses.

"From the ground up" is a fitting expression, for most of us not Only picked and seedes the cotton, but alsogathered thr bark and berriesn to make our dyes, and dug the shale or slate rock, as we knew it to make the copperas with which to set the color of our dye. This rock was heated in a large oven until soft enough to be pulverized a dn was then ready for use.

When the cotton had been seedes by hand-this was done at nights chiefly it was washed in strong soap suds,squeezes into large cakes, and placed on p planks to dry in the sun. An occasional pounding and loosening of the cake hastened the drying and made the lint fluffy and light. Whwn thoroughly dry, the cotton was carded, withhand cards, into soft, white, downy rolls to be spun on the old spinning wheels, some of which had been in our families for a hundred years.

There were two kinds of thread: the chain, or warp, which was made hard by double-twisting, and the filling, a soft, loose thread. All of it was wou wound into hanks on a machine called a reel, which measured the cuts of one hundred and forty-four threads. Four of these cuts made a hank ofthread. One hank of filling made a yard of cloth threequarters of a yard in width. All of the thread was boiled after being hanked, to make it soft enough to dye wall.

We could make five colors of non-fading dyes: purple, copperas, green black and purplish gray. A great deal of white thread was used with these colors in weaving the patterns of the cloth.

The purple dye was made by boiling the bark of the sugar maple tree and setting it with copperas. This made a clear bright color, either a light or dark shade, according to the amount of dye used, of course.

To make the copperas dye, we boiled the shale and set the color with a weak solution of lye made by wood ashes in an old time ash hopper.

The green dye was made by boiling hickory bark orpeach tree leaves and using a bit of alum to set the color. But the cloth was first dyed a copperas color and then boiled in the green dye. This made a clear, bright green color.

The black dye, we boiled black sumac beeries andused the copperas to make the first color fast. However, the threadwas dyed purple first, and th then dipped inot the sumac mixtyre.The resulting color was a rather dingy, weak black, but brave enough not to run.

Cedar tops were boiled to make the gray dye, and copperas was used with it. The color produced was a mixture of purple and gray.

After the thread was dyed, the warp was dipped into a cornmeal starch called sizing, which made it smooth and slick, to keep it from fraying in the weaving.

When dyed and sized, the hanks of thread were put on the winding blades and from these wound on to corn cobs, spools, home made, also.

A WAR TIME DRESS (CON)

From these spools the warp was laid on warping bars, a process almost as complicated as the weaving. From these it was removed by looping the knotted meshes of thread on the weaver's arm. Then began the tedious placing of this knotted warp in the loom. After this was finished, the long, weary hours of running the shuttle to and fro to waeve in the filling continued until the web of twenty-five yards was made.

The warp was made up of all different colors, according to the pattern preferred, also the colors of the filling made the check material.

Seven yards of this heavy cloth was used in a dress with plain, full skirts, blouse waist, and coat sleeves.

We fashioned our own patterns and stitched our dresses by hand with the thread that we also spun and twisted.

Our years supply of clothing consisted of two of these homespun dresses two suits of underwear of whitehomespun, a woolen balmoral petticoat, a knitted scarf andhome made shoes cobbled by the neighborhood shoemaker.

(Mrs. R. G. SMith(nee Myra Anne Mitchell) was a native of Cannon County, Tenn where she lived during the war and thedaughter of Daniel West Mitchell. She was the mother of Austin W. Smith, for many years Dean of the Tennessee Polytechnic Institute atCookevillem, Tenn. It was Dean Smith who furnished this copy.)

LETTER TO MRS. GEORGE ANDERSON TAYLOR FROM DR. AUGUSTINE C. Somervell
RECORDS OWNED BY MRS. BENTON TERRY, COOKEVILLE, TENN.

University of Virginia
Jan 18, 1857.

Dear Sister Fannie:

Your letter of Jan 4th was recieved yesterday togather with one from cousin Elen & another from young Jimmy You may imagine how much plesed I was at the reception of so many niceletters from friends at home and especial one from elder Ssiter when I tell you that I had been in bed with chills all the past week I was so much perplexed & feeling so much depressed by the enevating effect of chills that I had the blues quite bad. I have lot so much time by being sick that I fear that I shall have to with draw my name from the number of candidated for graduation my first examination will be in Chemistry int 5h month of Feb the 20th of that month it will be the intermediate examination & I fear my stand in that branch will be bad I have missed eight or ten lectures or more in that one study this has all been doneby chills & you may know that my animosity fir them is great they are very mischievous little varments & If I had it in my power would banish them from the earth in short order. I should like to have been at home to have enjoyed the meeryn Xmas with the young folks. Elen & Jimmy gave me a detailed account of the frolics & fun But as it was impossible for me to be there I am sure glad thatthey enjoyed themselves & hope all that want to marry may o do so.

I am not a marrying man now at all. If cousin Fannie Green likes Mr. Geo Terry" & he loves her I hope they may do well &Mary I understood that d Hodge was out in Tennexpressly to see "Mollie Taylor" & her neggers hurraw for Hodge he is as independent as a wood sawyer I glory in his spunk as the oldfellow said when he fell of the Bridge and broke his neck. Old Skutes goe like hot cakes among College boys. Jobe Williams if he marries Miss Baby wil be pitied by me certainly. I have read and heard of snow storms but I never saw one before today, it has been snowing & the wind has been blowing as old Alobus had become mtoycated & they had all gotten from under his controle & blowing from every possible direction it has been snowing and the wind has been blowing for more than 18 hours more rapidly than I ever saw it the snow isnow more than three feet deep in manyplaces & five in others it has been so bad all day that it was impossible to see more than twenty yared before you in any direction Oh the cold; cold; it is bitter cold, I would not be surprised if it killed all the snakes in the CountryI hope you have had nothing of this kind in Tennessee it is now nearly eleven o(clock & I have been sick & it is so cold I will endeavor to finish tomorrow the cars did not run tiday on account of the snow storm, I was speaking of Dr. Roan to Dr Davis yesterday & he told me that Dr Roan was fine young man & that he graduated with more honers than any other young man had ever done before or since at this place in 15 years, that was speaking a great deal was'nt it; Goodnight I will finish To morrow.

January 19th.

It is nwo Monday morning & the bell has rang for lecture but it is an extremely cold & very windy day & as I have recovered from being quite sick, I deemed it prudent not to venture out today, Therfore Iavail myself of the present time to finish my epistle tomyou. the snowis banked up to my window this morning & is drifted 5 or 6 feet deep in many places. The boy has not broght me any breakfast this morning & I assure you that I am quite slank as to my appetite and oh, how much I should like to have some of the nice break fast that is brought to your table this morning. Some of your nice sausage

LETTER TO MRS. GEORGE ANDERSON TAYLOR (CON)

or hash and biscuits & coffee howmuch more would I enjoy it Jonny has just returned from latin lecture & is well the exception of a cough & he sends his love and says we will write to you in a few days. I recieved two lettes from Arks last week onr from Cousin Fannie & other from myfriend Billy Smith who is despertly in love with Miss Fannie & says he loves her to distruction he has gotten it into his head that I am in love with her & is quite difficult for me to convince him that he is misteken Your Uncle's family were all well & were very much disappointed by the relations in Tennessee not paying them the expected visit Give my love to Cousin George & the children& Grandma & Uncle Fent & to all the home folks when you see them & tell them we are well at present & hopr they are better Write to me soon & believe me to be your fond attached but absent brother,
     Augustine C. Somervell
P. S.
  Love to all yhe servants I have not recieved a letter from Eli in a month but I correspond with one sweet cousin who lives in Warrentown & I hear from her regular she is wel & is attending school again.
         Gus.

LETTER TO MRS. GEORGE ANDERSON TAYLOR FROM DR. AUGUSTINE C. SOMERVELL

RECORDS OWNED BY MRS. BENTON TERRY, COOKEVILLE, TENN

University of Va,1857
Mar, 2nd

Dear Sister:
Your kind letter of the 9th of Feb. was recieved saveral days ago and would have answered long before this But for the fact that I had the misfortune to be sick all of last week with chills & was not then in a state of bodily or mental composure which I cinsider a requisite in order that one may write with the hope ofbeing some what pleasing to therecipient of his letter & with more satisfaction to the writer. To day is a genuine March on or daughter (no sense) I can not say which it is but one thing I know that its a very windy & disagreeable day indeed & a good fire seems quite a blessing being very cold, Last week we had beautiful weather, it was fine Spring warm sun all this week, but oh; to day and yesterday seem to be cold enough to pay for it allWell Jammie I stoped writing a few minutes ago & put my pipe in my tobacco bag & filled it with a portion of that much abused plant I am now smoking whilst I endeavor to write Lem Tarry has just come in he has been to the office and says there was nothing for the Somervells Tarry told me a day or two ago that his cousin Mollie Tarry was to be married to a Capt. Jeffres ofMechlinburg Va Soon; Tarry is a very good boy I like him very much indeed Mr Arnell of Tenn Columbia) Johnney's friend has just been in & him and myself have had a dispute abput the merits of a book which Jonnie has (Whilem Merster) It is a book which wastranslated from the Germans I think it is a very interesting book though it does not give a very enviable character to the German Ladies or at least should feel sad indeed if american Ladies H had the character which the orthers hives the Germans perhaps you have road the book. I have been very much entertained whilst reading the book as it was written by a German Virginan thatit portrys the charatters of the German Lad ies he certainly gives them an unenviable character.
News of very scarce at the Universitythere is a great deal of tak about the innorguation of M. Buckhanan and a great many of the students are going to Washington in the morning about 50 left here yesterday & to day I should have liked to have been in Washington on the 4th myself very much, but fate have decreed other wise I was very muchsurprised to learn that Uncle Jim had lost his little baby andfeel very sorry for him andAmelia Weldon Claiborn was at my room a night or two since and told me that his mother is dead. She died about three weeks ago. he seemed to be quite grieved to speak of her. I noticed he was wareing crape and ask him if his familyand all were well when he told me concerning his mother But all mankind must taste of the bitter cup which fate has mixed" I was no less surprised to learn that the Esqr's banished daughter had returned to her Fathers house, and that all was well and Christianlike I hear that cousin Kate Somervell of Ark's is tob be married soon now that is pleasing I like to hera of the like and hope that she may have a felicitous deliertaion (delightful) time indeed. It is gettig late & I must finish I hope you may have fine weather in Tennessee this Spring & that there may be elegaht crops made & that the farmers may get 10cts around for cotton Jony has been down to the Gymnascum to excersize but found the wind too sharp that there was so little comfort while out in it that he has taken a wise conclusion and return to his room, he is busy reviewing his Mathematics he has an examination on th 11th of this month,

RECORDS OWNED BY MRS. BENTON TERRY, COOKEVILLE (CON)

and I have one at the same time in Materoa Medica Tonight a week ago the wash Society had a celebration on Washington birthday, address was made by E. K. Harris of Meclinburg it was a very nice affair they employed a band & had everything went on very nice the ypung men promenaded about three hours with

LETTER TO MRS. GEORGE ANDERSON TAYLOR FROM DR. AUGUSTINE SOMERVELL

RECORDS OWNED BY MRS. BENTON TERRY, COOKEVILLE, TENN.

University of Virginia
Apr 2nd 1857

Dear Sister:

Yours of the 26ult was recd today And I avail myself of the prseant opportunity of writing to you in response to your much suprised letter; we did recieve a letter from you about a week or ten days ago, but as it is always tge case a duty posponed is seldom or ever complyed with as thus your letter was not answered. I promised to be more punctual in the future When ever we recieve letters in conjunction, Jonny waits for yme & I for him & Time for neither of us however I have no objection s to you writing to us in conjunction If you prefer to do yourletters will be answered more punctually in future I was quite sorry and very much surpried also today to learn ffom your letter that Ann Eslenor was unwell I had not heard before that she was atole sick when you see her again present me kindly to her if you please-I was pleased to learn that cousin George yourself & the childra were well & that the farmers are blessed with a good & Early spring I do hope that htey may all may make large crops of cotton & corn & that cotton may sell for 12½ cts a lb you said that cousin G. & myself had been fishing & had very good crops for Fale I was much surprised tho hear that it is cold in htis region that I magine fish cant live on the waters before July I recieved a letter from Jinny yesterday saying that all were well at home, & that he had found my last dog. I was quite vexed when ma told me that a fellow Hulit had stolen my T. Q, if Hulit had been comeatable I htink he would have felt my stick laid on his coput, with some emphass, And Tome Taylor is going to move to Deer Creek, well joy go with him I hope he may do well-The inhabitants of old Tipton are moving to otherparts of the country & some to their long home & everything is changing according to the Laws of nature so materially that it is probable that I will not be at all home when Iget back home again oh;how mutable are all things ni this world, if I get the blues very bad this summer you all must not be surprised if you see me at home I read a lettervfrom Cousin Will yesterday saying that his Parents desired him to return home this summer And that in about 2½ months he would be at home in Tenn, which made me feel s good deal like seeing my Parents and kin too, Therefore if I come home thissummer you all must not reproveme for it. I am very anxious to see you all again-I do not believe there is one particle of News in College a good many of the students have become Werried & some hav gone home & others speak of going shortly. The examination come of in Annatormy today But I did not stand it in account of not being able to review Anatomy with out loosing a good many of the regular lectures on subjects that I wishe dto know more about & which are important I understood from one of my correspondents that cousin George Terry was discarded by Miss Fannie Green whilst in Tenn, I suppose that you have heard that Miss Mary Torry was married last month to Col. Jeffries Uthey have gone south on a bridal tour, I heard some time since that Miss Kate Arks was to be married to Mr. Eaton they have my wishes for their happiness in life may their paths be strew with flowers of all kinds I have received a letter from Eli myself since Xmas, though I have written to her several times during that time, I reckon she is very busy & has not the time to write I intend to conyinue to write to her u untillshe writes to me. Tis late & I must close give my best respects to

RECORDS OWNED BY MRS. BENTON TERRY, COOKEVILLE, (CON)

cousin George & and the children to grandma Uncle Ted & to my other kin give my love to all at home when you go to pas Love to the Servant , write to me agan soon & excuse all mistakes in this & in previous & suceeding letters I remain as ever your brother,
    In closed you will fine a ticket to our intermediate celebration ,
                              Gus A Claiborn Somervell.

LETTER TO MRS. GEORGE ANDERSON TAYLOR, FROM DR. AUGUSTINE C. SOMERVELL
RESORDS OWNED BY MRS. BENTON TERRY, COOKEVILLE, TENN

University of Virgina, Aprile 24, 1857

Dear Sister:
  Your last has been recd and I have some lisure time to day I have concended to write you a few lines in answer to your grateful letter.
  We have had winter weather during the present week, & the mountain tops have been white with snow for three or four days past. I never saw or heard of such weather this month, There has nothing very interesting transpired here for several days, lastSunday there was a tremendous row among the students the cause of which was ; a little Jew shopper on Saturday night shot two students one of whom was wounded severely in the head- But is better recovering. About 300Students assembled in front of his Jew Shop Sunday morning broke open his door & played the mischief with his merchandis & C. After searching for the Jew several hours, he was found under the bed of one of his neighbors he was taken out in the street by the students &b tied to a tree where the vote was taken wheather or not he should be Linched It is my opinion that the little "Isaac Of York" would certainly have met wiht a severe castigation if not with his death, But for the Thuonstrautes of Dr. Maupin & a few sensible students who were not so much exceted The jew was take to jail sitting on a rail where he is now, I believe his trial is tomorrow.
  There are some very heatted men University of Virgina, The ioght of of an celebration some onewho surely must have been acquainted with a young man of mt state Mr Barr Tenn, whilst Barr was at the public Hall attendin the celabration A man I say who must have been well acquainted with Barr to took the liberty of going into his room & trunk and from thence he carried $35. dollars of Barr's money?And a few days before this took place some rascal shot at W. Claborn from the street whils A, Claiborn was preparing to retire for the night Therefore I say that there are some rascal Villians in College.
  I read a ticket to Cousin Mary Caths wedding some time since done up in very recheche stile indeed I hope that she may nevervrepent of her selection & that they may live a long and happy life && C I read a letter from Will, day before yesterday he will be at home about the middle of June. I wish you would send me something nice by him when he returns as I will be sure to seehim either inWarrentown or at C. H. N. C. this summer. I do want to see you all at home so much & if I cant see you you must send me something fromhome by Will I shall write to him & intrust him to bear tO me any thing which the old folks at Home may burden him with for me, He is a good boy & I know he will take pleasure in obliging me I heard from Ealie last week & through Willies letter she was well & doing well except that he does'nt like to write letters very much One of my cousins promised to exert her influence in persuading her to write to me I expect a letter from her daily. I read a most charming & fasinaying letter two of them this week. one from my cousin Fannie Somervell & the other from my cousin Fannie Gres. they both write beautifully, as Jonnie wishes to write on this sheet I must close Give my best love to your oldMan & to the children Kiss them for me & to G. Ma & my kins in general write soon to yourbrother May you ever be happy
        Farewell Farewell,
        A. C. Somervell.

LETTER TO MRS. GEORGE ANDERSON TAYLOR (CON)

To Mrs. I. F. Taylor, Tennessee

This young man promised to leave me this whole leaf but while I was out he has written not only all of the paper, but I fear all of the news. I wrote Elylas night I have not recieved a letter from him in several months, was much pleased to hear Sickly- I expect that much of your enjoyment will be destroyed by Wills going home next summer I hope that he will have much pleasure He is one of the greatest boys I ever saw. How is cousin George getting on with his farm? I hope finely The weather has been bad for more than 3 weeks Glad it has moderated and today is very pleasant. A young man here from the Isle of Wight, and who is acquainted with Dr. Peek family recieved a letter from his brother, who is at a Military School not far from his fathers he wrote in fine Spirits and was perfectly well .He fodd opened a letter recieved in the same mail from home and learned that after a few hours writing his brother had been accidently shot by a pistol which he had in his pocket while out with some of the other boys and throwing rocks The young man is very lively generally and is the life of our Range his brother was about 15 I don't believe he has more than smiled since he heard Of his death. The session is now on faston the wave and the time will soon come for us to layaside our study gowns for awhileI much pleasure ever in the prospect of meeting one of my sisters thissummer and think that will must feel pretty good in looking forward to the meeting of all of his relations in Tennessee. Nevertheless I think that it is much better not to go home than I should hate to leave home again. Give much love to all excuse mistakes &ct. I am well but have several Lectures to prepare.

Write Soon tomyour affectionate brother,

John W. Somervell

LETTER TO MRS. GEORGE ANDERSON TAYLOR FROM DR. AUGUSTINE C. SOMERVELL
RECORDS OWNED BY MRS. BENTON TERRY, COOKEVILLE, TENN.

Univ of Virgina
May 30th 1857

Dear Sister:
Your much valued letter was recd several days since having been quite unwell for the past 4 or five days I hope that you will excuse my seeming neglect I said that I had been unwell for the past few days But am much better this evening I have felt extremely Billious & also have suffered with a bad head ache However I took 12 gr calomel last night I feel much better to night.

As I did not feel entirely well tonight, I did not attend Society, therefore will improve my time by writing you a few lines in answer to your before mentioned. The weather has been very pleasant here for two orthree weeks And every one hascome out in white clothes,

I was much surprised this morning to learn that Prop "Bledso" & family were all in mourning for Miss Bledsowho died last night no one knew what was the disease with which she died Her death was certainly very sudden & unexpected indeed Please excuse all mistakes I have to entertain company and write during the time.

One of my friends have justinvited me to his room to eat fried chiken tonight that is good isn't itp a great many students have with drawn from college and gone home & they continue to leave every day. The time will soon be here for us to depart we will soon be with ourfriends in Hicksford & Greensville Oh; Have you heard that, Loraster Fane & Dr. George Stark, They are marries At last I was very glad to hear of it George has been courting Miss Loe for about10 or 11 years I hope that they may live long and be happy I read a very nice letter today from Cousin Fannie Somervell shespoke of the enjoyment at her sisters wedding Oh; how shecompliments Uncle Dick forbeing so good to visit themH, H, Mr Leiper & cousin Lou Eaton waited togather And every one enjoyed them selves finely-Also had a nice letter from Cousin Fannie Green she writes a very nice letter, and I think is one of the most accomplished& keenest ladies of my acquaintance I must beg that you write excuse this short & indifferent letteras I do not feel in the moode of writing to night. If you do not write to us before the middle of June you must direct your letter to Hicksford where we expect to be the last of June or first of July.

My love to all the family & kiss all the children for me.
Your brother and ever time friend,
A. C. Somervell

LETTER TO MRS. GEORGE ANDERSON TAYLOR FROM DR. AUGUSTINE SOMERVELL

RECORD OWNED BY MRS. BENTON TERRY, COOKEVILLE, TENN.

                              Univ of Penn Phila
                              Feb 27th 1858

Dear Sister:

    Your letter of the 9th instanthas been recieved it gave me much pleasure in communicating that you & your little tribe were all well & happylong may you live thusI suppose in this time that money matters in Tenn a are in a much better condition than they have been during the fall and winter InPhila the Banks are paying apesil I believe & business is going on as well as ever and I am convinced that the people of the North look more to h their interest inn banks and money mattersgenerally than those of the South There has been a deep snow here for several weeks, & there is yet remaining a quantity in the Streets. Manypersons have been enjoying sleigh riding in abundanceseveral young gentlemaen myself among the number procured seats in a 6cent omnibus sleigh last Saturday evening & rofde out to the girard College-There were several ladies aboard & we had a very gay time indeed I have not felt rich enough as yet to hire a single sleigh at $5.00 an hour 7 ride out any of my lady friends or acquaintances & do not think I shall feel so. John as perhaps you have learned was in the City a few weeks agince he saw all of the sights that was to be seen & was very much pleased I believe I took him to the Italian Opera to hear MRd Legrange & Domfre Td Trovator was the opera,& tis very grand & striching opera. The house in which they acyed is one of the finest in the world Academy of Music on Broad St(John was verymuch pleased with the buildingsperhaps more than with the opera & the magnificantly dressed ladies who were present on the occasion in white silk and satins low necks & short sleeves Whilest I had on my over coat & was not at all uncomfortably warm Tis indeed surprisa ing to see how a pretty woman will expose herself in order to exhibit her t charms-Vanity thy name is Woman You are very sure that I have been disappointed in Love; Not so Oh nono, woman has wver flirted with me or ever wil as long as I am in sane mind I defy the race of women I do not wish you orn any one else to think that any lady everflirted with me, for such is not the sace . I have merely come to the conclusion that loving and addressing the ladies is not a very profitable business I don't want to marry& therefore I entend to say as many hard things about the sex as they deserve & b independent I do not say it and bost at all But candidly I will say to you that I never have addressed a woman so far who did notn confess that she loved me & would marrie me if the trooth must be told frequently thoughtless young men court ladies whom they think at the time that they love. and after tis too late they repent of having placed themselves in such a positi ion Yet don't infer from this that I would repent or flirt with a lady after going so far. No I would never let her know that Iregreated having courted her. In fact I have no grounds for complaint against any woman. But have becomeowearied with love if this is possible.

    My first examination will be held next Saturday week on Chemistry The a old mais that I am boarding with have just gor a piano and they worrie me no little practicians I think of quitting the premesis soon or after the examinations are over Tis too boaring to listen to her bang till ten o'clok at night on a piano. Give my bes & respects to cousin George & the children as well as to Grandma Uncle Bert & Charley to your Brother,
                                                 A. C. Somervell

Write soon

RECORDS OWNED BY MRS. BENTON TERRY, COOKEVILLE, TENN.

Cora Arnold   Virgina Records.

          Rev. J. J. Somervell & Lady
               Compliments
       Tuesday, 11, Oct., 6 P. M. 1859
DR. A. C. S mervell   Miss Mary B. Somervell
       " North view "

To Mrs. Ann H. Clement & Daughter
        Present
 To Mr. Wm. Sometvell & Lady
   & Daughter.
The pleasure of your company
is respectfully solicited to meet
Mr. J. W. Williams at a Soiree,
at Sam Taylors Residence on
 the evening of the 10th inst
at 7 o'clock.
    Tipton Co. Ten June, 1, '52

Wm. Somervell & Lady Compliments
Requesting the pleasure of your Company
on Wednesday Evening, Nov, 17, 1852
 at 5 o'clock
     Bobby H. Hamier, Tenn

TO CAPT. JOHN W. SOMERVELL A. A. GEN. JACKSON DIVISION.
RECORDS OWNED BY MRS. BENTON TERRY, COOKEVILLE, TENN.

Feb 1864.

My Dear Uncle:

This is the Second letter I ever write, the first was to cousin Bettie Claiborn. I went to grandma's Friday and carried it with me and they thought it was very nice Aunt Mamie recieved two letters lately from Uncle Walter saying that he was well.

Mr. McCall lost all of his Soldiers Clothes but Uncle Walters Servant Bill saved his, Some Negroes stole two bales of cotton from Uncle Tom but he found it at A.M.Archers to whom they had sold it, but he sold it for a high price than he would have gotten here Aunt Kate and Bet are going to Covington to school to morrow and grandma says they must go there two years. Uncle Jimmie says that he is very glad that they are going. I knew all my lessons this morning and am getting on very well with my studies. Ma was at grand mas yesterday and it rained so I do not think she went home MissHenrien sends her tobacco bag and says she hopes you accept it as a token of remembrance Uncle Jimmie had a dining on his birthday. There were a great many gentlemen there and he enjoyed it very much . Aunt Mary's mules foot was sore and she did not go. I wish you should answer this letter.

from your affectionate neice
Mary H. Taylor

RECORDS OWNED BY MRS. ALTHA VADEN, COOKEVILLE, TENN

This Indenture made the 18th of March 1815 And in the Year of Our Lord one thiusand eight Hundred and twenty five Between Benjamen J. Blackburn and of the county of Jackson and State of Tennessee of the one part and Samuel Hardester of the County and State aforesaid of the other part witnesseth that for and in consideration of the sum of one hundred Dollars to him in Hand paid Benjaman J. Blackburn hath Bargained and Sold and delivered a tract of Land containing thirty seven and a half acres Lying in Jackson County in the first District on the waters of Pegeon Roost Creek Baginning at two Blackoaks this South 80 poles to the Black oaks and Blackgum thence East to a stake thence North 80 poles to the beginning Including Blackburns Improvement Surveyed the 26th day of November 1813 by James Tousansend S.d. Day of November 1813 by Hames D. S Sd Blackburn oath Bind himself his heirs and executors administrators to warrent and forever defend the Sd tract or parcel of Land whom ever claimimg or to claim whereunto I sey my hand & seal Wednesday and Date above written

        Attest   Benjaman Blackburn (SEAL)
  Reubin Perkins
  Alfred Hardyster
  X his mark

PROPRTY OF MRS. ALTHA DENTON VADEN, COOKEVILLE, TENN.

State of Tennessee------No 3967.

To all to whom these presentd shall come Greeting, Know Ye, that for and in considerstion of twelve and one half cts per acre, on the htird day of July 1824pursuant to the provisions of an Act of General Assembly of said State 6 Tennessee on the twenty second day of November, one thousand eight hundred and twenty three by No 275 there is granted by the said State of Tennessee unto Patsy Embry, a certain tract or parcel of Land containing one hundred and fourteen and a fourth acres , a certain tract or parcel , by survey bearing datethe 6th day of August, 1825 lying in said county on the South fork of Mine lick Creek waters of the Caney Fork and bounded as follows to-wit, Beginning at a white oak on the south west corner of a thirty acre survey belonging to the said Patsy Embry running South by fifty poles to a white oak thence East crossing the creek at a ten poles ain all ninety poles to a poplar in John Harris west baundry line of his 50 acres tract, Thence North with said line one hundred and seventeen poles to a white oak in the S& South boundry line of John Hensleys 10 acre tract, Thence west with hisline fourteen poles to a Sour wood stump, the south west corner of said tract, The thence North sixty poles to a black gum the North west corner of said tract ,Thence west one hundred and thirty eight poles to a black oak and Chestnut , Thence South one hundred and twenty sevenpoles to a chestnut, ThenceEast sixty two poles to the Beginning, including and exceeding the 30 acre tract on which the said Patsy Embry now lives.

With the hereditaments and appurtenences To have and to hold the said tract or parcel with its appurtenances to the said Patsy Embry, and her heirs forever. In witness whereof William Carroll, Govnor of the State of Tennessee, hath hereunto set his hand and caused the Great Seal of the State to be affixed at Nashville on the Eleventh day of Sept. in the year of Our Lord one thousand eight hundred and twenty six and of the Independance of the United States the fifty first.

By the Govnor, Wm. Carroll.

Danial Graham, Secretary.

Recorded in the Registers office Westv Tennessee, February, 28, 1827.
Stith Harrison, D. R.

No 3967 Patsy Embry, 1144 acres, Jackson County.
Patsy Embry is entitled to the within mentioned tract of land.
T. M. McGavock, Register,West Tennessee.

RECORDS OWNED BY MRS. ALTHA VADEN, COOKEVILLE, TENN.

State of Tennessee No 940-
To all to whom these presents shall come Greetings: Know ye that for and in consideration of the sum of one cent per acre paid into the office of the Entry Taker of White Countyand entered on the 30th day of January 1827 pursuant to the provisions of an Act of the General Assembly of said State passed on the 3rd day of December one thousand eight hundred and twenty five by No 1270 there is Granted by the siad State of Tennessee unto Joseph Hunter a certain tract or parcel of Land ontaining fifty acres by survey bearing date the 20th day of June 1828 lying in said County and on the Falling Waters oand boundes as follows, Beginning at a stake and pointer the poles East of the South corner of a survey Eight and one half acre made in the name of Joseph Hunter Running thence south Twenty four poles to a white walnut Thence West one hundred poles to a Lynn Thence siuth fifty six poles to the Beginning With hereditaments and appurtenances To have and to hold the said Trust or parcel of Land with its appurtenances to the said Joseph Hunter and his heirs forever.
In witness whereof Sam HoustonGovnor of the State of Tennesseehim hereunto set his hand and caused the Great Seal of the State to be affixed at Nashville on the 20th day of September in the Year of Our Lord one thousand Eight hundred and tewnty eight of the Independance of the United States the Fifty third
By the Govnor
Daniel Graham
Recorded in my office in Book B. Pages 368-369
R. Nelson Register of the Mountain District
No 940.
Joseph Hunter 50 acres White County
Joseph Hunter is entitle to the within described tract of land
R. Nelson Register of the Mountain District

This Indenture made this the Thirteenth day of December in the year of Our Lord one thousand eight hundred and fifty three by and between James Dodan seign of the County of Jackson and the State of Tennessee of the one part and James Brockof the County and State aforesaid of the county other part witnes that for and in consideration of the sum of sixty five dollars to me in hand paid by the 3rdBrock the receipt where of is hwerby acknowledged hath bargained sold and by the presance do bargain sell and deliver unto said Brock one peace or parcel of landthat he the srd Dodson bought ofAbsolem William Supposed to contain sixty acres he the same orless cituated being and lying in Sd county of Jackson on the waters of Peigeon Creek Beginning at a stake in h the West boundryline of a Sd corner between I sd James Brock and James Dodson Runningthencewith the calls of said deed of conveyance and the condition line between sd Brock and him the srd Dodson laking one half of the Spring that the srd Dodson makes use of including the srd sixty acres more or less to haw and to hold his the srd James Brock his heirs and assigns forever and the srd Dodson do herrby warrent and forever defend the same from allpersons whatsoevr from holding claiming or onany wise lawful demanding ant part thereof in witnessI have hereunto set myhand and affixed my seal This day and date above written signed and sealed and delivered in presence of us
Attest J. P. Dearing , Stexenson D Ward
James Dodson(Xhis mark)
(SEAL)

RECORDS OWNED BY MRS. ALTHA VADEN, COOKEVILLE, TENN

This Indenture made this fifteenth day of September in the Year of Our Lord one Thousand Eight hundred and Thirty six Between James Brown of the County of Overton and State of Tennessee of the one Part and George McGhee of the Coynty and State aforesaid of the other part witness That the said James Brown for and in consideration of the Sum of Three Hundred and seventy five Dollars in hand paid by the said George Mc-Gheethe Receipt whereare of in here by acknowledged Hath given granted Bargained sold delivered in fuaffed(?) Conveyed and confirmed and by these presents doth give grant Bargain sell alein in puff(?) convey and confirm unto the said George McGee his heirs and assigns forever in the following tact or parcel of Land situated Lying and being in the County and State aforesaid on the Thence West with a tract originally in the name of said Murphree and John Ramsey fifty one poles to a hickory and Dogwood Thence North with Lornes Borne Line to a dogwood thence west with said Line passin Bornes and Wm A Savages corner and with Savages line to a popolar and two white oaks and Beach Pointers Thence Siuth with Savages Line Passim his and Fowles and Wm Marchbanks corner with said Fowlers and Marchbanks Line to the Beginning in the whole one hundred and Fourteen acres to be the same more or less to have and to hold and to hold the before Receted Tract Or Porne Sabd with all and singular the rights and Prefits emoluments hereditaments and appertainances of inand to the same Belonging or in any wise appertaining to the only purpose use and behalf of himn the said George McGee his heirs and assogns forever and the James Brown for himself his heirs Exicutors and Administrators doth covenant and agree to and with the said George McGee his heirs Exicutors & C that the before Renyed Land and Bargained Premises he will warrent and forever Defend against the wright till interst or claims of all persons or manner of persons

Bever Creek Containing one Hundred and Fourteen and one quarter of Acres Running as follows to wit, Beginning ata stake and dogwood pointers the Northern Boundry Line of Josiah Marchbanks tract Tence East with hsi line one hundred and fifty poles to a elm Enock Murphree South West corner of a twenty acre Tract thence north with Murphree line fifty seven and one half poles to Stake and Buckeye.

Whatever in Testimony where are he the said James Brown hath hereunto set his hand and affixed his seal the day and year first above Written

Signed Sealed and Delivered in presents of James Brown (Xhis mark) State of Tennessee Personally appeared Before me William Gore Clerk of th County Court of said County James Brown the conveyor in a degree of conveyance of George McGee for 113¼ acres of said land in said County with whom I am personally acquainted and who acknowledged that he dult executed the said delivered for the purposes therein Contained witness my hand at office on 27thday of Oct 1837

The foregoing is a correct transcript of the office recovered made on the acknowledged the within and subjoined deed

Attest William Gore Clk

State of Tennessee, I hereby certify that hhis deed and the certificate hereon are truly Registered in my office inLeger F. Pages twenty seven and eight In witjess whereof I John Kennody Registeredfor the County of Overton in said state have hereunto set my name and privet seal on Public official seal being provitted for this officedone at office on the eith day of Mar one thousand Eight hundred and thirty nine

John McKenney Reg for Overton Co

PROPERTY OF MRS. ALTHA DENTON VADEN, COOKEVILLE, TENN.

This Indenture made and entered into this twenty first day of Sept in th the Year of Our Lord, One thousand Eight hundred and thirty eight between Charles Sperry of the one part and Henry Frasure of the other part both of htetown of Sparta in the County of White and State of Tennessee-Witnessed that the said Charles R. Sperry for and in consideration of the sum of one hundred and two Dollars current money by the said Henry Frasier in hand paid to the saidCharles R. Sperry the receipt whereof is hereby acknowledged and thereof acquitted and foreverdischarged that by these presents doth bargaine and convey and confirm unto him the aforesaid Henry Frasier his heirs and assigns forever, One certain lot or parcel of land containigg forty eight Square perches situated lying and being in the town of Sparta in the County of White and State of Tennessee itbeing part of the lote No 73 and 74 as laid down in th eplan of said town and the same price of ground which was conveyed on the 12th day of June A. D. 1834 by Madison Fisk & Robert Montgomery to the said Charles R. Sperry and which was conveyed to them on the 13th March, 1829 by the Representatives of Doctor Lawson Noussa Dec. which is bounded as follows to wit; Beginning at a post standing at the intersection of thelines of Back ally and turn pike street on North sideof said stret it being the South west corner of lot No 73 andwith the line of said Back e allyrunning twelve poles Northward by the full breadth of Lot No 73 and 74 to the intersection of theline of a crop stand thence with the line of said c cross Street Eastwardly four poles to a stake thence by a line Southwardly paralelled with the stakes twelve poles to a stake in the line of Turnpike streetthence with said line westwardly four poles to the beginning Togather with the appurtenances belonging or in any wise appurtenances to have and to hold the the above describedlot or parcel of ground or land with its hereditaments and appurtenances to the only propr benefit andbehalf of him the afore said Henry Frasier his heirs or assigns forever And the aforesaid Charles R. Sperry hereby covenants and agrees to and with the said Henry Frasier the right titke interest claim and demand of in and out to the above described lot or parcel of land which its appurtenances will warrent and forever defend unto him the saidHenry Frasier his heirs and assigns forever against the rihjt title interest claim and demand of all manner name and affixed my seal the day and date above written signed sealed and entered in the presence of

        N. Owham,& C. R. Sperry (SEAL)
        A CKD 20, Sept, 1838

State of Tennessee, White County Personally appeared before me, Nicholas Owham, clerk of White County court, Charles E. Sperry the within named conveyor with whom I am personally acquainted and acknowledged the due execution of the within deed for the purposes therein contained which is recorded witnessed my hand at office the 20th Sept. 1839.
        Test N. Owham, Clerk, White County Court.
State of Tennessee, White County, I hereby certify that the within Deed and above certified was on the 21st May, 1839, Registered in my office in Book L, Pages 292 and 293.
        Test N. Owham, Deputy of
        Jo W. Roberts, Register of White County.

DEED
RECORDS OWNED BY MRS. ALTHA VADEN, COOKEVILLE, TENN.

Charles Cook
Robert D Allison
Chairman of County Court

I Charles Cook have this ady bargained and sold and do hereby transfer and convey unton Robert Allison Dallisro chairman of the Putnam County court and his Successors office forever for the consideration of a and for hundred dollars to me in hand paid certain tract or parcel of land in the State of Tenn Putnam County District No 1 containing by estimation forty acres and bounded as follows to wit, Beginning on a black oak and black jack pointer in a conditioned line between said Cooks and George and James Ramsey runningSouth sixty two poles to a Stake and Black oak pointer fufty two poles to a stake and black oak pointer thence West eighty four poles to a stake in the glade thence North twenty eight poles to a stake in the glade thence east twelve poles to three hickorys and Black Jack pointers thence North sixty six and one twelfth poles to a stake and blck Jack pointer thanc east twenty two poles to a black Jack and pointer in said conditioned line thence South with said line thirty two and one twelfth poles to the beginning to have and to hold unto said Robert D. Alliosn and his successor in office foerover I do civenant with the said Robert D. Allison that and Lawfully seized of said land hhve a good right to convey it with that the said unincumbered I do covenant and bind myself my heirs and representatives to covanent and forever defend the title to said Land and ebery part of to the said Robert D. Allison and his successors in office against the lawful clems of all persons whatsoever this the 6th day of June 1854

          Charles Cook (SEAL)

Exicuted and delivered in the presents of us this day 6th of June 1854
Sign Jihn Terry
 Robison Dyer

Stateo fTennessee Personally appeared before me Putnam Co. Russell Moore, Clerk of Putnam Co Court Charles Crook with whom I am personally acquainted and who Acknowledged that he ececuted the within Deed for the purposes there in contained which is recorded witnessed my Hand at office this day 6th of June1 1854

          Russell Moore (Clk)
          Putnam County Cpurt

The foregoing deed was Received for registration Augist 10th A. D. 1854 at 1o o'clock A. M. and Registered
          W. Baker

State of Tennessee, Putnam County , I. M. Scarlet register of Putnam County b hereby certify that the above are foregoing is a true & correct coppy A Deed executed by Charles Crook to Robert D. Allison chairman of the County cpurt of Putnam Gounty and regis tered in Book A. On Page 9-10
          by William Baker
          M. N. Scarlet (Regs) of Putnam Co

PROPERTY OF MRS. ALTHA DENTON VADEN, (CON)

Thos. J. Poteet is entitled to the within described Tract of Land.

John F. Voss,
Reg. of the Mountain acre rtact.

Recorded in the Registers Office for the Mountain District in Book No 10, pages 669.

John F. Voss,
Reg. of the Mountain District.

Grant No. 11573, Thos. J. Poteet, 145 acres , Putnam County, 20th Dec,1855.

PROPERTY OF MRS. ALTHA DENTO VADEN, COOKEVILLE, TENN.

    I, James W. McDaniel have this day bargained and sold and do hereby transfer and convey unto I. W. Crutcher his heirs and assigns forever for and in consideration of forty five dollars to me in hand paid a certain town lot in the town of Cookeville, Tenn and situated in Block No 3 North and lot No 4 of said block in the plan of said town to have and to hold the same to the said I. W. Crutcher his heirs and assigns forever against the lawful claims of all persons whatever. I further covenant with the said I. W. Crutcher that I à lawfully seized of said land have a good right to convey it and that the sam same is unincumbered. I further bind myself, my heirs and representatives to warrent and forever defend the title of said land to the said I. W. Crutcher his heirs and assigns forever against the lawful claims of all persons whatever. Given under my hand and seal this 5th day of Dec. 1859

                                J. W. McDaniel (SEAL)

Test-R. B. McDaniel
C. R. Ford

  State of Tennessee, Putnam County, Personally Appeared before me Russell Moore Clerk Of Putnam County Court S am W. McDaniel the with in barganer with whom I am personally acquainted and who acknowledged the due execution of the writtendeed of conveyance to be his act and deed for the purposes and things therein contained which to is Recorded Written by hand at office this 5thday of Dec. A. D. 1859.

                              Russell Moore, Clerk

State of Tennessee, Putnam County, I, Stephen W. Brown Reg. for said County do certify that the written deed of conveyance was filed for Registration on the 6th day of Dec. 1859 & was noted on filation Book A. pages 104 &105 at 4 o'clock P. M. & was Registered on Book D. pages 28.

                              S. W. Brown, Register.

  I. W. McDaniel
    To
  Deed lot I. W. Crutcher.
  State Tax-----50
  Clerk fee------25
  Reg. fee   1.05
      Ack. 5th Dec. 1857

  We, James McKinny, Robert D. Allison, Joseph Hyder, James W. M. Daniel and W. H. barnes, commissioners of Putnam County for the consideration of Thirty threeDollars & 75 cts to us in hand paid by Joseph W. Crutcher have this day bargained and sold and do hereby transfer and convey to said Joseph W. Crutcher his heirs and assigns forever for the consideration above named the following described Town lots known and designated in the plan of the town of Cookeville, 1st as S. W. Block No 3 Lot No 2 bounded on the south by Spring Street & on the South by South Street 2 other lots known & designated in the plan of saidtown as lots No 1 & 4 S. W. Block No 3 Bounded on the North by South Street , on the South by by the land of JohnDitty, To have and to hold the above described town lots to the said Joseph W. Crutcher his heirs and assigns forever and we hereby convey& transfer for the said Joseph W. Crutcher hsi heirs & assignes & all the right title & claim that the County of Putnam has in and to said Town lots in as full and ample manner as we as commissioners of said county can, or ought to convey not further or otherwise.

    Witness our hand and seal this 13th day of Aprile 1857.
    Ack. by McKinny, W. H. Barnes & J. D. Hyder.

PROPERTY OF MRS. ALTHA DENTON VADEN, (CON)

	Robert D. Allison	(SEAL)
Test	J. D. Hyder	(SEAL)
	J. W. McDniel	(SEAL)
	W. H. Barnes	(SEAL)

Joseph W. Crutcher
   FROM Deed ----3 town lots , Commisiioners of P. C.
State Tax---------1.20
Clerk Fee ------- .25
Recorded on page 4 Book of Putnam County, Tenn
                    Russell Moore , Clerk.

Reg. Fee----1.50 Paid
   State of Tennessee, Putnam County, Personally appeared before me, Russell Moore,Clerk of Putnam County Court, James M. McKinny, Joseph D. Hyder, & W. H. Barnes Sr. commissioners of Putnam County, the within bargners with whom I am personally acquainted and who acknowledged the due execution of h the within deed of conveyance to be their act and deedfor the purposes and things contained witness myhand at office the 7th day of June,A. D. 1858.
                    Russell Moore, Clerk.

   THE STATE OF TENNESSEE*---To all to whom these presents shall come,Greetings:
   Know ye, that by virtue of Entry No 26, made in the office of the Entry Taker of Putnam County and entered on the 10th day of February 1855 pursuant to the provisions of an Act of the General Assembly of said State paper on the 9th day of January, 1830, there is granted by the State of Tennessee unto Thomas J. Poteet, A certain Tract or Parcel of Land containing One hundred and forty five acres By Survey bearing date the 17th day of Mar. 1855 lying in said county of Putnam , it being five acres less than the location calls for on the head waters of the little Caney Fork and on the Mountain Beginning on a sugar tree and sugar tree pointer the North east corner of the Tract on which the Poteet now lives, Running thence South with said line eighty eight polesto two white oaks another of his corners, Thenve West with his line eighty one poles to a black oak dogwood and black gum, another of his corners, Thence South with another of his lines thirty poles to a chestnut . Thence East fourteen poles to a hickory Wilkerson's corner. Thence South with Wilkerson's line seventy two poles to a corner, Thence South with Wlikerson's line seventy two poles to two dogwoods and maple pointers, Thence East one hundred and eighty poles to two white oaks and two maple pointers, Thence North with a line of a survey in the name of Clark eighty six poles to a chestnut in Coopers line, Thence west two poles to a black oak and hickory, Coopers corner, Thence North with Cooper's line forty six poles to a poplar Coopers corner, Thence west with his line sixty poles to a double dogwood and Pointers on a bluff of Rocks, Thence Northfirty five degrees west with Coopers line sixty two poles to the Beginning , including a part of said Poteets Improvements. With the hereditaments and appurtenences , To have and to hold the said tract or parcel of Land with its appurtenences to the said Thomas Poteet and his heirs forever. In witness whereof Andrew Johnson , Governor of the State of Tennessee hath set his hand and caused the great Seal of the State to be affixed at Nashville on the day of the Twentieth of December, in the Year of Our Lord, One Thousand Eight Hundred and fifty five and of the Independance of the United States the 80th year,
           By Governor, Andrew Johnson,
                    T. N. W. Brown, Secretary.

LETTER TO MALINDA JARED, FROM RODA BYRNE YOUNG.
PROPERTY OF MRS. EFFIE BOYD YOUNG, COOKEVILLE, TENN.

Nawvou, Ill. Jan. 25th, 1845.

Dear Mother:
it is with feeling of no ordinary kind that I take my pen in hand , this Sabbath morning to address you this letter. We are all well at present, and have been ever since we sent the last letter, which was to David Nichols except little Samuel he was very sick a few days with the hives, but he is now harty as ever. All the children or more fleshy yhan ever they were before. I hope this letter will find you all well. we have not heard from you since we received your letter of the 28th of July we want you if you have not written since to write as soon as you get this letter for we want to hear from you very much indeed. Write everything that you think might be interesting to us, yousaid in your last letter that we should render each other all the satisfaction we could bywriting. I am some what at a Loss to know, what would be the most satisfactory to uoi, howeverI will tell you a li ttleabout Nawvau Mormonism so called . Nawvou is a city of Saints gathered from many parts of the world as the old Prophet said two of a family and one6 of a city to do the commandments of God even to build a house to his name, with a few exceptions I believe they are the best people in the world, all is piec and quietness the people are industrious, virtuous and temperate but upon this is the words of St. Paul verified that they live Godly in ChristG shall suffer persecutions for the hand of persecution has been heavily laid on us and now the world it seems is making preperations to put the iron hand of oppression , Still heavier upon us By enventing the most abominable false hoods ever thought of Either by man or devil and publishing them abroad by this influence, the Charter of this city has been taken away, the next attempt may be to take away our lives the mobers in hancock County is still prowling around like so many blood hounds , or like so many hungry wolves howling over the blood of some innocent sheep which they have murdered to gratify their ravenous apetite they cry thieft and robbery, when it is indeed that the grater part of thieft they speak of really does not exist, while on the other hand beegums have been stolen and the gums found by the Mormons house and the honey in th house of a mobacrat and many such like circumstances they do this in order to justify them selves in the eyes of the people, for murdering Joseph andHiram for they know that thay cannot make it appear that the Mormons did it. they gathered up the chips whereon Joseph bled and sent them one to another, hundrecd of milesas a token of triumph, My verySoul shudders at the th ught of the unlimited wickedness Especially when I think how soon the rath of God will be pored down on them. Shurely all manner of eveil is spoken of us falsely for Christ Sake but we know that through much tribulation we must enter into the Kingdom, but in the mists of our afflictions our hearts are made to rejoice, for we put our trust in that God, who is able to light up a smile, in the aspect of Wo, yea, his Spirit is better then the juice of the grape and is a probation preferable to the Smile of Princess, his favor is richer then the f finestgoald and his wisdom transcendeth all humon understanding his power is Surpreme his plans is founded on wisdom, he will perform his work and accomplish his purpose. Man cannot prevent it, principles ofhis kingdom are princ$ iples of truth and truth is everlasting as him self therefore his Kingdom wil stand and those that abide its laws will come up before him to dwell in his presence, therefore we will adhere to his statutes we will win out in the new everlasting covenant, not counting our lives dear unto us.
Mother, I often ask ,yself this question, Why am I here alone, withou

LETTER TO MALINDA JARED, (CON)

any of my connection, why do they not come into this work, the ans is suggestd to my mind they worship God and they think that is all that is required of them if this is the case I wish to refer you to the 8th Chapter of the Acts where a man of Ethiopie had been to Jerusalem to worship and was returning, reading his Bible when Phillip came to him and preached to him and the first water they came to, they went down into it and he was baptized, also in the 14 thbchapter of Act worshiped God yet she gave heed to the Gospel preached by God though the Lord ppened her heart that she might receive his word. Now if the Lord has not opened the eyes of you understanding to see the necesity of his Church, being organized according to the New Testament pattern I entreat you to pray that the Lord in the infervency of your Soul, that he wouldopen your heart to receive thetruth of all that he has designed for our Salvation. Mother tellme your mind upon tjis subject in the next lwtter. I must begin to come to a close give my Love to Grandmother Byrne, and Mother Young and to all inquiring friends. I beg to be able to be excused for my bad writing and Spelling for the children was very noisy and little Samuel was hanging around my lap. I call the children up around me and asked them what I should tell you about them. Francis said she wished I would put her in the office with the letter & send her to Tenn for to see her Grandmother, Now said she if you write that it willt tickle them. Vivian sends her love to Grany Byrne, Anna & Martha syas send mim two. We remain as ever,

               Yours in love untill death,
               R. B. & A. D. Young.

LETTER TO L. BYRNE, ESQ. FROM BRICE BYRNE & ANN BYRNE.

OWNED BY MRS. EFFIE BOYD YOUNG, COOKEVILLE, TENN.

                                                        Crooked Creek, Ark.
                                                        June, 8th, 1851.

Dear Brother:
        I embrace the present oppitunity of informing you that we are at this time in the enjoyment of reasonable health. We have had sickness in the family and death has visited us. Our Dorcus is no more she departed this life on the 13th of last month, at 12, o'clock. She was taken about twenty days The physician that attended her Termed the disease congestive fever, since her death but thiught before it was caused from exposure, and had taken cold, he had notconsidered her case serious .the health of my family has not been very good for the two last weeks. Mary Ann & L. V. has been unwell, but are up agai n Williams helth is not improving this summer, thereappears to be more sickness this spring and so far this summer than has been since we have been in Arkansas. The prevailing disease is called congestive fever. By some called winters fever And has proved fatal in several instances. I have been anxiously looking for a letter from you in answer to one sent you sometime ago. I hope you will not neglect writting much longer. I am always anxious to hear from you and f amily and all the connection. it has been a long time since I have heard from any of the connection in your section. None of you seem to bother yourself to keep up a corespondance with us. I want you to understand that htese lines reach you-Malinda and Joseph Jared And will expect a corespondance from each of you as though I had directed to you seperately. I wrote to your son, Alex and requested a more frequent corespondance . he answered me ametiately and said hw was well, he gives me much pleasure in his communication, all was in goof helth the last news from him.

        Harvest has just commenced here and the prospect is flattering, the wheat isbetter than I ever saw, if we shoo have a favorable time for saving there certainly will be more wheat in the country than ever in this country in any former season, so think all the oldest settlers. There was considerable wind and some rain passed last night. I fear it has done damage. I have not heard from any yet. There is an apperance of more rain , the season has been very dryhere, but last winter and spring the crops of corn and oats look very well n buy a little backward. The price of corn is 50cts a bushel, wheat will probably be worth about 50cts,corn crops having been so short last year, bacon is worth about 8cts per lb. A dommon cow and calf is worth about $8.00, beef will be woth about 2cts, coffee is worth from 16 to 20cts. Sugar 10 to 12. Dry goods a little on decline but dear enough yet. I have no political news that is very interesting, not being the year of our election. Save that a member of Congress, the Democrats nominated Johnson for reelection and I presume he will have no opposition. Please allow your selves time to write me as soon as convenant give me the helth of the country, the family news without stint,, Deaths, marriages the commercial political and All interesting news. I will also inform you before concluding that the families of the son- inlaws are in reasonable helth as near as could be reasonably be expected. Miariam has a daughter two months old and Elizabeth a daughter borned the same eve that Dorcus died. They have named them both for our dear lamented child. I nowconclude with a hope of good news from you and that these lines when they reach you may find you all enjoying good helth. Please accept of the Respt. and well wishes of myself and Ann and all the children to you all.
                                            Brice Byrne& Ann Byrne.

Larance & Sarah By me & family
Joseph Jared & family
Malinda B. Jared & family

LETTER TO WILLIAM JARED, FROM BRICE BYRNE.
PROPERTY OF MRS. EFFIE BOYD YOUNG, COOKEVILLE, TENN.

Crooked Creek Arks
May, 4th. '53

Dear Nephew:
    I avail myself of the present opportunity to inform you and your mother that we are all at present in the enjoyment of reasonable health. The conection here are generally well, I hope Providence will bless you All with equal health and prosperity.
    I don't know that I have any interesting news to write, Though if I fail to write you might think I would be treating you with infifference or neglect which is far from my intention. I take as much delight in hearing from my friends , particularly my connection as any personliving, You know that there are only three of the old stock left, and I think a more frequent communication would be better proof of our filial feelings toward each other, tho if there has been neglect on the part of the old ones I am glad to see the young ones unwilling to follow the examples and from yourpromise in your letter to me I shall expect letters frequently from you. Your Uncle Lorance boy have written to me frequently and take great pleasure in receiving their communications. I received a letter lately from Alexandria he informed me of his trip to your neighborhood. I was truly glad that him self and family that was i with him, enjoyed themselfs with so pleasant a trip, as he states and found al well at home on his return. I am looking by every mail for letters from my young friends, jog their memoriesa little. I wish you to inform your mother a and Uncle Lawrence & your Uncle Joseph Jared that I would like to read a great long letter from either or all of them, give them all the contents of thisconsideration as though it had been directed to them.
    You wished me to hive you some information respecting this country rather a describe I am not a good hand to describe tho proceed to tell you something about it would have done so sooner, but thought I would be better prepared after returning from an expected Tour of surveying in different parts of the country, I have been in the upper part of the county two trips surveying the Northern and Western part of the county, in Praitie Town Ship North of this I found a beautiful country, it was aboutthe first of Aprile, the prairie just beginning to make its grass appear, the Land generally lies wellTimber tolerably scarce, and not so very good, consisting of PostOak, black Oaks, black Jacks and Hickory, the black jack in this country denotes Strong land such as will bring with a favorable season, 50 bus of corn per acre, or from 20 to 25bh wheat, large blackjack groth denote Strongest of land. Water is tolerable plentiful, some verygood springs, and excellent summer rains. I was also on a water course called Osage, a tributary of White River the bottoms there are excellent and lie very well, the hills are also very rich and not very scarce, The timber , Oaks, of every description, Hickory, Hackberry, Lyn, Sugar tree, walnut cherry, box elder & blue and black ash& Shrubbery or undergrowth huge pawpaw, Spin wood & Sumak, range for horses and cattle not so good as in the Prairie or barrens. Tho I think hogs do very well. Again I was on Kings River anothet tributary of White River. I surveyed some very good land, some bottom land and some very good barrens generally Oak and hickory timber out from the bottom and shumak and hazel undergrowth, Springs some what scarce, pretty good range this part of the county where I lived on Crooked Creek consists of Prairi barrens and some bottom lands, generally very good timber, tolerable scarce. w water is to be had in Spgs. frequently very good. Some have to dig the well. Water is generally very good thispart of the county, hard to beat in its general aperance, the grass is excellent, Milk cows fill the pails to over flowing

they can get grass plenty with out going out of hearing the soil here is adapted to the growth of almost everything I ever knew to grow any where, corn, wheat, oats, cotton & tobacco, Irish and sweet potatoes, cabbage, onions and garden vegetables grow better here here than you would suppose, or even conjecture in a northern latitude.

There is a great deal of broken hilly country here some mountains and ridges and some places very stony and gravelly, but the cleanest country of mud and stagnated water I ever saw, the streams generally runs swift and are as clear as crystal. I can't see any local cause for sickness, not withsatnding last year was very sickly here, and in some parts of the county, typhoid fever as the physicians (termed it) proved very fatal , now as respects my opinion concerning the exchange of your country with this I hardly know what to say though if I were a citizen of Indian Creek or owned no better than one of the little farms above Uncle Bills old place as it used to be called , I certainly would be facingfor Arkansas, I suppose it depends on, presumably on our taste, contentment is said to be the best fortune. I would be glad , how wise a choice you would make and would be mighty glad to fine you my neighbor with your mother and many other of our friends. We have had a favorable winter somewhat changeable, very dry and so has the spring been untill now , Monday evening and the rain came in torrents and the water rising fast, so goods and Groceries that are lying on the river below will be up imediately, theprices of produce and stock are as follows, hogs from 50cts to $1.00, cows & calf from $10 to $20 , yoke of Oxen $40 to $50 , corn 20 cts per bushel, wheat 50, flour $2 per hun

I will here state before concluding, Elizabeth Gillen has a son, call him name Brice H. Miriam has a daughter, calls it Malinda. I and The Respects of all my family to you all and all the cousians, also the respects of your Uncle,

               Brice Byrne.

LETTER TO MALINDA JARED, FROM M. J. NICHOLS, SOLDIER IN CIVIL WAR
PROPERTY OF MRS. EFFIE BOYD YOUNG, COOKEVILLE, TENN.

                                                        Camp Trousdale,
                                                        July, 1, 1861.

Dear Grandmother:
            I seat myself beneath the clamors of the drums and bugles to drop you a epistle full of confabulation it is with gratitude that I am granted the great privilege of addressing one by dexterity whose integrity glitters before my imagination as bright as the most precious jewels, you have ever treated me with great respect and I will ever feel grateful towards you for so excellent works.

      Oh, but that I had mental ability sufficient to paraphrase my sincere thanks to one so great and kind I perhaps would have been reckless character if it had not been for the expostulations of my beloved friends who have been instruments in keeping me from nefarious acts.

      When I look back on my past life and meditate my opportunities of culture it makes tears run down from my glimmering eyes as they did from Nebuchadnezzer in his sorrows but then I have one consolation, that is I am permitted the glorious privilege of enjoying a bountiful share of good helth. John is in good helth and is now on drill today is my time to staneguard and I write your letter during my time to rest. there are fifty eight sick in the Hospital with the measles and many other contageous diseases one man died last Saturday in Numans regiment, and they buried him yesterday in honor of war. I happened to be over there when they statted with him I went to the burying (dis, 4 Ms) when we got there we found a camp ground surrounded with tombs. The Funeral was preached by a very able minister, who is the Chaplain of that regiment, yhe harbor under which the sremon was preached was about 50 yds from the grave of the warrior and during the sermon I, (being tired) layed down to sleep and when I awoke I found myself alone, but ran up to the graveyard and they were just putting him in the grave, they covered the body slightly with dirt and then fired twenty four guns over the grave, which seemed to carry up honor to the God of battle. I would not like to be berrid here if I were to die but would want to be brought home. I am peculiary anxious to see you all and miss you to visit us When Father & Mother come to see us, we are all allowed 40 day during the year, and I will spend mine at home Mrs. West and her daughter are here on a visit they say rain is needed at Cookeville. I want you all to write soon and tell me all about the Farm and stock and helth of your community. I received your kind letter on Saturday morning which gave me much satisfaction.

                                              With Love Yours Truly
                                                 M. J. Nichols
                                                     To
                                             Malinda Jared

P. S.
     Father I will respond to your add soon, Write me soon
                      And with accuracy,
                      Yours Truly,
                            M. J. Nichols
                        (Moses Joseph Nichols)

LETTER TO D. H. NICHOLS, FROM JOHN H. NICHOLS,

OWNED BY MRS. HAYDEN YOUNG, COOKEVILLE? TENN.

Bristol Virginia,
July, 28, 1861.

Dear Father:

I wrote to Mother two ago when we got orders to stop and go back to Mo. I wrote that we were going to stay at that place some days, amediately after I had written we got orders to go on to Virginia we had left the Rail-road, somedistance and had pitched our tent but we took them down amediately and proceeded to execute the command We then got on the cars, that have conveyed us to this point where we have to change cars. When we changed the fact was assertained that the trains was not sufficient to take the whole regiment so part of the regiment have gone and our company with one more is left to go on another train. We wil not get off till morning. Father you know that we did'n anticpate faring as well on the Road as we did at Camp Trousdale, but that was a mistaken idea for we fare better the way we do is we do not have to the fatigue of drilling and we are as wellsupplied with provisions we with at the Camp. In my other letter I told you of the battles which had already been fought, but they are now recruiting for another battle which I am sure will be much more
 terable than those of which I gave an account but we are 300 miles from the place where the battle is to be fought so I fear it will be fought before we get there. Father Do not mistake me and understand that I want to get in a battlefor I never have said that for if this great and solemn craïs could possibly be settled without a single battle I would snatch eagerly at the settlement, I would lay fast hold with both hands and cling with more than filal affection to that compromise which would save the spilling of the most precious blood that ever flowed in the veins of the American people, but as the divisions and subdivisions of the people in to parties both political and religious has gone into such measure that it must be settles at the point of the bayonet, I as one who loves liberty as one who feels it ny duty to help sustain the liberty due us at the expense of the blood of our Fathers, am ready at any moment to carry this thing into effect, and you may never be unesay about me, butwhen you think of me let these words comfort me , if in battle I am slain I shall die at my post, It is true enough Father that I would be proud to see
 you all before we go into battle but at the same time that love for our real Southern rites which first prompted me to leave my home and happy fireside , still prompts meto go on in the grand andGlorious cause . Tell Mother that no matter where I go the burning words she spoke to me two days before I started still hum with me in heart and I know that her words were true when she promised me her tenderest sympathies and most humble prayers and Father let me beg of you and Mother to never cease instructing my younger brothers and sisters in the right way for on such an occasion as this your words of instruction arise in their minds as words of comfort, then they as I now do, will thank you for your words of instruction given us in a proper time. I beg too be excused for this advising although my condition enables me to feel the good of pleasant words spoken in time. This makes me feel that it is my duty to do so. You need not write to me without me Stationed at some point. I shall write often, whih will be gladley handled bt you. Farewell, this leaves me well,

From your Son, JohnH. Nichols

To D. H. Nichols

LETTER TO DAVID H. NICHOLS, FROM ROBERT F. JARED.

OWNED BY GRANDAUGHTER, MRS. EFFIE BOYD YOUNG, COOKEVILLE, TENN.

Sparta, Tenn. White County,
Aug, 8, 1861

Dear Cousin:
    Your letter came to hand July, 2oth, I and Pa was glad to here from you. We are all well at present but Pa he is in very bad helth, he is out at the Mountain now 12 miles from Sparta, he has been there two weeks and he aint coming home till frost, Crops looks very well here at this time, we have not suffered for rain but little there has been more wheat raised here this year than has been raised for many years. Wheat is worth 75cts here corn a dollar.

    There is canstant talk here about the war, some of the people is scared half to death I aint scared. I never think about it much. I go about my business like I allways did. I hope these few line find you all well so far a I have no more to write at present I will bring my letter to a close, excuse my bad writing, and look over mistakes and as I am in a hurry so no more at present, I remain
    Your friend untill death,
    R. F. JAred to D. H. Nichols

LETTER TO DAVID H. NICHOLS, from M.J. NICHOLS, SOLDIER IN CIVIL WAR.
Property of Mrs Effie Boyd Young, Cookeville, Tenn.

                 Camp Chattanoogia,
                 Aug. 3, 1862.

Dear Father, Mother & Grandmother:
  I again avail myself of an opportunity which I am always glad of Happy am I to inform you that I have the consoling privilege of sitting beneath the shade of Tennessee Oaks while I endeavor to communicate my friendship to you with quick steps and glad hearts, we put our feet to Tennessee soil on the 27th ult, all glad to find enough uninvaded ground to strike camp on, also to find water pure and cool. We find the weather to be much more pleasant here than in Miss, the weather, water and people seem so delightful that we feel like we have emerged from a land of despair to a land of felitity, a great change has taken place among the Tenn troops, they were then thought to be of the bravest species in Virginia, South Carolina, ans Miss, but since the move they all seem to frown with madness and bravery the thought of enemy being among our friends and relatives is sufficient to promt every country loving man to action amediately, here we are within one hunded miles of home, but of fear of being troubled by the cannon invaders of our State we dare not visit home, and frie nds. They are wickedly infesting our vicinities destroying privet property and like roaring lions they are traversing Tennessee seeking whom they may devour, they even rob poor helpless women and children of their provisions and leave crying infants reaching their weak hands for bread bread. What is to be done with the Murders of women and children? It recurs to all at once that they should be treated likewise. this is a thing hard for us to endure without vigorously rushing forwarde and snatching them from their positions, as an aegle does her prey . We are expecting to have Gens Buel and Mitchels supplies cut off in a short time, when it will be that we will liberate Tennessee. After we get them cut off from their beef and crackers, they will fail to get backers and we will drive them off as a shepherd drives his herd only we will be little rougher than they usually are, we will generally order them out of our premisesc and if they fail to respond fairly we will slightly put our bayonets to them and push them Northward until they strike their own soil, and when they are convinced that we are getting in good killing plights(sspirits?) they surely will get cold in their cause as some has already gotten, Before we get done with them we will make them men of consideration and cause them to think seriously on the subject of war. the whole Northern army consists of poor deluted scoundrels, who cares for nothing but money and something to eat, Lincoln has made another call for troops, but finds them slow to act they have found out the grilling shame by which the hireling were dragged into the field. If he gets them at all he will have to raise their wages. All that we have to do now to achieve liberty is a gene eral forward movement with sabers in front pointing at the hearts of those God-forgetting invaders who so much hars (hate?) us and who curl the lips of deri at Southern rebellion, let us be co-workwer in this struggle and add golden feathers to our gleaming laurels which we have so vigourously (victoriously?) won on goery fields of battle if the victories we have gained heretofore is not sufficient to prove our intentions, the be-holders is hardb to convince, i it pught to prove all at once that we will die fighting for freedom, rather than be conquered by so unworthy Co-horts. Independance is a thing worth working for and we must work with the whole heart and have spirits, if we accomp plish our design and unless consolidated forces, it will take years

LETTER TO DAVID H. NICHOLS, (CON)

to effect peace the thing has to be settled, some way in a short time, or we will have a debt hanging over us for ages, but the debt is nothing compared with the object of our design we had rather have a debt hanging over us throu life, than be brought under the tyranical laws of the North, we will take death before subjugation, and debt before Northern laws, there cause must be an unjust one and they can never complete there boasted Determination, which they so clamorously difused among nations, in the out set, they boasted of things they cannot stand up to, and are thisday sorry that they bragged so strenously fo their power and ability A few more good overthrows such as those at Manassa, Shiloh, and Elkhornand Richmon and manyother points, wil their line so much, that it will be hard for them to form a line of battle, after we getour conscriptions in the Field they had better make their wills for they must surely die or flee from our sdil with celerity, they have already been running from their post at several points which fulfills our passage from the Scripture, (the gilty fleeith when no one persueth)they have no human regard for civility, but go in for a wicked contest entirely and one thing is certainly true if they do not change their notions they will undoubtedly fall in to oblivion with out mercy at their down fall we will endeavor to thrive ande njoy freedom. The Glittering Monuments of Southern liberty is fast building the day is near at hand for us to reap ourrteward on earth which will be pure satisfaction through life, and cause has proven to the world, to be trulyjust, Nations abroad looks on us as soldiers, laboring for pur just deserts England and France are expecting us to be successful in the out come, not long from this day. We will be free from the North and Northern oppression there is enough at stake to call forht all friends of Liberty to working for their country and firesides, the soldiers all seem to be on the right side of the question, while there is some men in the dungeon of unionism, In a few days we will complete the work in Tenn and free the prople as well as those portley fellows who could nto muster up courage to take their own part in the National struggle, Good for Nashville in a short time. Father we are near enough for you to come to see us by land, and I want to see you so much as ever I want to see perticularly at this time try to come soon andI think you will never regret the trip. Stock is in fine demand at present, beef is worth 10per lb, horses are selling very high since the armyyczaame in, a drove of b beef cattle would pay very well if you could get them cheap. Mother I would love to see you and Grandmother, and all the children but I rather you would not come to camp for this is no place for women wait a while and we will get a chance to visit you this leaves us all in good helth and fine spirits give my best love and respects to all inquiring friends, tell them all to write me and be sure and write soon, giving the news in general. I am dear Father, Mother and Grandmother your dutiful son and will ever remain so,

          M. J. Nichols.
         (Moses Joseph Nichols)

www.ingramcontent.com/pod-product-compliance
Lightning Source LLC
Chambersburg PA
CBHW080551230426
43663CB00015B/2798